The Dove in the Consulting Room

Psychoanalysis began over a century ago as a treatment for hysteria and it has recently turned its attention to hysteria once again. Provocative and original, *The Dove in the Consulting Room* engages critically with psychoanalysis – and in particular with the phenomenon of hysteria's return to analysis – from a Jungian perspective, asking such questions as:

- What role does the concept of hysteria play in psychoanalysis?

- What does it say about the concept of the soul, and about analytical culture?

- Does the spiritual aspect of the unconscious have any place in psychoanalysis – the dove any place in the consulting room?

Drawing on the works of Jung, Freud, Hillman, Giegerich, Bollas, and others, the author provides a lively and compelling Jungian analysis of analysis itself – both Freudian and Jungian.

The Dove in the Consulting Room is illuminating reading for the professional analyst and for anyone interested in the spiritual and cultural importance of psychoanalysis and analytical psychology.

Greg Mogenson is a graduate of the Inter-Regional Society of Jungian Analysts. The author of many articles in the field of analytical psychology, his previous books include *God Is a Trauma: Vicarious Religion and Soul-Making* (1989) and *Greeting the Angels: An Imaginal View of the Mourning Process* (1992). He is in private practice in London, Ontario, Canada.

The Dove in the Consulting Room

Hysteria and the Anima in Bollas and Jung

Greg Mogenson

Brunner-Routledge
Taylor & Francis Group

HOVE AND NEW YORK

First published 2003 by Brunner-Routledge
27 Church Road, Hove, East Sussex, BN3 2FA

Simultaneously published in the USA and Canada
by Brunner-Routledge
29 West 35th Street, New York, NY 10001

Brunner-Routledge is an imprint of the Taylor & Francis Group

Typeset in Times by Regent Typesetting, London

Printed and bound in Great Britain by T J International Ltd,
Padstow, Cornwall

Paperback cover design by Amanda Barragry

British Library Cataloguing in Publication Data
A catalogue record for this book is available
from the British Library

Library of Congress Cataloging-in-Publication Data
The dove in the consulting room : hysteria and the anima in
   Bollas and Jung / Greg Mogenson.
      p. cm.
   Includes bibliographical references (p.) and index.
   ISBN 1-58391-258-4 (alk. paper) – ISBN 1-58391-259-2
      (pbk. : alk. paper)
   1. Jungian psychology. 2. Psychoanalysis.
 BF173 .D625 2003
 150.19'5–dc21

                                          2002034504

ISBN 1-58391-258-4 (hbk)
ISBN 1-58391-259-2 (pbk)

For
Angela Sheppard
Ross Woodman
Wolfgang Giegerich

Contents

10 The Advent of the Notion   **159**

Foreword

If it had not been such a great tragedy, it would have been a supreme irony. The letters between Vienna and Zurich crossed in the mail. Both had been posted on 3 January 1913. Freud had said in his letter to Jung, "take your full freedom and spare me your supposed 'tokens of friendship'." Jung, taking back some of the earlier harshness that had prompted Freud's comment, wrote that he was "offering . . . friendly wishes for the New Year." But when Jung received Freud's letter on 6 January, he typed on a postcard: "I accede to your wish that we abandon our personal relations, for I never thrust my friendship on anyone." The rest, as one says, is history.

The tragedy was more than personal, more than an unhappy rift between two great men, two pioneering thinkers. It produced a tear in the modern soul, a war between what James Joyce called the Swiss Tweedledee and the Viennese Tweedledum, a rivalry of psychological siblings who embodied the hysterical neuroses that they themselves diagnosed and healed. Each was able to see the stick in the other's eye, but not the log in his own.

Unfortunately the psychological traditions that have followed have contributed to the rift and have widened and deepened it. Latter day Freudians and Jungians continue the war with one-sided caricatures of the other side's positions, like some Cain and Abel or Jacob and Esau. Their distancing of theoretical perspectives in psychology has produced a split between science and religion, sex and spirituality, body and soul, fate and destiny, diagnosis and prognosis, making for a travesty of dogmatic one-sidedness in the practice of therapy.

There was thus a sort of *anima interruptus* in 1913, which produced an either/or: psyche represented as the soul of body, or psyche represented as the soul of spirit. There are exceptions in the tradition, to be sure. There are those who are more dialectical in their logic of the psyche than they are dualistic. One thinks of James Hillman and Wolfgang Giegerich in the Jungian tradition and of Jacques Lacan and Christopher Bollas on the Freudian side. There are others as well. But it is in relation to Hillman and Giegerich, on the one hand, and Lacan and Bollas, on the other, that Greg Mogenson positions himself in this provocative work. By locating himself betwixt and between these major perspectives, the author begins to minister to the harm done to the human soul by a tragedy early in depth psychology's history. He manages what he calls, in the language of Jacques Derrida, a supplement of reading, supplementing both Freudian and Jungian perspectives in terms of each other.

Mogenson notes that the split between Freud and Jung was itself psychological, even archetypal. It had already happened with Plato (Jung) and Aristotle (Freud), and perhaps it is always already happening. Jung might have known this. During the four years following his typing of the fateful postcard, he had worked on a book that would be published first in 1921 under the title, *Psychological Types*. In the epigraph to this work, Jung cited the German poet Heinrich Heine, who had written:

> Plato and Aristotle! These are not merely two systems, they are types of two distinct human natures, which from time immemorial, under every sort of disguise, stand more or less inimically opposed. . . . Although under other names, it is always of Plato and Aristotle that we speak. Visionary, mystical, Platonic natures . . . [and] practical, orderly, Aristotelian natures . . . keep up a constant feud.

In the book that follows this epigraph, Jung applied the typology to Alfred Adler and to Sigmund Freud. He failed to see himself in his own vision.

Mogenson's strategy is to take the two sides of the split into the self, so that the psyche is at once Tweedledum and Tweedledee. This move enables one to see the rivalry of Freud and Jung, and of Freudian and Jungian, as a lovers' quarrel. The book is a sort of mating dance or dating game between Freudian and Jungian perspectives, especially as these perspectives are exemplified in the writings of Christopher Bollas and Wolfgang Giegerich. It represents a *rapprochement*, an engagement, a coming back together and a thinking anew of what nearly a century ago was torn asunder.

There are fundamental differences, to be sure, between Freudian and Jungian perspectives. The author does not blink or gloss real differences. In his critical analysis Mogenson demonstrates the vulnerability of each side. However, in spite of what the author calls "the polarizing rivalry between them [Freud and Jung]," the book demonstrates compellingly that their "visions complement each other," that they need each other for the sake of the human soul. And so the book moves toward an integrated theory of psychology combining Freud's and Jung's views by way, especially, of Bollas and Giegerich.

The clue to Mogenson's argument lies in what Freud and Bollas call "hysteria" and what Jung and Giegerich call "anima" (soul). These terms have feminine overtones in both Freudian and Jungian theory. For a hundred years – from Freud's *Interpretation of Dreams* in 1900 to Bollas's *Hysteria* in 2000, from Jung's *Symbols of Transformation* in 1912 to Giegerich's *The Soul's Logical Life* in 1998 – it is the hysterical and animating soul that has been the ground of psychological theory. Juliet Mitchell, writing recently about hysteria, has argued that "hysteria," the conversion of psychological events into behavioural and physical symptoms, is the dynamic that has been disguised as many other diagnoses, as if soul seduces by way of other names. All the more interesting is it that hysteria and soul (even with the popularity of this latter term in New Age circles) have tended to be slighted increasingly during the past century of psychologizing. Mogenson's argument refocuses theory on what psychology was fundamentally about. The book is not so much an example of the return of the repressed (hysteria and soul) as it is a testimony to the return of repression, and especially repressed sexuality (not only in Jungian tradition, but also, if surprisingly, in Freudian tradition as well).

Not only has sex been repressed, but so also has religion. In what follows in this book the reader will be introduced to a theoretical deconstruction of one-sided psychological dogmatisms; but she or he will also be allowed to be, in Mogenson's felicitous phrase, a "fly on the wall" of the intimate dynamic of the analytic process. This book is about the practice of theory with special focus on the messy situation of transference and countertransference. What Mogenson calls to the reader's attention are the non-personal and trans-personal dimensions in the analytic process, that which he calls the "dove in the consulting room."

It is not only the ghostly and sometimes ghastly dove that informs a person's experience non-personally, haunting experience unconsciously. In Mogenson's skilful writing, other metaphors and myths of religion, and especially the religion of Christianity, also contribute insight into hidden dimensions of analytic experience: immaculate conception, Mary's ear, the stable at Bethlehem, holy family, Herod, flight to Egypt, annunciation, virgin birth, Joseph's (the father's) non-role, Pharisees, Magi, Gabriel the angel, trinity, Pentecost, star. Mogenson is following up on his earlier books – *God is a Trauma* and *Greeting the Angels* – by continuing to show that *post mortem Dei*, whether we like it or not, whether we are religious or secular, we still live in the shadows of a culturally assimilated Christian mythos and theology. In the author's hands, religious narrative gives psychological insight without becoming spiritualizing, which could lead analytic practice into the ether that Freud appropriately, long before the New Age, called a tidal wave of the black mud of occultism.

Mogenson's tracking of psychological theory to religious metaphor has a radical implication. It implies that we are all hysterics. We are living literal lives out of fantasies, and these fantasies have become converted into postmodern realities. Hysteria today, as Mogenson demonstrates compellingly, takes the surprising form of globalization, terrorism, down-sizing, profit maximization, fundamentalism, political correctness, infotainment, internet and cyberspace, an unstable market economy, and money. And this is only a partial list of where the tear in the soul is experienced today.

Mogenson cites the songwriter Leonard Cohen, concerning the tear. In the song, "Anthem," Cohen wrote: "There is a crack, a crack, in everything." Freud and Jung were as clear about this as Cohen is. Freud insisted on the idea of "the fundamental ambiguity" of the self. Similarly, Jung called this nature of the psyche by the Latin phrase *complexio oppositorum*, a "complex of opposites." Like Cohen, both psychologists said that finally we will be "never free." Freud, in the famous last line of *Studies in Hysteria*, wrote: "The goal of analysis is to change neurotic suffering into ordinary human unhappiness." Likewise, in *The Psychology of the Transference*, Jung said: "Like the alchemical end product, which always betrays its essential duality, the united personality will never quite lose the painful sense of innate discord." If psychoanalysts and analytical psychologists who followed their founders have softened or repressed this basic viewpoint of depth psychology, Lacan and Bollas have not, and neither have Hillman and Giegerich. By way of these radical psychologists, Mogenson leads the reader into the "crack" about which Cohen sings with insight and understanding, allowing him or her to have the experience that Goethe must have had when he put these words in Faust's mouth: "Two souls, alas, dwell within my breast!"

After reading this book, these two souls can be named "Freud" and "Jung." Seeing these two figures as within the self not only re-imagines past psychological perspectives, but it thinks them forward, beyond the literal Freud and Jung, and beyond Freudian and Jungian literalisms, in a fundamentally new way.

David L. Miller
Watson-Ledden Professor, Emeritus, Syracuse University
Core Faculty Member, Pacifica Graduate Institute

Acknowledgements

For their encouragement and support along the way as I wrote this book I wish to thank David Miller, Michael Mendis, Wolfgang Giegerich, Angela Sheppard, Michael Adams, Rita Mendis-Mogenson, and Andrew Samuels. I am also grateful to James Hillman for the inspiration which his writings have provided me through many years, and to Paul Kugler, John Desteian, Judith Savage, Peter VanKatwyk, Don Kalsched, Marion Woodman, and Ron Schenk for the roles they have played in my professional life at various times. I am especially grateful to Ross Woodman for his generosity of spirit and speculative strength during the course of countless discussions and fruitful exchanges during the past twenty years.

Permissions

Introduction

Hysteron proteron

A further development of myth might well begin with the outpouring of the Holy Spirit upon the apostles, by which they were made into sons of God, and not only they, but all others who through them and after them received the *filiatio* – sonship of God – and thus partook of the certainty that they were more than autochthonous *animalia* sprung from the earth, that as the twice-born they had their roots in the divinity itself. Their visible, physical life was on this earth; but the invisible inner man had come from and would return to the primordial image of wholeness, to the eternal Father, as the Christian myth of salvation puts it.[1]

C. G. Jung

Needing to adapt to reality – in order to fulfil the other's desire for socialisation – the hysteric hates [the internal father,] a structure that progressively separates the child from the open arms of the virgin mother. The maturational logic of the self – its destiny drive – is ambivalently regarded and true self realisations, through use of the object world, are retarded in order to signify loyalty to a past meant always to repudiate the future. Mother-past and father-future are a couple, the primal scene of which is intended to create a holy ghost in the present, who can magically move back and forth between maternal and paternal orders. This is the picture [of hysteria][2]

Christopher Bollas

It has been said that the history of Western thought is a series of footnotes to Plato and Aristotle. Psychoanalysis and analytical psychology are no exception to this dictum. Their differences as traditions of analysis and schools of thought originate in the contrast between Plato's idealism and Aristotle's empiricism. Jung, with his theory of the archetype, is akin to Plato, while Freud, with his emphasis upon causality and deductive reasoning, is heir to Aristotle. Little wonder, then, that these two men became the progenitors of rival traditions of depth psychology. Whatever their famous parting of the ways was about in their minds during their time, it had, in another sense, happened already. Long before they ever met, their colleagueship was doomed. Though the persons they were had wanted it otherwise, neither could withstand the logic of the God-terms playing through them. And so it was that their names, no less than those of their ancient Athenian precursors, came to be figurative of that rent in the Western soul which they each, at the same time, felt called to heal.

At cocktail parties during the early years of the last century, when psychoanalysis was in the ascendant, Freud and Jung were regularly the topic of polite and nefarious conversation alike. Identifying themselves as introverts or extroverts, people confessed to having complexes and pounced with delight upon one another's slips of the tongue. When news of the bitter split between Freud and Jung reached the same parties, constituencies of opinion spontaneously arose as guests debated which of the two men was right. Reduced in this way to a lowest common denominator, Freud's name became synonymous with sex and aggression, Jung's with humanity's spiritual dimension. Those who believed in the basic goodness of man and in the creativeness of his soul said as much, forming thereby (more by rumour than by reading) the image which Jung has come to have in the popular mind. Those, on the other hand, who were more pessimistic about human motives, or who regarded religion to be an oppressive tyranny, contributed to the popular image of Freud by expressing these sentiments whenever his name, or that of his rival, came up. Long before the psychological theories which are rightfully attached to their names had been fully worked out, "the Swiss Tweedledum" and "the Viennese Tweedledee," as Joyce dubbed them, were popularly acclaimed as spirits of their age.[3]

ψ

Serious students of depth psychology also had to take up the question – Freud or Jung? – at least in the early days of the psychoanalytic movement. One of these, the Protestant minister and lay-analyst, Oskar Pfister, is especially noteworthy in this regard. A Swiss living in Zurich, Pfister was an early member of the psychoanalytic circle in that city. As such, he enjoyed collegial relations with Jung. When Freud and Jung brought their collaborative effort to an end, however, Pfister was forced to work out his own response to the Jungian question. The difficulty here was not over whom to side with; Pfister's loyalty to Freud was unwavering. But as a minister committed to applying analysis to the cure of souls he had more than a little in common with the reprobate Jung. Or so, at least, it might have been thought. Writing to Freud to dispel this impression, Pfister declared himself "finished with the Jungian manner. Those high-falutin interpretations which proclaim every kind of muck to be spiritual jam of a high order and try to smuggle a minor Apollo or Christ into every corked-up little mind simply will not do."[4] Though Pfister never abandoned his commitment to blending analysis, ministry, and education, his repudiation of "the Jungian manner" paved the way for many years of friendly debate with Freud regarding the value (denied to the end by Freud) of religious forms and ideals.

ψ

In his insistence that religious values are compatible with psychoanalysis, Pfister was something of an oddity within the psychoanalytic movement. Heirs to Freud's views on the subject, the vast majority of psychoanalysts, down to the present day, have been thoroughgoing atheists. Eager to show themselves free of that "squeamish concern" for the "higher things in man," which Freud regarded as "unworthy of an analyst,"[5] some even went so far as to wage an unholy war against religious traditions, taking prisoner as many thoughts for the Oedipus-complex as Christianity ever took for Christ.[6]

In this connection we may recall the work of Ernest Jones. In two papers, "The Madonna's conception through the ear"[7] and "A psycho-analytic study of the Holy Ghost concept,"[8] Jones demonstrated his own lack of squeamishness by exposing the Holy Ghost to be nothing but a "displacement from below upwards" of a childhood sexual theory wherein conception is brought about (miraculously enough), through an Oedipally triumphant fart.[9] Applying this interpretation to the Annunciation story, Jones further suggests that within the perverse imaginings of the Christian unconscious, the ear through which Mary is traditionally represented as having been fructified by the Spirit of God is not an ear at all, but rather an anus into which the "intestinal gas" of the castrated father's "lower alimentary orifice" has been expelled.[10]

Within analytical psychology, the attitude taken toward life's religious dimension is exactly the opposite of such psychoanalytic atheism. Following in Jung's footsteps, analysts in this tradition have tended to be spiritually oriented individuals who conceive of the psyche as being animated by a religious instinct. Scholars of myth and religion (if only amateurishly and in their spare time), Jungians turn to the symbolism of world culture in much the same way that Freud turned to what he called "the Witch, Metapsychology."[11] In the symbolism of fairy tale, myth, and religion, they see, as Jung put it, "the whole range of the psychic problem [portrayed] in mighty images."[12] It is only when these "mighty images" are presented within therapy in a haphazard or ham-handed fashion that Pfister's charge of "smuggl[ing] a minor Apollo or Christ into every corked-up little mind" applies.

ψ

From the cocktail parties of the 1920s to the analytic institutes of today, the false dichotomizing of the psyche under the aegis of the Freud–Jung split has had deleterious consequences for analysts and patients alike. As the distinguished British psychoanalyst Nina Coltart has pointed out, "many people who are religiously observant and value their spirituality turn naturally to Jungians when looking for analytic help . . . [with the] secondary result . . . that analysts and therapists in the Freudian tradition do not have experience of dynamic work with religious people sufficient to broaden their views intelligently from the dismissive prejudices which Freud himself undoubtedly harboured."[13]

Within the world of Jungian analysis, a complementary concern has been raised as to whether Jungian practice, for all the attention it pays to the spiritual aspect of the unconscious, is sufficiently differentiated as a clinical enterprise. In the past twenty-five years, much work has been done to remedy what truth there was to this assertion, so much, in fact, that many within analytical psychology now find themselves wondering if their tradition has become so subject to foreign motions that it has lost its own.

ψ

The present book, as its title suggests, is about the spiritual dimension of the psychoanalytic enterprise – the dove in the consulting room. It is also about hysteria; hysteria and the anima in Bollas and Jung. What religion has called soul, and psychoanalysis has called hysteria, Jungian tradition, with a nod to the figure of the inspiratrix or muse, has called the anima. Heir to the "narcissism of minor differences"[14] that alienated Freud and Jung almost a century ago, these are the terms that must be revisited if psychoanalysis and analytical psychology are to renew themselves at their origins for the century to come.

The connection between these several themes is best indicated at this point by means of a bold statement of the book's thesis. Succinctly put, in the pages that follow, we shall be reflecting upon psychoanalysis and analytical psychology in the light of the assertion that *hysteria is the anima, or Madonna even, of the therapeutic psychology that came to prominence during the last century of the Christian aeon.* Our touchstone in this effort will be Christopher Bollas's year 2000 book, *Hysteria*, which we shall attempt to read through Jungian and post-Jungian glasses.

ψ

In a filmed interview given in 1957, an animated if grandfatherly Jung (he was over eighty at the time) made the following statement concerning his concept of the anima (and animus). "The archetype," he explained,

> is a force. It has an autonomy and it can suddenly seize you. It is like a seizure. Falling in love at first sight is something like that. You see, you have a certain image in yourself, without knowing it, of woman, of *the* woman. Then you see that girl, or at least a good imitation of your type, and instantly [Jung's voice rises expressively] you get a seizure and you are gone. And afterwards you may discover that it was a hell of a mistake. A man is quite able, he is intelligent enough, to see that the woman of his "choice," as one says, was no choice, he has been caught! He sees that she is no good at all, that she is a hell of a business, and he tells me so. He says, "For God's sake, doctor, help me to get rid of that woman!" He can't, though, he is like clay in her fingers. That is the archetype, the archetype of the anima. And he thinks it is all his soul, you know! It's the same with the girls. When a man sings very high, a girl thinks

he must have a very wonderful spiritual character because he can sing the high C, and she is badly disappointed when she marries that particular number. Well, that's the archetype of the animus.[15]

Of the many accounts Jung has given of his anima/animus concept, this one, intended for a general audience, is doubtless among the simplest. The merit of this simple account in the present context is that it immediately brings our complicated thesis about hysteria and analysis to life in a familiar way. Just as a man falls in love through a choice that is no choice at all, but rather an *a priori* or archetypally conditioned seizure, so psychoanalysis (here used in a sense inclusive of analytical psychology) owes its existence and much of its subsequent differentiation to its having met, in the syndrome called hysteria, "that girl" in which its own interior image, unconscious trajectory, or implicit logic is outwardly figured.

"Falling in love again, can't help it. Falling in love again." Like the professor enchanted by the cabaret singer in *The Blue Angel*, psychoanalysis, whether it knows it or not, is smitten with that anima it calls hysteria.

Blue angels are one thing, the Madonna another! What could the Divine Mother have to do with analysis and hysteria?

By a flight of ideas (or on the wings of a dove) it would be possible here to present a nexus of interrelated ideas in support of this connection. Hysteria, meaning literally "wandering womb," would remind us (if we were to allow it) of Mary, wandering across Palestine, great with child. In the same associative flash we would recall Breuer's analys and Anna O. The first patient to be treated by the psychoanalytic method, Anna O. developed an erotic transference to her doctor, becoming hysterically pregnant by the force of the "unconscious." And then there are Dora's associations to a dream set in the Dresden art gallery, a place where, as Freud put it, she had once "remained two hours in front of the Sistine Madonna, rapt in silent admiration."[16] But, lest we fall foul of Pfister's derisive comment about turning "every kind of muck into spiritual jam," we shall defer explication of this theme until that time in the book itself when it arises in a more convincing manner by coming of its own accord.

ψ

In the chapter, "Observation of method," of his *Pagan Mysteries in the Renaissance*, Edgar Wind states that "the commonplace may be understood as a reduction of the exceptional, but the exceptional cannot be understood by amplifying the commonplace." Elaborating this point further, Wind adds that "both logically and causally the exceptional is crucial, because it introduces . . . the more comprehensive category."[17] Applied within the present context, these statements indicate something of the approach upon which the current book is based. In the pages that follow we, too, shall insight the commonplace from the perspective of the exceptional. In this venture, as we shall see, the anima and the Holy Spirit will prove to be the crucial terms. For, like necessary angels, they present more comprehensive categories than do those commonplace terms which analysis and hysteria become when taken literally (i.e., as identical with themselves).

ψ

The consulting room as place of the dove is a theme with a multitude of resonances in Jung's thought. In the index to the *Collected Works* there are no fewer than sixty-five listings under the heading "Dove," while 194 are given for "Holy Ghost" and "Holy Spirit." And this is to say nothing of the discussion of these and related themes which can be found in Jung's many letters replying to the queries of theologians and others interested in his psychology of religion.

When discussing these matters, Jung always took great care to protect himself from the charge of psychologism. Again and again he stresses that he has no intention of reducing the spiritual status of figures such as the Holy Ghost or the Madonna to the "nothing but" formulas of personalistic psychology. His aim, rather, is to free psychology from the reductive personalism which has alienated it from the "mighty images" in which its outer circumference and inner infinity are figured. As this is expressed in one of his many essays dealing with religious symbolism, "if Christ and the dark nature-deity [Mercurius] are autonomous images that can be directly experienced, we are obliged to reverse our rationalistic causal sequence, and instead of deriving these figures from our psychic conditions, must derive our psychic conditions from these figures."[18]

The Christ Jung refers to in this quotation is not the historical Jesus, but the symbolical Christ, a mythical personage expressive of what Jung, translating the archaic speech of myth into the terms of our more recent mythologem, psychology,[19] variously calls the collective unconscious, archetype, psychic non-ego, superordinate personality, and self. To derive our psychic conditions from this Christ is to recognize that the psyche, far from being a merely personal affair, has a transpersonal structure which conditions the way we experience everything that happens to us. As Hermann Hesse puts this in a novel based upon his experience in analysis with a pupil of Jung's, "In each individual the spirit is made flesh, in each man the whole of creation suffers, in each one a Saviour is crucified."[20] In his 1937 Terry Lecture, Jung makes much the same point: "Since the life of Christ is archetypal to a high degree, it represents to just that degree the life of the archetype. But since the archetype is the unconscious precondition of every human life, its life, when revealed, also reveals the hidden, unconscious ground-life of every individual . . . what happens in the life of Christ happens always and everywhere. In the Christian archetype all lives of this kind are prefigured. . . ."[21]

ψ

Edward Casey, a philosopher of imagination who has made many significant contributions to the post-Jungian school of archetypal psychology, has said that an image is not what we see, but how we see.[22] When read in connection with Jung's statement about deriving our psychic condition from figures such as Christ and Mercurius, this adage succinctly sums up Jung's psychologically intensive, and yet non-reductive, approach to religion. In contrast to the likes of Ernest Jones, Jung does not study religious symbols with the aim of interpreting or explaining them with reference to something more substantive, objective, literal, or common-place. Rather, he looks through religious symbols as one might look through a lens or magnifying glass. When viewed in this way – not as what we see, but how – religion ceases to be merely an object of study. A lens that is seen through (if only by seeing through itself; *religio* = linking back), its logical form enters the status of the subjective, the status of psychology. This is not to say it has been *reduced* to psychology. On the contrary, through being reflected more deeply into itself, it has been transfigured into the psychological mode of thought which it always already latently or nascently was.

The psychological move, as Jungian analyst Wolfgang Giegerich has recently argued, is always a move against positivity and into reflection.[23] Reflected into itself, religion sloughs off its positivity – its institutional facticity as this or that variety of religion – and becomes psychology. While still there, of course, in its bricks and mortar, rites and rituals, it is read differently now, metaphorically, psychologically. As Giegerich puts this, inasmuch as it is based upon the negation of empirically-based consciousness, and thus has no referent outside the all-encompassing sense of the "inner" which it brings, psychological consciousness takes religion (as well as science and medicine, etc.) up into itself as a sublated moment within its more comprehensive vision.[24] Far from being reductive with respect to religion, psychology (here to be distinguished from the behavioural science that everywhere takes its name in vain) is a new dispensation, not of religion any more, since the logical status has changed, but of "sublated religion."[25]

That this is so is particularly evident in the case of the Jewish and Christian traditions out of which both psychoanalysis and analytical psychology have emerged. The statements of the historical Jesus (to take but one example) already bear witness to the interiorizing process, the move against positivity and towards reflection, that constitutes psychology. Almost everything that the gospels report Jesus as having said during the course of his life has a deliteralizing, interiorizing effect on the matter at hand. One thinks immediately of his Sermon on the Mount. In this sermon, he takes up the laws of the Mosaic Decalogue one by one, re-articulating them in a more subtle and internally binding manner. Even more important is Jesus' teaching regarding the mystical (i.e., inner, subjective, psych-ological) form of himself (or successor to himself) that he will leave within the Christian psyche after his death. Speaking to the disciples at the Last Supper, Jesus said, "It is for your own good that I am going, because unless I go the Advocate [Paraclete], will not come to you; but if I do go, I will send him to you" (John 16:7).

Are we to conclude from these thoughts and associations that psychology itself is the Paraclete which Christ's death (or conceiving this more broadly, the decline of Christian symbolism generally) has left in its wake? Is this loss of symbolism the greater transference which our lesser transferences have been conceived to

resolve? Tertullian said that the soul is naturally Christian. Further to this statement (and leaving to one side the issue of the other faiths), is it not more accurate
today to say that both psychoanalysis and analytical psychology alike are in a
similar sense post-Christian?

ψ

Jung, as we have seen, honours religion by turning to its symbolism for perspective. His manner of doing so, however, differs considerably from that of the
theologian. The crux of this difference lies in the special, interiorized meaning
that he gives to the word "transcendent." In theological discourse, the term
"transcendent" is used mainly in an ontological sense. When, for example, a theologian speaks of God as being transcendent, he or she affirms the existence of
the deity as a metaphysical *entity*. Jung's use of the term, by contrast, is strictly
epistemological.[26] That is to say, in Jung's view, it is the mind itself that is
transcendent, if only in the negative sense of its "structure . . . [being] responsible
for anything we may assert about metaphysical matters."[27]

   Jung's position here may remind us of Lacan's notion of the letter in the unconscious.[28] Because all experience is psychically mediated, there is a gap, or
fissure, between the psychic image or signifier and its transcendental signified,[29]
between the God-image(s) and God. As Jung puts this:

> It is only through the psyche that we can establish that God acts upon us, but
> we are unable to distinguish whether these actions emanate from God or from
> the unconscious. We cannot tell whether God and the unconscious are two
> different entities. Both are border-line concepts for transcendental contents.[30]

In this passage Jung does not reduce the God of theological discourse to the unconscious. As a psychologist, he has nothing to say, one way or the other, about the
existence of God as a metaphysical entity. However, in making the point he does
about our inability to distinguish between the actions of God and those emanating
from the unconscious, he deconstructs those texts of theology which, from time
immemorial, have positivized "God" within a metaphysics of presence. The result
of this is that the God-image is released from the hegemony of theologically
approved meanings, becoming perceptible within ourselves once more as that
(referent-free and, yet, all-referring) negated or floating signifier which tradition
has called the Holy Spirit or Holy Ghost.

ψ

But how, then, does God, in this "inner, transcendental"[31] or psychological sense
figure in analysis? Or, to ask the question in another way, how is the dove in the
consulting room to be recognized as such?

   In his 1951 book, *Aion: Researches into the Phenomenology of the Self*, Jung quotes a passage from the second-century Gnostic writer, Monoïmos, which sheds much light upon these questions:

> Seek him from out thyself, and learn who it is that taketh possession of every-thing in thee, saying: *my* god, *my* spirit, *my* understanding, *my* soul, *my* body; and learn whence is sorrow and joy, and love and hate, and waking though one would not, and sleeping though one would not, and getting angry though one would not, and falling in love though one would not. And if thou shouldst closely investigate these things, thou wilt find Him in thyself, the One and the Many, like to that little point . . . for it is in thee that he hath his origin and his deliverance.[32]

In keeping with the spirit of this passage, Jungian analysis may be described as an interpretative vision which constitutes itself by means of an interminable process of discrimination wherein the subjective will of the patient, analyst, or analytic couple is again and again differentiated out from and confronted with the will (if we may call it that) of that ego-transcending, and hence God-like, "Other," the unconscious. The purpose of this discriminative process or interpretative vision is to facilitate a dialectical relationship between the ego and the unconscious.

The expression, "dialectical relationship with the unconscious,"[33] like the older idea of a conversation with one's good angel, refers to the healthy middle-road between the pathological extremes of alienation and identification. People who are alienated from the unconscious tend to experience symptoms such as depressive moods and depersonalization. They complain of feeling empty, listless, or bored. Life for them has become quite meaningless. Those, on the other hand, whose consciousness is identified with, or possessed by, one or another of the principalities and powers that potentiate the unconscious tend to become manic, obsessional, or paranoid. Life for them can be said to be too meaningful. In both cases, it is equally crucial that the individuals in question come to recognize that their experience is not something that they have fabricated, but something that happens to them.[34]

ψ

"What mankind has called 'God' from time immemorial you experience every day," declares Jung in a letter written the same year that his *Aion* appeared.

> You only give him another, so-called "rational" name – for instance, you call him "affect." Time out of mind he has been the psychically stronger, capable of throwing your conscious purposes off the rails, fatally thwarting them and occasionally making mincemeat of them. Hence there are not a few who are afraid "of themselves." God is then called "I myself," and so on.[35]

In an interview given in 1955, Jung makes a very similar statement concerning the psychological application of the term "God."

Without knowing it man is always concerned with God. What some people call instinct or intuition is nothing other than God. God is the voice inside us which tells us what to do and what not to do. In other words, our conscience. . . . Consciously or unconsciously [mankind today] is once more groping for God. I make my patients understand that all the things which happen to them against their will are a superior force. They can call it God or devil, and that doesn't matter to me, as long as they realize that it is a superior force. God is nothing more than that superior force in our life. You can experience God every day.[36]

Jung's intention in these passages is not to say what God *is*. Speaking as the founder of a contemporary school of depth psychology, his aim, rather, is to convey the essence of his analytic attitude. This attitude, as we have seen, is based upon the recognition that the subject in the diminutive sense, the ego-personality or "I", is utterly transcended or negated by a greater subject. This greater subject, it is important to stress, is not a positively existing entity.[37] On the contrary, like that *deus absconditus* of Lacanian theory, the phallus, it exists within and brings to bear the status of negation.[38] We could also say, the status of reflection, the status of thought. Just as the "spirit," according to Rilke, "loves in the swing of the figure nothing so much as the point of inflection,"[39] so Jung's greater subject, especially when thought of as the unity-in-difference of whatever happens to us and "God" (or "devil"), inflects, deconstructs, and logically negates the more rationalistic God-terms we assign to such events but otherwise tend not to see through – "affect," "instinct," "conscience," "intuition," "I myself," and so on.[40]

Neti-neti: as each of these too-knowing terms for the unconscious is rejected (even as Freud rejected the seduction theory) a new, *psychological* register of experience is constituted. Initiated by his or her symptoms into psychology, the patient learns to "let things happen in the psyche," to "not know beforehand," to live a "symbolic life." What our pious forebears, living within a religious onto-logy, had called the "outpouring of the Holy Spirit," "the baptism in the Holy Ghost," and by still other names, the contemporary analyst and analysand, living within psychology's parenthetical "ontology" and speaking in its God-terms, call the "autonomous," and therefore "numinous," "reality of the psyche."

In symptoms, dreams, and transference/countertransference enactments, the psyche asserts its imperatives, even as in earlier times God had visited his people with tribulation and deliverance and was himself changed in relation to their suffering of him.[41] What the analyst and/or patient had previously identified with as *their* subjectivity, reveals itself, theophanically, to have an objective, transper-sonal aspect. Likewise, the cultural form of this subjectivity, therapeutic psych-ology itself, is shown to be, as Jung put it, "a sphere but lately visited by the numen, where the whole weight of mankind's problems have settled."[42]

ψ

But what about God in the sense of traditional belief? God in the sense of a wholly other, absolutely transcendent deity? Is depth psychology, as the theologian Martin Buber worried, an eclipse of God?

Like it or not, our age is a psychological one, and under these conditions God can only be known immanently, as an image, emotion, or idea in the soul. Heir to the religion which preceded it, psychology itself has the character of a theophany. While such an assertion will, no doubt, arouse the resistances of those who can construe it only as a confinement of God within human limits – so small is their notion of psychology – it may also be understood as a deepening extension of God along the axis of human experience.

Jung's psychology of religion is not a discarding of God, but a deeper surrender to that "most certain and immediate of experiences" which Jung considers God to be.[43] Indeed, from his point of view, it is quite as if the God from whom the author of the 139th Psalm cannot flee, no matter in which direction he travels, extends into us as well, such that the epistemological cul-de-sac which psychological criticism reckons the psyche to be, far from eclipsing God,[44] is but another expression of the inescapable presence of God – hence Jung's repeated reference to the *imago dei* and his coining of the term "immanent–transcendent."[45] As Jung expresses this at the end of his *Answer to Job*, "even the enlightened person remains what he is, and is never more than his own limited ego before the One who dwells within him, whose form has no knowable boundaries, who encompasses him on all sides, fathomless as the abysms of the earth and vast as the sky."[46]

ψ

The emphasis which Jung and subsequent analytical psychologists have given to the religious dimension of the psyche should not lead us to conclude that the spirit's dove is exclusive to the consulting rooms of Jungian analysts – or even that it is *necessarily* to be found there at all. "The spirit," as Jesus said to Nicodemus, "bloweth where *it* listeth."[47] It cannot be cooped up. Not even in theories and doctrines that have been inspired by its recognition. Archetype, wholeness, individuation, and Self – these notions, for all their importance, have long been positivized within the discourse of analytical psychology. Even the term "un-conscious," in both its personal and collective senses, seems to designate something familiar and known to us now. The same can be said of the God-terms which underpin the discourse and practice of contemporary psychoanalysis. Perhaps this is why many within analytical psychology and psychoanalysis find that they have a more meaningful second analysis with an analyst from a rival school – this despite, or rather because of, the resultant confusion of tongues.

ψ

But how does the spirit that "bloweth where it listeth" come to manifest itself in the consulting room of analysts of the Freudian tradition?

In a letter to a correspondent Jung writes that "just as through preconceived opinions [one] can hold back or actually stop the *influxus divinus* [divine influence], wherever it may come from, it is also possible for [one] through the suitable behaviour to come nearer to it and, when it happens, to accept it. [One] cannot force anything; [one] can only make an effort to do everything that favors this and nothing that goes against it. . . . What can, but not necessarily will, then come about is the kind of spontaneous action arising from the unconscious that has been symbolized by the alchemists, Paracelsus, Böhme, and modern students of the unconscious as *lightning*."[48]

From a Jungian perspective, Freud's reductionistic theory, so hostile to the higher things in man, would seem to be itself a most pernicious example of the "preconceived opinions" that one would expect to "hold back or actually stop the *influxus divinus*." However, as Jung himself frequently noted, Freudian interpretations may also be used against the complexes that foreclose the patient's relationship to the spirit (however this is referred to), thereby facilitating what Jung, in another letter, calls the "approach to the numinous."[49] And this is to say nothing of the many contributions that Winnicott, Bion, Lacan, and others working within the Freudian tradition have made with respect to the analysis of pathological structures and the welcoming of that uncanny guest, the unconscious. Winnicott's concept of the "true self," which he also refers to as "the spontaneous gesture" and distinguishes from a "false self," merits special mention here, especially in light of its subsequent development in the writings of such third-generation analysts as Michael Eigen and Christopher Bollas.

As for the psychoanalytic correlate of Jung's statement about doing everything that favours reception of the *influxus divinus* and nothing that goes against it, in this connection we may think, first and foremost, of the "fundamental rule" of psychoanalytic practice as set out by Freud. The requirement of the patient, that he or she say whatever comes to mind, no matter how irrelevant, embarrassing, or difficult it may seem – this, when combined with the special kind of diffuse listening on the part of the analyst that Freud characterized as "evenly-hovering attention,"[50] creates a potential space in the consulting room in which the spirit that "bloweth where it listeth," i.e., the sudden ideas that erupt from the unconscious, may manifest themselves in that lightning flash of awareness or insight of which Jung spoke. "*Freier Einfall*," or, as this is known to English-speaking analysts, "free association": it is through the practice of this technique above all others that psychoanalysis becomes what Emily Dickinson said art aspires to be, "a house that tries to be haunted."[51]

ψ

Besides free association and evenly hovering attention, there is another fundamental feature of psychoanalysis that favours reception of the *influxus divinus*, or as we might also express this, the eruption of the unconscious. We have already mentioned this in passing in our earlier discussion of psychology as being constituted by the move against positivity and into reflection. I refer, of course, to Freud's so-called rejection of the seduction theory. Wandering about in that womb of wonders that his consulting room was turned into by his hysterical patients, Freud first came to believe that their illness was a result of their having been sexually abused during childhood. This view, which psychoanalysis would push off from when Freud rejected it, was already (nascently) psychological insofar as it deliteralized the earlier aetiological theory that attributed hysteria to the passing on of a hereditary taint. Freud's project, however, became still more psychological as the result of his subsequent rejection of this view too. Expressing this in the Hegelian language of Giegerich, we could say that with this doubling up of negation, reflection came home to itself. Hysteria was now regarded as having an immanent, i.e., psychological, cause. Fantasy, not fact, was recognized as the principle aetiological factor. As Freud wrote to Fliess, "there is no 'indication of reality' in the unconscious, so that one cannot distinguish between truth and fiction that has been cathected with affect."[52] With this insight, gleaned from his work with hysterical patients, the notion of psychical reality was parthenogenetically born.

Of course, the phrase "rejection of the seduction theory" is really a misnomer. Freud did not reject the seduction theory, or even its predecessor, the inheritance theory. On the contrary, he rescued and retained (Hegel's *aufgehoben*) both these explanations within the wider view that resulted from their deliteralization and interiorization. Psychoanalysis (and analytical psychology, too, for that matter) unfolds its notional life through an infinite series of just such acts of deliteralization or interiorization. Indeed, just as Freud negated the seduction theory (while retaining his interest in sexual trauma), so those who follow after him must reflect *any* positive fact or theory into itself in order to stay the psyche's course. Nothing outside the psyche may be permitted to explain the psyche. For "psychoanalysis," as Freud said, "goes by itself."[53] Drives, the breast, family dynamics, social inter-action – though all of these "positivities" may come to symbolize psyche (inasmuch as the unconscious appears first in projected form) or be objects of psychological reflection, none has the status of an explanatory principle or psychic cause. In order to create that freedom for itself that it wishes to afford its patients, psych-ology must say to itself again and again what Freud wrote to Fliess as he pushed off from the seduction theory into psychoanalysis proper: "Initially I defined the aetiology [of hysteria] too narrowly; the share of fantasy in it is far greater than I had thought in the beginning."[54] No matter what aetiological account is given of hysteria, this statement bears repeating. Indeed, reflecting Freud's statement into itself, we could say – and will in the pages that follow with reference to both Christopher Bollas's and Juliet Mitchell's theories – that, for all the aetiological accounts of itself it has inspired, hysteria, that *femme fatale* of psychiatry's positivizing mind, has no aetiology itself – hence our designation of it as the anima of psychoanalysis.

ψ

But what has that empty sepulchre of a concept – logical negativity – to do with hysteria? Doubtful that what has been suffered in the flesh by a patient can overcome itself to live again as theory, a positivistic Thomas in us wants to touch the symptoms in this notion. Is it truly they, he asks, the stigmata of hysteria, that have been sublated into psychoanalytic thought?

Summarizing the observations of Charcot, Janet, Myers, Breuer, Freud, and other investigators of his day, William James notes that "one of the most constant symptoms in persons suffering from hysterical disease in its extreme forms consists in alterations of the natural sensibility of various parts of the body." These alterations, he continues, are usually in "the direction of defects, or anaesthesia."

> One or both eyes are blind, or color blind, or there is . . . blindness to one half the field of view, or the field is contracted. Hearing, taste, and smell may similarly disappear, in part or in totality. Still more striking are the cutaneous anaesthesias. The old witchfinders looking for the "devil's seals" learned well the existence of these insensible patches on the skin of their victims, to which the minute physical examinations of modern medicine have but recently again attracted attention. They may be scattered anywhere but are very apt to affect one side of the body. Not infrequently they affect an entire lateral half, from head to foot, and the insensible skin of, say, the left side will then be found separated from the naturally sensitive skin of the right by a perfectly sharp line of demarcation down the middle of the front and back. Sometimes, most remarkable of all, the entire skin, hands, feet, face, everything, and the mucous membranes, muscles and joints so far as they can be explored, become completely insensible without the other vital functions becoming gravely disturbed.[55]

Anticipating the psychology-constituting move from positivity to reflection, hysteria negativizes the organs of sense, through which the world in its positivity is empirically known. The eyes become partially or even entirely blind. In other cases, a similar "anaesthesia" occludes one or another of the other perceptual organs. When, however, it is shown that none of these defects has a basis in the pathology of the actual physiological systems involved, the medical mind is turned back upon itself and forced to think in non-medical ways about the illness. Positive physiological explanations give way to negative, psychological ones. Disorder appearing in the body is recognized to point in another direction, to the order of the *un*conscious. Hysteria's essence is reasoned to be mental. For these reasons alone hysteria may be regarded as the positivistic precursor of logical negativity.

ψ

Another question must be considered if we are to set out as we must, *hysteron proteron*,[56] from that end-point or final insight which the present book unfolds: why Bollas?

A straightforward answer to this question would lead us to consider Bollas's many contributions to psychoanalysis. In the course of such a discussion, appreciation for the lucidity of his thought, the meditative richness of his prose, and his many insights would pave the way to critical appraisal. Succumbing to the temptation to speak personally, I might even attempt to convey something of what I, as a Jungian analyst, have learned from this contemporary psychoanalytic author. And on the basis of this, a comparative study might then be made of Jung and Bollas. In the course of such a study, Bollas's notion of the destiny drive would in all likelihood be compared to Jung's notion of individuation, his concept of the transformational object to Jung's ideas concerning the transformative symbol, and so on. Such a venture, however, will not be undertaken in these pages. On the contrary, and consistent with the tenor of our discussion so far, our interest is, rather, in what might be called the *negative* Bollas.

While it is certainly true that Bollas in his positivity is the author of the theories that the commonsense and academic mentalities alike attribute to him, it is also possible to "inflect" or "see through" the positivized contributions of the positive Bollas to the universal that he, as the author of this or that idea, exemplifies. Viewed in this way, as being the signatory of all that he in addition to himself is not, a lens or metaphor, the "Bollas" of these pages stands for, or better said, *as*, the more inclusive or embracing category – psychoanalysis itself at the Millennium.

"Theories of mental life and human behaviour will come and go much as they have since the beginning of psychoanalysis," writes Bollas, embracing the negativizing process that theory-making in psychology essentially is. "What will not change is the deeply evocative effect of the psychoanalytical situation and its method."[57]

But still the question remains: why Bollas and not another theorist? Winnicott, Bion, Lacan, or Klein – why Bollas and not one of these analytic giants upon whose shoulders his work stands?

Simply put, it is because he, or rather through him, psychoanalysis itself, has met "that girl" we heard about earlier from Jung.

"You have a certain image in yourself, without knowing it, of woman, of *the* woman," Jung told his audience.

> Then you see that girl, or at least a good imitation of your type, and instantly you get a seizure and you are gone. And afterwards you may discover that it was a hell of a mistake. A man is quite able, he is intelligent enough, to see that the woman of his "choice," as one says, was no choice, he has been caught! He sees that she is no good at all, that she is a hell of a business, and he tells me so. He says, "For God's sake, doctor, help me to get rid of that woman!" He can't, though, he is like clay in her fingers. That is the archetype, the archetype of the anima.[58]

Psychoanalysis has wrestled with that siren of psychic reflectivity, the anima, through few contemporary analysts as cannily as it has through Christopher

Bollas. Railing against her in some of his writings, he has been her poet-philosopher in others. Beginning with the first of these engagements – Bollas's effort to free the analytic mind from the treacherous seductress that the anima can undoubtably be – we shall, towards the middle of the book (in the spirit of analytic play), bring out the anima-friendly aspect of his work by staging a production of "My Fair Hysteria," in which the part of "Bollas" is played by Professor Higgins and that of the hysteric by Miss Doolittle. Throughout these ventures, a "supplement of reading" will be provided, drawing upon the perspectives of analytical psychology. The effect of this reading will be, in the first place, to negate Bollas's personalistically conceived theory of hysteria (and by implication, psychoanalytic theory generally), if only to then rescue and retain these under the wider perspective of that "stone which the builders rejected," analytical psychology. In the course of this effort much will be said further to the issues introduced here with regard to the spiritual dimension of analysis. And finally, in the last sections of the book, the various themes and subthemes discussed along the way will be considered in the light of that further move against positivity and into reflection which psychology is only beginning to reckon with: the sublation of the anima's sensuous, object-determined imagining mode, or, as this might also be figured, the negativization of the dove. For, as Giegerich has recently shown, it is through the negation of that form of negativity or reflection that the imagination constitutes with its images that the spirit's life asserts its sovereignty in our day.[59]

Chapter 1

"That Girl"

As with the Siren seducing Odysseus, [the] hysterical [patient's] narrative-performance is meant to entrap any self that would assume its intended journey. Knowing that psychoanalysis is his or her co-invention, the hysteric assumes possession of the psychoanalyst, and demands that the analyst sacrifice his or her own personal ambitions to the violent charms of the other. The analyst is meant to be spell-bound and shipwrecked. He or she is meant to give up the profession. As we shall see . . . the hysteric becomes addicted to the transference. . . . [H]e or she insists that analysis become sexualised and the analyst become its victim.[1]

Christopher Bollas

[I]t costs [people] enormous difficulties to understand what the anima is. They accept her easily enough when she appears in novels or as a film star, but she is not understood at all when it comes to seeing the role she plays in their own lives, because she sums up everything that a man can never get the better of and never finishes coping with. Therefore it remains in a perpetual state of emotionality which must not be touched. The degree of unconsciousness one meets with in this connection is, to put it mildly, astounding.[2]

C. G. Jung

Leda and the analyst

What does the future hold for psychoanalysis? Time itself prompts the question, the centenary of the movement coinciding, as it has, with the end of the millennium. Will the beginning of a new century, the dawn of a new aeon, bring with it an essential change in the spirit of the age? And, if so, will psychoanalysis continue to have relevance? Or will the new era before us require entirely different perspectives? Our practices are down. Will psychoanalysis go the way of the dinosaur and the dodo?

Freud completed his *Interpretation of Dreams* in 1899, but had it released in its first edition with a publication date of 1900. With this simple gesture he distanced the science he hoped to found from the nineteenth century, which would soon pass, and placed it at the cutting edge of the twentieth.

In light of this history, it is reasonable, I believe, to assume that a psychological treatise bearing the publication date of the year 2000 might be especially pertinent to the question of psychoanalysis and the future. Such a book, we might expect, whatever it purports to be about, would be inspired, to some extent, by the millennialist fears to which we are all subject with respect to the possible end of (our psychoanalytic) history.

These reflections, which I am sure are not latent in myself alone, became manifest to me as my eye fell upon the publication date of Christopher Bollas's new book, *Hysteria*: "First published in 2000. . . ." How bold, I thought, to publish a book with *that* date. And the title! Psychoanalysis began with hysteria. And here is a book, a *clinical* book, which addresses that syndrome again.

What I had surmised at a glance was borne out when I came round to reading the book. The science of soul that began with hysterical neurosis at the beginning of the last century is reaffirmed in its pages for the century to come with reference to hysterical character. Like Freud before him, Bollas discovers or, rather, rediscovers the significance of infantile sexuality in the formation of personality in Western culture. Repressed sexual ideas, indifference to conversion, and over-identification with the other – these and other hallmarks of hysteria are not, in Bollas's view, yesterday's symptoms. On the contrary, hysteria (now in its characterological form) is as ubiquitous as it ever was. Perhaps, it is even more prevalent today insofar as it can now be recognized as readily in men as in women.

But how can it be, after a century of the sexual revolution, that we still suffer the consequences of repressed sexual ideas? Was the hysteria with which psychoanalysis began not merely a pathological spin-off of the prurient mores of the Victorian times in which Freud worked? Can we still credit the significance of repressed sexuality in the age of the rock video, the sitcom, and Dr Ruth?

As influential as cultural attitudes are in the shaping of our relationship to sexuality, their aetiological significance with respect to hysteria is quite secondary, in Bollas's view, to that of sexuality itself. Simply put, with its first appreciable appearance within the family during early childhood, sexuality has a traumatic effect upon *all* children insofar as it "'destroys' the relation to the mother, transfiguring her from 'mamma', the infant's caregiver, to 'mother', the child's and father's sex object."[3] While many children, with their parents' help, are able to navigate this fall from innocence into sexual knowledge, achieving adulthood with the passage of years, others tenaciously resist this development, becoming hysterical, pseudo-adults as a result. As Bollas puts it,

> The hysteric elects to perpetuate a child innocent as the core self, endeavouring to be the ideal boy or girl throughout a lifetime. He or she is always performing this child through the body of the adult, impishly undermining the ostensible effect of the biological maturation of the self. He or she is the 'child within' who castrates the self's achievements in the real by periodic uprisings that shed the self of the accoutrements of accomplishment. This psychic position is to serve as the fountain of youth, driving off ageing and death, and conferring upon the hysterical character a sense of immortality.[4]

In working out his thesis, Bollas displays abundantly the penetrating insight, clinical acumen, and therapeutic brilliance that has earned him the distinguished place he holds in contemporary psychoanalysis. Reading the book, the practising clinician, I am sure, will learn something from nearly every page. Technical considerations related to the use of countertransference in diagnosis (to name but one example) are adumbrated with generous lucidity. Many patients, we learn, who are currently regarded as suffering from borderline personality disorder, dissociative disorder, anorexia nervosa and still other illnesses are, in fact, hysterics in disguise. Among hospitalized patients, too, Bollas opines, there are many hysterics tragically living out their lives misdiagnosed as manic-depressives and schizophrenics.[5] Hysteria, in short, is a great mimic, able to manifest the clinical features of many maladies. And it is this, in Bollas's view, mimicry and misdiagnosis – not a reduction in the incidence of actual hysteria – that has led to the widespread but erroneous belief that hysteria is largely a diagnosis of the past.

But what of the millennialist anxieties that I suggested might be found in a book bearing the publication date of the year 2000? These, I believe, are in evidence when one considers the tenor of the book as a whole. In his earlier works, Bollas hospitably welcomes the reader into the meditative richness of his thinking process. When he presents a thesis or introduces a new concept, one feels its authentic origins in the evenly hovering attentiveness of analytic listening. In this powerfully presented and passionately argued book, however, one finds something else – *irritability*.

The originator of the concept of the "unthought known," Bollas, I am sure, needs no lesson from me on "negative capability." Indeed, his earlier works are exemplary of an analytic attitude that can be "in uncertainty, Mysteries, doubts, without any irritable reaching after fact & reason."[6] And yet, in the case of his latest book, *Hysteria*, I am struck by the presence of precisely that spirit of irritability that Keats touches on in this line.

Although ostensibly a work of clinical psychoanalysis, Bollas's *Hysteria* reads like a manifesto. In chapter after chapter, there is a driving quality, a nailing down, an interpretative violence. It is as if Bollas is fed up with the wily innocence of hysteria and with the collusive willingness of contemporary psychoanalysis to believe that hysteria has all but disappeared. The hysteric, he points out, is violent too, violently innocent.[7] Well, the gloves are off. No more will Bollas put up with psychoanalysis playing cuckold to the coquettish allure of this most autoerotic of patients. If, after a century on the couch, hysteria remains "the still unravished bride of quietess," it's high time that her virginity were tried. In the Name-of-the-(Lacanian)-Father, if not of Zeus, Bollas descends upon hysteria like the swan that ravished Leda. With Yeats, we are left to wonder:

> Being so caught up,
> So mastered by the brute blood of the air,
> Did she put on his knowledge with his power
> Before the indifferent beak could let her drop?[8]

Anima hystericus

The analytical psychologist, reading Bollas's *Hysteria* as part of an effort to integrate something of the perspectives of contemporary psychoanalysis into his practice of Jungian analysis, will be put in mind of the contributions of his own school to the problematic discussed in its pages. While admiring the clinical differentiation that the tradition Bollas draws upon has achieved in its hundred-year span, and perhaps even feeling a little wanting beside the immensity of this achievement, he will also sense that analytical psychology's *less* may well be *more* insofar as the lens provided by its concepts allows him to see the psychic forest, which his colleagues in mainstream psychoanalysis would seem to have missed, so acute is their perception of its trees. This, at least, has been my experience as a Jungian analyst working my way through Bollas's book.

Reading the literature of psychoanalysis in general, and Bollas's *Hysteria* in particular, I have been struck by the attention that is given to the classification of psychopathology. Subject, evidently, to a medical model, patients in this tradition are diagnosed as suffering from a particular illness, such as hysterical, borderline, schizoid, or depressive character disorder, etc., and treated with reference to the enormous compendium of clinical knowledge that has been built up during the past century.

The literature of analytical psychology, by contrast (with the notable exception of the developmental school), has given far less attention to diagnostics. Nor has it adumbrated anything comparable to what psychoanalysis has contributed in the area of methodology and technique – at least not in its written tradition. Patients are not regarded as hysterics, paranoiacs, or depressives, etc., requiring treatment in light of the positivized findings of prior experience with these syndromes. On the contrary, the patient is conceived, first and foremost, to be an *individual* whose suffering, for that very reason, may be discontinuous with what we in psychology already think we know about it. This is so even when the patient would seem to be a classic case of this or that disorder.

What is true of the patient is true of the analyst as well. He or she, too, is an individual first, the practitioner of a particular method or technique second. "Experience has taught me," writes Jung,

> to keep away from therapeutic "methods" as much as from diagnoses. The enormous variation among individuals and their neuroses has set before me the ideal of approaching each case with a minimum of prior assumptions. The ideal would naturally be to have no assumptions at all. But this is impossible even if one exercises the most rigorous self-criticism, for one is *oneself* the biggest of all one's assumptions, and the one with the gravest consequences. Try as we may to have no assumptions and to use no ready-made methods, the assumption that I myself am will determine my method: as I am, so will I proceed.[9]

But how then, if not through diagnosis, does analytical psychology understand the various manifestations of psychopathology? This question, born of the contrast between psychoanalysis and analytical psychology, was simultaneously raised in my mind and answered as I read Bollas's *Hysteria*. The lucid discussion in that book of the various transferences and countertransferences with which the analyst must struggle when treating patients of different diagnostic types reminded me of another seminal book, one from my own tradition, *The Psychology of the Transference*. Writing in 1946 (but some fifty and more years ahead of his time at that), Jung speaks in this work, not of hysteria, perversion, multiple personality, and all the rest, but of the anima and animus. Regarded from within the purview of analytical psychology, the various character disorders may be subsumed under the names of these archetypal figures, at least insofar as the clinical encounter and the transference are concerned.

But what did Jung mean by anima and animus? There are many avenues one might take with respect to this question. Popularly understood, these terms refer to the contrasexual side of the personality – the anima corresponding to the so-called "inner woman" in a man and the animus to the "inner man" in a woman. More deeply comprehended, however, the anima and animus are mediating figures which personify the innate potentials of the collective unconscious. In contrast to the familial complexes, which tend to bring a more or less oppressive sense of repetition and fate (being rooted, as they are, in one's actual developmental history and object relations), the anima and animus, with their roots in the "timeless" or "eternal" world of the archetypal psyche, inspire our lives, at times to a dangerous degree, with a sense of purpose or destiny. In this connection we may think of the princess of a fairy tale, an anima-figure who frequently presents the heroic masculine ego with challenging tasks or difficult trials which open new vistas of experience while, at the same time, transforming him. The same motif may be conceived in terms of the transformation of the feminine ego that occurs as a consequence of putting the masculine, animus-hero to work.

Of course, in our day and age any theory that is conceived in terms of gender differences is highly suspect. And the anima/animus notion has been given short shrift in contemporary discourse on this account. To clarify the concept in light of this situation, it is important to stress that the gender of the anima/animus is not a function of the "facts" of literal gender.[10] Rather, it is as the negation of these. Just as the phallus, in Lacanian theory, is not to be confused with the penis, so too the absently-present femininity of the anima and the absently-present masculinity of the animus are not reducible to the masculinity and femininity of men and women in their biological, sociological, and anthropological positivity. On the contrary, the concept was first developed by Jung as a way of reflectively containing and imaginatively comprehending aspects of the self's otherness that appear in the form of projections that distort perception of the opposite sex. Pushing off from the literalness of gender, while at the same time retaining the gender opposites under sublation as a mode of imagining, we may understand the contrasexuality of the anima and animus as a radical metaphor of the Otherness of the psyche as well as of that non-identity with ourselves and with one another that is one of love's main lessons. Just as many languages have grammatical gender, so too has the language of symptoms and dreams, attachments, and desires.

When projected onto the persons, places, and things with which we live, the anima/animus engenders a sense of spirited aliveness, or, as James Hillman – the main contributor to the differentiation of this notion since Jung – would put it, soul.[11] Subjected to the sublating influence of these inspiring and, yet, tricksterishly de-literalizing and negativizing agents, perception changes. Objects – internal or external – are no longer perceived as being simply identical with what they positively, empirically, or literally are. On the contrary, they are apperceived in terms of something else that they are like – suffused, we might say, with the light of nature or life of metaphor.

Finding himself the recipient of such a projection, the analyst may believe that he is being presented with transferences derived from the patient's early childhood. Though he may, to be sure, have to deal with such transferences, those issuing from the anima/animus have a very different background. Born, not of the personal unconscious, but of the collective unconscious, the productions of the anima/animus infuse the experience of even the most intact and mature adult with precisely those energies of life and imperatives of wholeness of which the facilitating environment of the developing ego has been largely unaware. Having reached the zenith of its assimilative power (we may think in this connection of the famous "mid-life crisis"), the ego, rather than continuing to "develop," is now relativized and transformed, often violently, by contents of the collective unconscious that are so remote from the subject's previous experience that they may be symbolized as culturally, geographically, historically, and sexually "foreign." It is this transformative process of ego relativization and enrichment (as opposed to the earlier, precursive stage of ego-development), that Jung referred to when he spoke of self-realization, personality integration, and individuation.

This bare-bones description of the anima/animus, I believe, is sufficient to support the comparison between their phenomenology, as archetypal figures, and the clinical phenomenology that Bollas describes with respect to the hysteric. It also goes a long way in accounting for Bollas's forceful style and irritability. These are typical countertransference reactions when the totalizing vision of a strongly accentuated interpretive consciousness must contend with that mistress of anomalies, the anima.

In the quotation cited at the outset of this chapter, Bollas likens the hysteric, with her extravagant narrative performances, to the mythological figure of the Siren, who would have lured Odysseus to destruction had he succumbed to her song. "Knowing that psychoanalysis is his or her co-invention," writes Bollas in this passage, "the hysteric assumes possession of the psychoanalyst, and demands that the analyst sacrifice his or her own personal ambitions to the violent charms of the other." "The analyst," he continues, "is meant to be spell-bound and shipwrecked . . . meant to give up the profession."

The clinical situation that Bollas describes with reference to the Siren and

Odysseus brings many further amplifications into play within the mind of the analytical psychologist. The seduction of Adam by Eve and the emasculation of Samson by Delilah are but two of the more familiar depictions of the destructive side of the anima. On the more positive side (though possibly experienced just as negatively by the frustrated heroic-ego), are motifs wherein the alluring woman simultaneously attracts and forestalls the amor of her hero, taming and sophisticating "the brute blood" of the passion with which he would master her. One thinks, in this connection, of the many further faces of the anima that Odysseus encounters during the course of his journey home to a Penelope besieged by restless suitors, of the tasks that the princess of a fairy tale sets as conditions for her hand, and of the thousand and one stories Shahrazad tells the enraged King Shahrayar to prevent his murdering her while at the same time curing him of his rage and misogyny. Other examples come to mind. One thinks, to take just three more, of the unicorn tamed in the lap of the virgin, of Theseus being wound through the labyrinth by the thread of Ariadne, and of the alchemical motif of "atomization of the bridegroom in the body of the bride."[12]

In *Hysteria*, however, Bollas writes as if he is entirely unaware of the anima's role in chastening, sophisticating, and relativizing the psychic hegemony of a consolidated ego. Indeed, in his book, what I, following Jung, have referred to as the anima is nothing but a hysterical cock-teaser, who retreats from the sexuality she ambivalently evokes, not for the higher purpose she presents with her ruse of spirituality,[13] but as part of an effort to reverse the maturation process and to find the caregiver, "mamma," in the lover.

Fixated in a childhood identity by a pattern of maternal care in which the self's being was affirmed while the body's genitals were effaced, the hysteric, even when promiscuous, unconsciously despises sexuality. In adult relationships, the genitals are skirted and intercourse avoided for as long as possible. Foreplay, on the other hand, tends to be a long, drawn-out affair and, in Bollas's view, too tedious for a normal partner to bear.

The background to this peculiarity of the hysteric's sexual life is, once again, the mother. Unable to welcome the sexual life that first appears in her child at age three (let alone to actively promote it through a wholesome maternal eroticism), the hysteric's mother, often an hysteric herself, lavishes attention upon toes, shoulders, and ears, etc., in an effort to avoid the genitals, with the result that the libidinal excitation that properly belongs to the sexual organs is distributed widely across the child's body. And so it is that the seeds for the conversion symptoms of later life are sown.[14]

But what about the father? Though Bollas devotes an entire chapter to the functions of the father, I can here mention only a few of his main points in passing.

In a brilliant revisioning of Freud's original seduction theory, Bollas argues that it is not the father's seduction of his child that causes hysteria, but the mother's failure to do so. In this scenario, the father, even in a healthy, non-hysteric-producing family, plays the scapegoat. Freighted with the sexuality that "mamma" and toddler are so loath to welcome, his role is to hold it in waiting, as it were, like some big bad wolf until it can be received and accepted. In the hysterical line of development, however, this time never comes. The father remains saddled with blame, sometimes even legally so, when years later sexuality's menacing dawn is falsely remembered as sexual abuse at his hands.[15]

Along with the rejection of the father, into whom sexuality has been projectively identified, comes a rejection of the entire adult order of life beyond the family which he mediates. While an especially strong father can, in his role of "family inseminator,"[16] so infuse the family with the values of the symbolic order that his children may yet be saved from becoming hysterics, many weaker men abdicate this role, leaving their children trapped, according to Bollas, in the maternal imaginary.

Looking back over their years of practice with Bollas's model of hysteria in mind, clinicians of all schools, I believe, will recall patients of their own who might easily have appeared in the pages of his book. Those of us practising in Jungian analysis, I am sure, are only too familiar with cases in which the anima and animus cannot be projected, nor life beyond the family eroticized, so encapsulated are these figures in the parental imagos. Indeed, I think it fair to say that the greater part of our bread and butter as analysts is earned working to free our patients, ourselves, and our theory from that archetypal drama which Jung referred to as "the secret conspiracy" between a mother and a child in which "each helps the other to betray life."[17] Turning to Bollas's personalistic account of this situation, the analytical psychologist will be grateful for the useful counterpoint it provides to his own more archetypal view.

There are other patients, however, for whom Bollas's model may not be as apt as it first appears to be. When the hysterical presentation is more indicative of the anima/animus than of the parental imagos, the analyst's reliance on a model that so emphasizes the latter may provoke mighty resistances in the patient. Faced with these, analysts of lesser subtlety than Bollas may feel more certain than ever that they are dealing with precisely those hysterical wiles that he has so powerfully – perhaps, too powerfully – explicated in his book. Compensating for the poor rapport that follows from this, the transference may well become sexualized. When this is then taken to be a hallmark of hysterical character, matters may easily turn from bad to worse. Transference neurosis may give way to transference psychosis. The patient may be regarded as a malignant hysteric when, in fact, the situation is one in which the anima/animus, provoked by the analyst's *mauvaise foi* (and, yet, true to their function for all that), orchestrate an epistemological critique of the analyst and of the theoretical underpinnings of psychoanalysis itself by means of the negative therapeutic reaction.

In "Little Gidding" Eliot speaks of the importance of discriminating between "conditions which often look alike/yet differ completely."[18] Bollas, obviously, concurs with Eliot on this point, offering much guidance to his readers with regard to how hysterical character may be differentiated from the other types of character pathology with which it is so often confused. It is a grave omission on the part of the analytic tradition from which he speaks, however, to have failed to distinguish between hysterical presentations that are anima/animus-based and the mother-fixated syndrome of hysterical character disorder.[19] As Jung put it, "Prakrti dancing before Purusha in order to remind him of 'discriminating knowledge,' does not belong to the mother archetype but to the archetype of the anima, which in a man's psychology invariably appears, at first, mingled with the mother-image."[20]

In this connection, I am reminded of a descriptive passage in Bollas's book in which ordinary rituals of courtship are presented in a depreciatory way as being nothing more than pathetic reenactments of "mamma's" avoidance of sexuality in a bid to return to her once again. Read in terms of the supplement of reading I have presented here, however, this same behaviour may be regarded more benignly and prospectively as an enactment of the soul-sophisticating dance of the anima/animus. In coming to terms with any particular situation, the clinician, to be sure, would be well advised to hold both viewpoints in mind.

"Hysteric lovers-to-be," writes Bollas derisively,

> may meet up for a film, stumble into rationalised need to visit one lover's flat, make tea in the kitchen, bump into one another like two internal objects cut loose, giddy with the oddity of their release into the real. They giggle a lot, and then talk and talk and talk. They may talk through the night. Other than the occasional collision there is no sexual touching. This would spoil the foreplay, the mutual presentation of innocence.

> All the while, however, like a Christmas tree with flashing lights, each feels the charge of erotogenic zones over the body from time to time, in polymorphous excitation. A kiss, a move toward intercourse, would prematurely bind the pleasures of auto-erotic movement – the charging of the body by the absence of touch. Indeed, the hysteric feels deeply bonded to an other who reciprocates [in kind], as this encounter fulfils the earliest terms of the hysteric's love relation to the other.

> Often enough the lovers-to-be do not have intercourse. Having spent themselves in speech – a dialogic avenue – they retire to separate dwellings, perhaps to meet again. The lingering questions – "Does she desire me?"; "Do I desire her?" – may verge on despair, carrying the child's forlorn feeling that he might not be the object of maternal desire after all.[21]

Completing this scenario, Bollas goes on to describe how when it happens that the hysterical lovers-to-be do make love, it is more as if they were the innocent victims of the sexual instinct than its mature carriers. "In the kitchen making tea, the one suddenly lunges for the other and they crash into one another, moving towards blind fucking."[22] This, according to Bollas's analysis, is an arrangement on the part of the hysteric that is meant to ruin the relationship so that the "labour of embodied existentiality"[23] that a sexual relationship brings can be avoided and the child's relationship to "mamma" reaffirmed. Though Bollas makes no reference to date-rape in his book, I think it is obvious that within the hysterical constellation at least, the accused rapist, where not guilty, may be regarded as playing the same scapegoat role as fathers are compelled to play when sexuality first makes its unwelcome appearance in the family life at the onset of the Oedipal period.

Petticoats and snake-skins

Bollas, I am sure, does not intend his account of the hysteric's dating behaviour to be used as a diagnostic protocol or assessment tool. If it were, most of us, I believe, would be fitted with the label. For who, it may be asked, has not been on a date that approximates to the one Bollas describes? The same can be said for much of the animal kingdom. Animals do not simply find an object and vent their drives. On the contrary, like humans they, too, have highly orchestrated mating rituals in which approach and avoidance, aggression and passivity, attraction and rejection are complexly interwoven.

While Bollas's example serves well his purpose of presenting his view of the hysteric's love life, it could, with different narration, be used with equal effectiveness to illustrate many other psychological constellations. As we all know, the same outward behavioural display may be underpinned by any of a multitude of unconscious motivational factors. Where Bollas tells the behaviour of his lovers-to-be into a story in which genital sexuality is rejected by a childish self intent on preventing its bond with "mamma" from succumbing to the fall, one could also tell their story, in the light of the comparative material I have offered above, in terms of anima/animus dynamics.

In this connection I am reminded of yet another amplification, a motif from the fairy tale, Prince Lindworm, which I have more than once found occasion to relate to a patient who was ambivalently, if not to say hysterically, engaged in a courtship scenario like the one described by Bollas. In the tale, a young woman is betrothed to a prince, who, due to bewitchment, has the form of a terrible snake. Fearing that she will be eaten by the prince on their wedding night, the bride-to-be appeals to her fairy godmother for help. The fairy godmother tells the maiden not to worry. All she must do is wear numerous petticoats to the marriage-bed and make sure that she allows only one to be removed after her new husband has removed one of his snake-skins. As he has nine skins, she must wear ten petticoats. Only when he has shed the last of his skins, and is, thus, no longer a snake, but a man, dare she remove the last of her garments. If, however, she is too hasty and removes all her clothing before her husband has been redeemed, she will, indeed, be eaten.

This fairy tale, it seems to me, addresses the same problematic Bollas illustrates with his account of the hysteric on a date. It is also pertinent with regard to the psychotherapeutic analogue of that date, analysis itself. For the complexes and transferences which underpin both these kinds of relationship are easily as numerous and varied as the snake-skins and petticoats which the couple in the fairy tale must work through. And, yet, to a fly on the wall the behaviour of one "analytic-couple" (as the analyst and patient are now often called) looks very much like that of another.

Of course, the fly is mistaken. Every case is different. There is never anything routine about analysis (although a snake-skin can sometimes make it seem as if there were). On the contrary, when viewed from within the associative stream, dream reports, and interactional exchanges, each relationship may be shown to be unique, often richly so.

This in itself can stir up resistances. Intuiting ahead to the end of the analysis, patient (and analyst) may be reluctant to actually begin the work. Like the hysterical lovers-to-be whom Bollas describes, they may unconsciously say to themselves that it is all just too complicated. For how will what they have created together in analysis be brought to realization by each of them apart from each other and beyond analysis? With this question, as much as with each other, patient and analyst wrestle from the beginning through to the end of treatment. In a successful analysis, it is usually asked and answered many times as each of a whole series of lesser transferences are worked through within the container of the greater, i.e., archetypal transference.

A romance of uniqueness, analysis is immensely challenging. As analysts we love our profession on this account. We also hate it for the same reason. Reading Bollas's caricature of hysterical "lovers-to-be" talking through the night over tea, it occurred to me that the current renewal of analytic interest in hysteria is an expression of the latter of these emotions. For, like the love-life of the hysteric, analysis is also a tea ceremony of sorts, in which genital contact is strictly forbidden, childhood passions are revisited, and the couple talk and talk and talk. Perhaps, I reflected further, diagnosis, for all its obvious merits, can also serve as a defense against the excessive love or hate to which all analysts are subject when their ability to tolerate the anima/animus phenomena, which can so hystericize an analysis, has reached what is for them its (ego-relativizing) limit.

Like the maiden in our fairy tale, the patients in our practice may be following the advice of that fairy-godmother, the unconscious, when they wrap themselves in the alluring petticoats of resistance. To be diagnosed by the doctor would be to be eaten by Prince Lindworm. And here we may ask: is it really any wonder that hysterics, or rather, those patients whom Bollas refers to with this term, have such renown as mimics of so many other psychiatric illnesses? If analysis, the "cure . . . effected by love" (as Freud put it in a letter to Jung[24]), is to be redeemed, its patient-of-patients, the hysteric, must wear as many resistances – and then one more – as there are diagnostic categories.

These reflections bring us back to the quotation, cited in the previous section, in which Jung recommends setting aside diagnosis and therapeutic methods in the interests of approaching each patient with as few assumptions as possible. In that same passage, it will be recalled, he goes on to point out the impossibility of achieving the ideal situation of having no assumptions, "one [being] *oneself* the biggest of all one's assumptions, and the one with the gravest consequences."

Analysis, when conducted in the light of this fact, is a dialectical procedure in which the assumptive identities of both patient and analyst are called into question as each encounters their own unconscious (as well as transpersonal dimensions of the collective unconscious) in the person of the other. While rigorously maintaining professional boundaries, analysts practising in this vein do not hide behind professionalism. Rather, by entering the process as fully as they expect their patients to, they take their own medicine even as their patients serve them back to themselves through various conscious and unconscious gestures and responses.

Sometimes our medicine is pure poison. It makes us ill. And so it is that we hate to take it. It is only by taking this poisonous *pharmakon*, however, and becoming sick of ourselves, that we can be transformed into the healing agent that the patient needs us to be.

Bollas speaks, in this connection, of the hysteric's uncanny ability to identify with aspects of the analyst's interior object world. This, he maintains, is an unhealthy "skill [which has] evolved from countless acts of fulfilling the imagined object of the other's desire, in which the true self is suspended whilst a stand-in takes its place."[25]In Bollas's view, it is by mimicking the analyst's unconscious in a coquettish bid to be mamma's child-beloved once again that the hysteric sings her destruction-wreaking Siren's song.[26]

Jung, on the other hand, with anima/animus dynamics in mind, conceives of the same process as an archetypal one, rooted in the coniunctio archetype. When analytic work proceeds in accordance with the instinctual imperatives of this archetype, a fabulous, if unholy, amalgam may be created out of the illusions originating on both sides. Compensatory to unconscious inner divisions within the patient and analyst as individuals, the affective union which has joined them together in mutual states of unconsciousness may become, with the passage of time, the crucible in which the characterological rigidities of each are dissolved. In the course of this process, resistances arise, complexes are discharged, and Siren songs are sung. Love gives way to hate and hate to love. One never knows, in any specific way, quite what to expect. But as each member of the analytic couple wrestles with what he or she finds of him or herself in the other, the personalities of each are united internally and a new attitude is born.[27]

Of course, not all that advertises itself as a new spirit is in fact that. And so, with Bollas we must question whether the child appearing in a dream, fantasy, or regressive state truly is the salutary *foetus spagyricus* of the alchemists, or, rather, something more demonic, the infantile shadow or demonic puer, referred to by Bollas as the "'child within' who castrates the self's achievements in the real by periodic uprisings that shed the self of the accoutrements of accomplishment."

The date that Bollas narrates in illustration of the love-life of the hysteric and the seductive resistances through which the hysteric attempts to turn analysis into an interminable love-affair may, to be sure, find their background in this figure. When this is the case, analytical understanding must work, as Jung put it, like a "corrosive or thermocautery,"[28] to destroy the unhealthy fantasies. Bollas's *Hysteria* is, I believe, a strong dose of this kind of medicine.

At other times or with other patients, however, similar fantasy-contents and transference/countertransference dynamics have an entirely different meaning. Here, when it is more a question of ego-relativization and individuation than of arrested development and false growth, a more "synthetic" approach is called for. With reference to this prospect, Jung writes,

> [The alluring sexual aspect] is always trying to deliver us into the power of a partner who seems compounded of all the qualities we have failed to realize in ourselves. Hence, unless we prefer to be made fools of by our illusions, we shall, by carefully analysing every fascination, extract from it a portion of our own personality, like a quintessence, and slowly come to recognize that we meet ourselves time and again in a thousand disguises on the path of life. This, however, is a truth which only profits the man who is temperamentally convinced of the individual and irreducible reality [as opposed to the diagnosable generality – GM] of his fellow men."[29]

Chapter 2

Sex and Religion

Looking at the Madonna, Dora would have directed her gaze up to the mother's face. In Christian theology, especially in medieval cosmologies, the upper part of the body suggests transcendence, as one looks *up* towards the deity. This is the food of Christian love, and it is based on the infant's dwelling in the eyes of the mother, who provides her milk and her love. It will be some time before something happens from below that creates a new order of things, disrupting the heavenly gaze. The Christian world assigns this rupture to the Devil, who embodies all that disturbs the sacred order. As Dora exemplified, and as Freud failed to see – so taken up was he in advocating the universality of human sexuality – sexual urges seem to destroy the self's relation to the sacred primary object, unless they can be transported from carnality to spirituality, with the soul as a stand-in for the genital.[1]

Christopher Bollas

In treating patients one is at first impressed, and indeed arrested, by the apparent significance of the personal mother. This figure of the personal mother looms so large in all personalistic psychologies that, as we know, they never got beyond it, even in theory, to other important aetiological factors. My own view differs from that of other medico-psychological theories principally in that I attribute to the personal mother only a limited aetiological significance. That is to say, all those influences which the literature describes as being exerted on the children do not come from the mother herself, but rather from the archetype projected upon her, which gives her a mythological background and invests her with authority and numinosity.[2]

C. G. Jung

Of mud . . . of occultism

In his memoirs, Jung discusses a conversation he had with Freud during their first face-to-face meeting in Vienna in March of 1907. It had to do, on the one hand, with what Jung regarded as Freud's antipathy toward the spirit. In Jung's estimation, Freud abhorred "virtually everything that philosophy and religion . . . had learned about the psyche."[3] Sexuality, on the other hand, Jung felt, was privileged by Freud to such an extent that in his theory all other aspects of psychic life were to be viewed in the light of its vicissitudes.

> Wherever, in a person or in a work of art, an expression of spirituality (in the intellectual, not the supernatural sense) came to light, [Freud] suspected it, and insinuated that it was repressed sexuality. Anything that could not be directly interpreted as sexuality he referred to as "psychosexuality." I protested that this hypothesis, carried to its logical conclusion, would lead to an annihilating judgement upon culture. Culture would then appear as a mere farce, the morbid consequence of repressed sexuality. "Yes," he assented, "so it is, and that is just a curse of fate against which we are powerless to contend."[4]

Reading Bollas's *Hysteria*, the analytical psychologist will be reminded of this famous exchange. While being as impressed with Bollas's sexual theory as Jung initially was with Freud's, he or she will also feel some of the same "hesitations and doubts" that Jung expresses in the passage cited above.

If he or she is familiar with Freud's writings, a passage in which Freud puts his own gloss on the intellectual controversy that divided him from his heir apparent, Jung, will come to mind. The passage to which I refer is taken from the long monograph, *On the History of the Psycho-Analytic Movement* (1914), a work that was written largely with the intent of drumming Jung out of the tribe.

> All the changes that Jung has proposed to make in psychoanalysis flow from his intention to eliminate what is objectionable in the family-complexes, so as not to find it again in religion and ethics. For sexual libido an abstract concept has been substituted, of which one may safely say that it remains mystifying and incomprehensible to wise men and fools alike. The Oedipus complex has a merely "symbolic" meaning: the mother in it means the unattainable, which must be renounced in the interests of civilization; the father who is killed in the Oedipus myth is the "inner" father, from whom one must set oneself free in order to become independent. . . . In this way a new religio-ethical system has been created, which . . . was bound to re-interpret, distort or jettison the factual findings of analysis. The truth is that these people have picked out a few cultural overtones from the symphony of life and have once more failed to hear the mighty and primordial melody of the instincts.[5]

All who read Bollas's *Hysteria*, I believe, will concur that he cannot be accused of "fail[ing] to hear the mighty and primordial melody of the instincts." Indeed, compared with the importance that he, like Freud before him, attaches to the appearance of sexuality in childhood, the discoveries that religion and philosophy have made with respect to the psyche are for him, as they were for our common forebear, but "a few cultural overtones picked out of the symphony of life."

Bollas's references to the Holy Family are a case-in-point. In this trio he finds nothing more than a burlesque metaphor for his theory of hysteria. Mary, the virgin mother of Jesus, who was herself immaculately conceived, is figurative of the hysteric's mother who has "withdrawn her love from the self's genitalia."[6] Joseph, likewise, is "the castrated sexual father" who personifies, by means of his castrated status, the sexuality that has been repudiated by "mamma" and three-year-old – Madonna and child.[7] And what of Jesus, the orienting sublime of the Christian West for the last two thousand years? When read in terms of Bollas's year-2000 theory of hysteria, the divinely conceived Son of God is nothing but the all-too-human casualty of an epiphany that is more sexual than divine, an hysteric of the ascetic variety who unwittingly touts his asexuality as if it were something spiritual. As Bollas puts it, "It was not only Jesus who left the earthly world to join his holy family; he paved the road walked by all hysterics, who renounce carnal interests to testify to their nobler existence."[8]

The irreverent use Bollas makes of the Holy Family is not merely a personal blasphemy on his part. It is part and parcel of a collective one. The "annihilating judgement upon culture" that he (or rather, the contemporary psychoanalysis exemplified by him) delivers in terms of these appropriated figures has been levelled by scores of others in much the same way. Irreverence (it is no longer even meaningful to say "blasphemy") is simply a sign of the times. The cinema, rock videos, and the arts generally – to say nothing of more academically conceived efforts – have all been making a farce out of religion for some time. That this is now done in such frankly sexual terms, I believe, indicates that we have now largely embraced the "curse of fate against which [Freud said] we are powerless [anyway] to contend."

Or perhaps, on second thoughts, it would be fairer to Bollas's thesis to say that we now act out this curse as never before. Acting out, after all, is not the same thing as embracing. To embrace something requires consciousness, for we are, or at least strive to be, conscious beings. Only as it is consciously embraced does fate cease to be a curse and become a destiny. In presenting Freud's sexual theory afresh at the brink of a new millennium (with amendments adopted from British object relations and Lacan) Bollas would have us face squarely the dark truth of our sexuality. For, from his point of view, it is only by coming to terms with the trauma that sexuality has universally and from time immemorial wrought in the lives of all children that culture can at last be liberated from the farce that it becomes when this is denied.

But what about the "black tide of mud . . . of occultism"? In that same 1907 meeting in Vienna that has been serving as a palimpsest for our discussion thus far, an emotional Freud is reported to have admonished Jung that a "dogma" must be made of the sexual theory, an "unshakable bulwark" against the "black tide of mud . . . of occultism."[9]

Jung, as he recalls in his memoirs, was aghast at this proposal. To his mind "the sexual theory was just as occult, that is to say, just as unproven an hypothesis, as many other speculative views." As he saw it, "a scientific truth was a hypothesis which might be adequate for the moment but was not to be preserved as an article of faith for all time."[10]

Jung, clearly, knew dogmatism when he met it. Neither he nor Freud, however, could have had any idea of what the "black tide of mud . . . of occultism" that Freud so dreaded would look like by the end of the century. What, we might ask, would these pioneers of depth psychology make of New Age spirituality and consumer greed, pop-psychology and the talk shows that dispense it? I'd like to think they would find in this embarrassment of riches that our times have become a common enemy. More likely, I suppose, is the prospect that they would blame each other for it.

Bollas, for his part, makes frequent allusions to the psycho-spiritual clap-trap in which the hysteric trades. That word "soul," so popular today, appears in his text, on the occasions that it does, in an ironic manner that exposes it as a euphemism for the disembodied, sex-denying self-state of the hysteric.[11] The "inner child," likewise, is shown to be redolent of the childish innocence that the hysteric is so violently reluctant to relinquish.[12] Though he does not mention the cult of the body, which so flourishes in our time, his critique of this can be readily deduced from his discussion of the role that "failed maternal libidinalization of the body" plays in the aetiology of hysterical character.[13] By the same token, a critique of New Age culture in general, and Goddess spirituality in particular, can be extrapolated from his account of the hysteric's failed "matriculation in the paternal order."[14]

This is not to say that Bollas is any more sparing when it comes to the traditional, so-called patriarchal religions. Indeed, in a discussion of St Francis, the saint is presented as an exemplar of a typically hysterical ruse wherein "the actual father" is repudiated in favour of a "spiritual father who is . . . an adored object of his culture."[15] "Christianity," he concludes,

> offers an hysterical solution to the problems posed by the sexual father. The story of Jesus, the separation of the sexes in the Catholic clergy and the renunciation of sexuality, the denigration of carnal requirements and the privileging of spiritual virtues, and the celebration of one's departure from earth to a joyful merger with spiritual beings in a better world – these teachings form a conduit for hysterical flight from the violation upon the self of sexuality.[16]

Though Christianity would seem to facilitate a passover to the father, even as Christ is said to have returned from the dead "in the glory of the Father," the opposite is the case in Bollas's view. In their apparent faith in the father-God, Christians like St Francis are but the minions of the maternal imaginary, or to use a phrase of Christ's, "eunuchs for heaven."[17]

Reading Bollas's account of hysterical spirituality, the analytical psychologist is liable to redden with both embarrassment and anger. Knowing only too well the vulgar uses to which the contributions of his own school have been put, he does not appreciate having his nose rubbed in it. How painful that the seminal works of analytical psychology have been virtually disregarded in the academic and psychoanalytic mainstream, while poppish tomes of "Jungian psychology" are sold, alongside crystals, pendulums, and other paraphernalia of the "inner journey," from the shelves of New Age bookstores. Must analytical psychology be forever damned, on account of its respect for the spiritual aspect of the unconscious, to such bad company? Surely there is something more to the religious function of the psyche than hysterical flight from the sexual father.

Spiritus sexualis

In the chapter of his memoirs dealing with Freud, Jung attempted to set the record straight with regard to his position on sexuality. Despite the theoretical differences that led to the break between him and Freud, Jung maintained that he "alone pursued the two problems which most interested Freud: the problem of 'archaic vestiges,' and that of sexuality."

> It is a widespread error to imagine that I do not see the value of sexuality. On the contrary, it plays a large part in my psychology as an essential – though not the sole – expression of psychic wholeness. But my main concern has been to investigate, over and above its personal significance and biological function, its spiritual aspect and its numinous meaning, and thus to explain what Freud was so fascinated by but was unable to grasp.[18]

Jung's views on this subject, as he goes on to explain, are presented in two late works, *The Psychology of the Transference* (a work from which we have already quoted) and *Mysterium Coniunctionis*. In the first of these works, Jung demonstrates the spiritual aspect and numinous meaning of sexuality as this is expressed and elaborated within analysis by means of the archetypal transference. The touchstone for this discussion is not a case study, but a series of erotic woodcuts from an alchemical manuscript, the *Rosarium Philosophorum*.

With its symbolism of emasculated kings, incestuous couples, and divine children, alchemy would appear, if read in the light of Bollas's work, to be an hysterical brew indeed. Jung, working with a fuller sense of archaic vestiges than Freud did, however, presents the spiritual meaning of this kind of fantasy material while elucidating the psychology of the transference at the same time. The picture that emerges is altogether different from that which Bollas paints with reference to case material in which similar images and motifs figure.

The crucial paragraph concerns a woodcut from the *Rosarium* series in which the divine siblings Diana and Apollo, dressed in royal attire, approach each other for betrothal. Apollo (the representative, for Jung, of the female patient's animus) stands upon the sun, while Diana (the complementary anima figure of the male doctor) stands upon the moon. In their right hands the two hold criss-crossing branches. Below this their left hands are joined. At the top of the picture, the Holy Ghost in the traditional form of a dove descends from a star with a third branch in its beak, which crosses with the branches that the couple hold toward each other.

"As regards the psychology of this picture," Jung writes:

> we must stress above all else that it depicts a human encounter where love plays the decisive part. The conventional dress of the pair suggests an equally conventional attitude in both of them. Convention still separates them and hides their natural reality, but the crucial contact of left hands points to something "sinister," illegitimate, morganatic, emotional, and instinctive, i.e., the fatal touch of incest and its "perverse" fascination. At the same time the intervention of the Holy Ghost reveals the hidden meaning of the incest, whether of brother and sister or of mother and son, as a repulsive symbol for the *unio mystica*. Although the union of close blood-relatives is everywhere taboo, it is yet the prerogative of kings (witness the incestuous marriages of the Pharaohs, etc.). Incest symbolizes union with one's own being, it means individuation or becoming a self, and, because this is so vitally important, it exerts an unholy fascination – not, perhaps, as a crude reality, but certainly as a psychic process controlled by the unconscious, a fact well known to anybody who is familiar with psychopathology. It is for this reason, and not because of occasional cases of human incest, that the first gods were believed to propagate their kind incestuously. Incest is simply the union of like with like, which is the next stage in the development of the primitive idea of self-fertilization.[19]

This is an important passage, but one, I think, that might easily be misread by contemporary analysts with an insufficient knowledge of Jung's writings. The idea, for instance, of "incest symboliz[ing] union with one's own being" might suggest to some an effacing of the object world or a withdrawal into a schizoid state. Likewise, Jung's reference to "self-fertilization" and "the union of like with like" might suggest a turning away from what Bollas has called "allo-erotic" object choice in favour of autoeroticism. However, the opposite is the case. In this passage Jung is very much concerned with what analysts since Winnicott have called "the use of an object." In Jung's view, relationship with others is the crucial catalyzing agent of the individuation process. Commenting in a later section of the same work upon the necessity of relationship for self-realization, Jung writes:

> The unrelated human being lacks wholeness, for he can achieve wholeness only through the soul, and the soul cannot exist without its other side, which is always found in a "You."[20]

Analytical psychology, approaching sexuality and object-use from an introverted perspective, finds in the image of incest a metaphor for the generativity of the subjective, psychic factor. While ultimately seeking outward manifestation through the use of what Bollas has called transformational objects, the subjective factor does so "incestuously," in terms of a projective strategy, which Jung has called "familiarization."[21] In *Hysteria*, Bollas presents a vivid account of incestuous familiarization in its lower form, while Jung, in *The Psychology of the Transference*, explores it in its higher aspect. Further clarification of the difference between the lower and higher forms of incest may be gained by thinking of these in terms of the distinction Jung draws between the personal unconscious and the collective unconscious.

It is an axiom of analytical psychology that "the unconscious first appears in projected form."[22] When applied to the object relations schemas and complexes that make up the contents of the personal unconscious, this axiom merely restates Freud's definition of the transference as "new editions of early [relational] conflicts, in which the patient strives to behave as he originally behaved. . . ."[23] In this connection we may think most readily of how familiarization, by drawing upon earlier experience, may complicate the current relationships it aims to simplify, as, for instance, when one puts one's "father's head," as the saying goes, on the shoulders of an important contemporary figure such as a spouse, employer, or analyst. In the terminology of analytical psychology, the imbroglios in which projections such as these enmesh us exemplify the lower incest. Because transferences of this kind often bring the conscious and the unconscious together in an inferior, retrograde, and poorly adapted way, they tend to be followed by a negativizing rupture or what alchemy called a "separatio." In analysis, both "Freudian" and "Jungian," such transferences are analyzed, i.e., taken apart.

Analytical psychology's axiom concerning projection can also be applied to the collective unconscious and its contents, the archetypes. The idea here is that of a phylogenetic or ancestral dimension of the psyche manifesting itself through familiarizing projections, such that life, for all its novelty and variety, is experienced in fundamentally human ways. From the cradle to the grave our lives are thematized according to adaptive potentials given by the archetypes. As these potentials unfold within us, becoming the imperatives we seek to fulfil, the world about us is apperceived in the light of their realization.

In Hindu thought, this projection-making, thematizing factor is conceived of as Maya, the spinning woman, who creates the illusions that entangle us in life. Jung, drawing upon a similarly mythical mode of thought, conceives of the projection-making factor in terms of the anima and animus. Contrasexual inner figures that personify the plurality of archetypes, the anima and animus, in Jung's model, mediate between consciousness and the collective unconscious while at the same time investing life, via projection, with the compelling significance that it comes to have.

The hallmark of the projections that spring from the collective unconscious is their numinous, larger-than-life quality. Archetypal transferences are predominately idealizing transferences. In the psychoanalytic situation, they correspond, on the one hand, to the projective processes Kohut discusses with reference to his notion of the selfobject, and, on the other, to the anima/animus phenomena described by Jung.

In contrast to personal projections, which give us the sense of being caught in the repetitive circle of fate, archetypal projections fill our sails with a sense of destiny. There is a feeling of having finally found the person through whom we can become who we are. When all goes well, a relationship develops in which the archetype is fleshed out with actual life experience. Expressed in terms of the woodcut discussed by Jung, we could say that in such relationships the divine siblings (i.e., the anima and animus) have come together to partake of that higher incest which is the prerogative of their divinity.

The higher incest, however, is not yet the greater *coniunctio*. To produce this latter state, other operations must be undertaken. These, as we know, have largely to do with disillusionment. In the *Rosarium* series, the woodcut imaging the betrothal of the divine siblings is followed by others in which a depressive process of mortification is represented. Fused together in the grave, the couple lose their soul, a development imaged by the figure of a child-like homunculus flying away from the hermaphroditic corpse that the couple have become. This low-point of the opus, however, is also its turning-point. In a subsequent woodcut, the soul, once again in the form of a child-like homunculus, returns and the lifeless hermaphrodite is resurrected in the form of a glorious androgyne. Compared to the pathologized image of the hermaphrodite, which is figurative of an interpersonal process dominated by projective identifications, the androgyne is figurative of the personality integration that may be achieved by each partner as a result of working through the projections, both personal and archetypal, with which their relationship to one another has been invested.

This brief account of Jung's alchemical model of the transference is sufficient, I believe, to indicate what he had in mind when he spoke of sexuality as having a spiritual aspect and numinous meaning. Sexuality, in Jung's view, plays a crucial role in the individuation process. Being rooted in the collective unconscious, even as the contrasexual imagos, the anima and animus, are conceived as mediating between the archetypes and consciousness, sexuality is a main conduit through which the innate potentials of our common human heritage incarnate themselves in the life of the individual. In this regard, sexuality is like the cosmogonic eros with which creation begins in Greek mythology, the projectile-firing Cupid of later myths, and the Socratic eros of Plato's *Symposium*: a daemonic power that entangles us in the great themes of existence as readily as it places us in each other's arms.

Bollas, I believe, would agree with Jung that sexuality has an important spiritual aspect. Indeed, from a number of statements in his writings it is clear that for him sexuality (in its "allo-erotic," object-seeking and object-utilizing form) is a numinosum, much as it was for Freud. The spiritual meaning he ascribes to it, however, lies more in the direction of Jung insofar as sexuality is seen as connecting one to those particular others who are significant for the elaboration and realization of the self's idiom. As he puts this in *Hysteria*,

A part of any self's idiom – which I see as the peculiar aesthetic of form true to our character – is the drive to articulate and develop this aesthetics of being, our destiny drive, as it were. The aim of such a drive is to present and re-present one's idiom, accomplished in part by selecting and using objects through which to develop. Understood as part of the life instinct, the destiny drive is the urge to use objects in order to come into being and relating expressive of one's true self, and this is the primary impetus behind the allo-erotic choice. By desiring the other – the objects in the world – the self finds a complex vocabulary of objects through which to speak the self, but auto-eroticism is a fundamentally different drive, more like the work of the death instinct – in which objects are selected in order to extinguish desire.[24]

The distinction Bollas draws in this passage between allo-erotic object choice and auto-eroticism is important. To my mind, however, he has drawn it in too hard-and-fast a manner. While he is certainly correct in emphasizing that allo-erotic object choice facilitates realization of the self's idiom by means of a sort of interpersonal process of amplification (in Jung's sense), his use of the term auto-eroticism, heedless as it is of the difference between the higher and lower incest, burdens psychoanalysis with a version of the incest prohibition that is too harsh and sweeping to be helpful in our day.

Jung, for his part, was also concerned with the deleterious effect of auto-eroticism. In a statement in which this concern is presented in terms of anima/animus theory, he characterized "the unconscious anima [as] a creature without relationship, an autoerotic being whose one aim is to take total possession of the individual."[25] The anima, however, can also promote relatedness. Indeed, as the personification of the archetypal potentials of the deep psyche, she is the animating factor that makes relationship to the object world possible. As Jung puts this, "the anima is the connecting link with the world beyond and the eternal images, while [at the same time] her emotionality involves man in the chthonic world and its transitoriness."[26]

Déjà vu. Once again we find ourselves re-enacting, at the dawn of a new millennium, an issue that divided Freud and Jung in the early years of the last century. In his memoirs, Jung states that "Freud clung to the literal interpretation of [incest] and could not grasp the spiritual significance of incest as a symbol."[27] When read in the light of Jung's theory of the anima/animus it is clear that the same observation can be made with regard to the contemporary psychoanalysis of which Bollas is a distinguished exponent. For, as we have seen, Bollas also insists upon the literal interpretation of incest, while disdaining its symbolic significance and spiritual meaning.

A most important casualty of this disdain is the inner child. Confining himself to a depreciatory interpretation, Bollas, as we have already noted, sees nothing more in this figure than an hysterical fixation to pre-sexual innocence. Jung, as we might expect, takes umbrage at such a view. While well aware that there is a figure that can have this meaning, he stands up, at the same time, for another child. The product of what I have been calling the higher incest, this child must not be pitched out with its bathwater, no matter how blackened with the "mud . . . of occultism" that bathwater may be. As Jung puts it, in a passage in which he anticipates the criticism he expects to receive (and did receive) from those who would commit such violence toward the soul's natural symbols,

The reader [of *The Psychology of the Transference*] should not imagine that the psychologist is in any position to explain what "higher copulation" is, or the *coniunctio*, or "psychic pregnancy," let alone the "soul's child." Nor should one feel annoyed if the newcomer to this delicate subject, or one's own cynical self, gets disgusted with these – as he thinks them – phoney ideas and brushes them aside with a pitying smile and an offensive display of tact. The unprejudiced scientific inquirer who seeks the truth . . . must guard against rash judgements and interpretations, for here he is confronted with *psychological facts* which the intellect cannot falsify and conjure out of existence.[28]

Fading symbols, falling stars

The sunken, derogatory analogy Bollas draws between the symptom-picture of hysteria and the symbolism of Christianity begs to be set alongside Jung's discussion of Christianity in *The Psychology of the Transference*. Most readers who delve into this work will, I am sure, find it odd that Jung devotes so much attention to topics such as Christian dogma and the Catholic/Protestant schism. What does the fact of Christendom's having been split into numerous denominational factions for over four hundred years have to do with the problem of the transference in psychoanalysis? Did the ageing psychologist just go off on a tangent here? Or is this a sign of how daft he in fact was? In a letter to Abraham, Freud said, "Jung is crazy."[29] In light of Bollas's account of how Christianity has provided hysteria with a collective sanction, are we to diagnose Jung as an hysteric?

The answer to these questions resides in still other questions. These Jung raises in the passage quoted at the end of our last section when he states that "the psychologist is [not] in any position to explain what 'higher copulation' is, or the *coniunctio*, or 'psychic pregnancy,' let alone the 'soul's child.'" Though he does not here presume to explain what these terms ultimately refer to or mean, he is at pains to affirm their status as the motifs through which questions pertaining to meaning are presented. Whatever their interpretation may be at any given time, the point that he wishes to emphasize is, I believe, the fact that they eternally exist. We meet them in the Christian story, in the guise of the Holy Family. We meet them again today in the form of psychodynamic processes and inner figures, such as the so-called "inner child." And it is their appearance in the psychotherapeutic process that leads us to speak of an *archetypal* transference.

Approaching psychology in general, and the problem of the transference in particular, with a greater estimation of what religion and culture have learned about the psyche than Freud had, Jung regarded "dogmatically formulated truths of the church," such the Immaculate Conception of Mary and the Virgin Birth of Christ, as "repositories of the secrets of the soul" in which "matchless knowledge is set forth in grand symbolical images."[30] At the same time, however, he recognized that symbolical images, even when stamped with the sanctity of a great religion, have a limited shelf-life and must again and again be updated and renewed.

Though the Protestant schism testifies to the vigour of Christianity's struggle to adapt itself to secular change through new interpretations, the fallout of its failure to do so adequately has filled the consulting rooms of psychotherapists for the whole of the last century. Where symbols operating on the cultural level had once mediated "that remnant of the primeval psyche" that is "pregnant with the future and yearning for development,"[31] we now – *horribile dictu* – conceive of individual patients as suffering from an inability to symbolize. And this is to name only one of the multitude of symptoms with which secular man is afflicted. As Jung puts this in another place,

> Since the stars have fallen from heaven and our highest symbols have paled, a secret life holds sway in the unconscious. That is why we have a psychology today, and why we speak of the unconscious. All this would be quite superfluous in an age or culture that possessed symbols. Symbols are spirit from above, and under those conditions the spirit is above too. Therefore it would be a foolish and senseless undertaking for such people to wish to experience or investigate an unconscious that contains nothing but the silent, undisturbed sway of nature. Our unconscious, on the other hand, hides living water, spirit that has become nature, and that is why it is disturbed. Heaven has become for us the cosmic space of the physicists, and the divine empyrean a fair memory of things that once were. But the "heart glows," and a secret unrest gnaws at the roots of our being. In the words of the *Völuspa* we may ask:
>
> What murmurs Woton over Mimir's head?
> Already the spring boils . . .[32]

The star *below* the stable

One especially important star that has fallen from its heaven in our era is the one that guided the Magi from the East to the scene of Christ's nativity. Confirming Jung's observation that psychology arises in response to the demise of such symbols, Bollas, as we have already discussed, finds a fallen form of the Holy Family within the syndrome of hysteria. But is hysteria the explanation of this great symbol, or is it rather, as Jung suggests, the other way around – the demise of the symbol that has disturbed the unconscious?

An important omission on Bollas's part lends credence to the latter possibility. In drawing the analogy he does between the Holy Family and the family of the hysteric, Bollas neglects to make any mention of the star that guided the Magi from the East to Bethlehem. Noticing this, the reader is left to wonder if what is missing from Bollas's account of the biblical story points to something missing in his theory as well.

The star above the stable would bring a more cosmic dimension to Bollas's theory. The Magi from the East, likewise, would bring in a transpersonal perspective, such as that conceived in analytical psychology, with its concept of the collective unconscious. Taken together, these missing aspects of the complete image are emblematic of the spiritual aspect of the unconscious – precisely what Bollas has so disdainfully left out of his account of hysteria.

Heir to the religious and cultural symbolism that passed into decline in the era that preceded it, psychology should ideally give living form once more to the primordial images of the soul. When there is a failure to recognize what we are heir to in doing psychology, however, the theories we make will be less life-giving, and sometimes even more hostile to life, than they otherwise would be.

Insight into this form of resistance, to which we all succumb when making theory, may be gleaned from a close scrutiny of our use of analogy. Analogies are impoverished forms of the living symbol. For all their usefulness in conveying what we mean, they may also serve as apotropaic defenses against the counter-position in the unconscious that they had themselves expressed before being forced into rhetorical service. In the midst of writing an article (or listening to a patient), an image comes to mind. In Bollas's case, it was the image of the Holy Family. At a conscious level this image appears to be nothing more than a useful metaphor that helps to convey what he means. Read in the light of the violence he does to it in the process of making it fit his cause, however, it appears, at an unconscious level, to be rather a defensive appropriation of a menacing anomaly. In Jungian parlance, we might say that Bollas here evades or throws off the compensation of the unconscious. The anima, reacting to his personalistic and pathologizing account of her as an hysteric, brings in the image of the Holy Family. It is as if she were saying, "Yes, yes, sexuality is a trauma to all children, and I would drive an analyst crazy, but what about the divine child, the transpersonal, and the spiritual? I, too, have something to do with these factors even as I bring these images to you now out of the birthing turmoil of your work." But Bollas's *Hysteria* is not the *Arabian Nights*. Or rather, if regarded as such, it is a version of that story that has a poorer outcome for Shahrazad. For where King Shahrayar was able to listen to the stories Shahrazad told, and (in some versions) even give up his murderous intent, Bollas no sooner thinks of the story of the Holy Family than he cuts it down to size and forces it to bear witness to his theory. And so it is that the living symbol that the Holy Family had become simply by coming to mind within the novel context of a psychoanalytic theory pales again, strangled by the death-cord of analogy.

Chapter 3

Nega-Nativity

The comforting illusion that mummy and daddy came together in order to bring a child into existence is now dispelled. Apart from Jesus (or 'the Holy Family'), the child did not enter existence through maternal immaculate conception. There was an intercourse. On the one hand, this actuates a narcissistic crisis, since the child is not only not the centre of the universe, but possibly an after-effect of parental sexual passion sought after for its own sake.[1]

Christopher Bollas

Once the personal repressions are lifted, the individuality and the collective psyche begin to emerge in a coalescent state, thus releasing the hitherto repressed personal fantasies. The fantasies and dreams which now appear assume a somewhat different aspect. An infallible sign of collective images seems to be the appearance of the "cosmic" element, i.e., the images in the dream or fantasy are connected with cosmic qualities, such as temporal or spatial infinity. . . . The collective [unconscious] element is very often announced by . . . dreams where the dreamer is flying through space like a comet, or feels that he is the earth, or the sun, or a star. . . .[2]

C. G. Jung

Modernity's manger

How different hysteria looks when we add the star back into the equation! And how much more valuable the Holy Family appears, even in its fallen, hystericized form!

Approaching the psyche in the light of his theory of archetypes, Jung writes of "revers[ing] our rationalistic causal sequence," when it comes to "autonomous images" such as Christ and Mercurius, and "instead of deriving these figures from our psychic conditions . . . deriv[ing] our psychic conditions from these figures."[3]

Applied to the Holy Family, this approach suggests a supplement of reading wherein Mary, Joseph, and Jesus (as well as the other figures of the nativity story) are not accounted for in terms of the personalistic psychodynamics Bollas describes with respect to hysteria, but rather, reversing this sequence, hysteria's psychodynamics are led back to them.

But how do we analyze such figures as these (or analyze by means of such figures) without reference to actual persons? Isn't psychology the science of the *human* psyche? Shouldn't we, here below, be the starting point?

This is not the place to explore the fallacy of psychology as the study of persons with such and such a psychology.[4] Suffice it to say that psychology's object, the psyche, is, to the discipline that would study it, what the economy and the political world are to the economist and the political scientist. While it enters or appears in people, even as Christ is conceived to have been incarnated and become a man, it is more apt to say that we are in it, even as we live within an economic and political climate. "[M]an . . .", writes Jung, "is enclosed in *the* psyche (not in *his* psyche)."[5] Or, as he expresses this in his monograph on the transference with reference to the anima/animus: "it often seems advisable to speak less of *my* anima or *my* animus and more of *the* anima and *the* animus."[6]

The same distinction applies to Mary, Joseph, and Jesus. As the epithet "holy" immediately conveys, the familial image constituted of these figures is not reducible to the empirical, i.e. profane, family – yours or mine. On the contrary, as a symbolic form rooted in the collective psyche, its referent (if we must conceive of it as having one at all) is the familiarizing, or even familializing, tendency of the soul itself.[7] Repeatedly in the soul's life, there is a moment in which a newly appearing value is wider or greater, at least potentially, than its facilitating environment, which may be experienced as inhospitable and even persecutory on that account alone – hence the nativity story and the vicissitudes of familiarization which are depicted in it.

Coleridge, the originator of the term "psycho-analysis" some one hundred years before Freud, referred to a hermeneutic technique which he called "tautegory."[8] More recently, Giegerich has brought this technique to our attention again.[9] Succinctly put, the tautegorical presupposition is a heuristic device which requires us to regard the various constituent parts of a myth or a story as "so many *different determinations* or '*moments*' of one and the same 'truth'. . . ."[10] No matter how contrasting or incommensurate these determinations or moments may seem to be, held together in the mind as one, they may be grasped as expressions of a single multifaceted thought.

It is this technique that allows us to "reverse the causal sequence" with respect to hysteria and its Christian cultural objects and to interpret life from the abjected vantage point of that "above" which those objects once were, but which has fallen into the unconscious in our time. Though we are ultimately enclosed within the psyche, yet may we differentiate it from within, bringing it to consciousness in the process.

Read tautegorically, the "grand symbolical image" of Christ's supernatural conception in the womb of the Blessed Virgin is not a function of the traumatic rupture which young children and hysterical mothers have felt from time immemorial when their bond of attachment and care is affronted by what Bollas calls the "sexual epiphany" of the Oedipal period. It is a function, rather, of the other images within the Christian story itself.

In supplement to Bollas's reading, I would especially emphasize the figures of secular authority and political power with which the Holy Family must contend. The fact that Mary is made pregnant, not in the ordinary way by Joseph, but miraculously by God through the agency of the Holy Ghost, and the fact that King Herod and the Romans are the ruling authorities while this is taking place, are but "different determinations or moments of one and the same truth." They belong together, these various figures, for each says the same thing from a different angle.

If the setup had been otherwise, if the Jewish nation, for instance, had not been subject to the *Pax Romana*, but was ruled by a vibrant Hebrew king who mediated well between the nation he epitomized and its God, there would not have been any need for the divinely subversive begetting of a redemptive culture hero. In such a scenario, Mary would not need to be the virgin receptacle of the Holy Ghost and Joseph would be the begetter of Jesus. Had the ruling dominant of collective consciousness been providing adequate interpretive expression in its cultural forms for the primordial images, there would have been no need to conceive a new value.

But the story of Christ, and especially the story of his nativity, is indicative of that occasion in the soul's life when a compensatory conception *is* called for. Occurring in Mary's womb by the Holy Ghost or Spirit, this compensatory conception is as new to the setting in which it has arisen as the Magi from the East are to that setting by their foreignness. Grasping the unity of these different and, yet, tautegorically identical images, we may say that just as the visiting kings bring gifts from a beyond imagined in geographical terms, so the Christ-child – God's gift to mankind – comes from a beyond imaged in heavenly terms. Joseph's removal, as earthly father, from his son's conception presents another determination of the same idea, as does Mary's being an unwed mother. The new value that Christ represents springs from a heavenly source (the unconscious in its greater aspect, i.e., the collective unconscious).

Resistance to the new value is yet another determination or moment within this archetypal scene of renewal. Symbolically figured in the image of there being no room in the inn for Mary to deliver her child, this idea is darkly reiterated in Herod's order to kill all Jewish boys under the age of two. The Holy Family's flight into hiding for fear of Herod's henchmen and the hasty departure of the Eastern kings without paying Herod the customary ambassadorial visit complete the picture.

Clearly, there is more to this child Jesus (and his fallen form, the "child within") than can be locally appreciated. Aside from a few lowly shepherds, the local surround, or as we now call it, the "facilitating environment," is unable to recognize him at all. The townsfolk, according to the story, cannot even see his star. At this we need not wonder. It is difficult to see much of anything when gazing up at the night sky from within the glow of a lighted city or town. The sighting of stars, as both astronomy and the Christian story attest, is the prerogative of those who dwell beyond the city walls – the shepherds tending their flocks by night and foreign kings from distant lands. That is why it is precisely these figures that appear at the scene of Christ's nativity. And by the same token, that is why the Christ-child must be taken off to Egypt (and the "child within" to God knows where). The village that it takes to raise this child must be a global one.

The phallus of denial

Bollas, in an earlier work, in which he gives the spiritual aspect of the unconscious greater credit than he does in *Hysteria*, speaks of a dream-making Other who "takes the subject's day narrative and transforms it into a night fiction, so that the subject is compelled to re-experience his life according to the voice of the unconscious."[11] The same notion, I believe, can be applied to a *myth-making* Other who takes personalistically conceived theories and transforms them into mythopoeic terms so that the theorist is compelled to re-experience his thoughts in accordance with the voice of the *collective* unconscious.

In this connection I think especially of what Bollas, with reference to the hysteric, calls "denial of the phallus" through "refusal of the father."[12] This aspect of Bollas's theory looks very different when the "rationalistic causal sequence" is reversed and it is read in the light of the tautegorically reconstituted symbol of the Holy Family.

Rejecting the father along with sexuality, the hysteric, according to Bollas, seeks to prolong his or her idyllic relation to the pre-sexual mother. Rejection of the father, however, Bollas regards as tantamount to a rejection of reality in general, insofar as the father is the representative of reality within the family imaginary. This, obviously, is not wholly tenable. The father exists; realities impinge. Resorting to a compromise solution, the hysteric makes a pseudo-alliance with an idealized, and yet denuded, father-image, resolving the Oedipus complex (if this may be regarded as a resolution) in hysterical fashion. Rather than fully engaging father (and reality, too, in the bargain), the hysteric ingenuously complies with the values and imperatives that the father mediates, bringing the paternal order, and its emblem, the phallus, down to the level of his or her own emasculated (and emasculating) littleness. The picture here is one of a good little boy or girl who play-acts a maturity that is never really achieved, even in actual adulthood, precisely on account of its being an act. Bollas, in connection with this, writes trenchantly of the hysteric's grudge against reality and of his or her violently sentimental wish to renounce the success that has been achieved in the realm of the father so that the paradise of the maternal imaginary may be regained.

But is the "denial of the phallus," which Bollas rightly decries, really the result of the hysteric's rejection of the *personal* father (through an object-demeaning kind of mock-idealization)?[13] Or is it rather a given of our times that even the healthiest of fathers is constrained within the status of the weak, ineffectual father mentioned so often in our case studies because the collective spirit he is entrusted to mediate is more inadequate than he? What was it Yeats said in "The Second

Coming" about a time when "[t]he best lack all conviction, while the worst/ are filled with passionate intensity"?[14]

These questions may also be put it terms of the Holy Family. What, we may ask, can the personal father be but an ambivalently loved Joseph when Herod and Caesar are in power? And by the same token, what can his son, the messiah or culture hero, be but an anti-hero, hysteric, or college dropout when the Name-of-the-Father is Nixon and Vietnam, Profit-Maximization and Downsizing, Globalization and Corporate Greed?

In a *fin de siècle* culture, the redundancy of the paternal order is announced by the appearance of the Rebel-Without-a-Cause, and the punker who wants to marry your daughter is a sign of the end times. Moral reformers, for all their apparent apathy, these figures herald a kingdom that, like Christ's kingdom, is not of this world.

Mythology repeatedly portrays situations in which the father must be rejected, the old king dethroned, and the dominant of collective consciousness renewed. In Gnosticism, this situation is figured in the image of Ialdabaoth, the ignorant demiurge. Grail mythology, likewise, revolves around the symbolical image of a wounded Fisher King, whose rejuvenation is almost immediately followed by (and tautegorically identical with) his death. Nearer to our time is the Romantic movement, God-is-dead theology, and modern (i.e., non-representational) art. Deconstruction and feminism must also be listed here on account of the witness that they, too, have brought to bear upon modernity's (or as we now say, post-modernity's) abjected nativity.

Addressing himself to the interpretation of the "seemingly nihilistic trend towards disintegration" that has figured so prominently in the development of modern art, Jung suggests that this "must be understood as the symptom and symbol of a mood of universal destruction and renewal that has set its mark on our age."

> This mood makes itself felt everywhere, politically, socially, and philosophically. We are living in what the Greeks called the καιρός – the right moment – for a "metamorphosis of the gods," of the fundamental principles and symbols. This peculiarity of our time, which is certainly not of our conscious choosing, is the expression of the unconscious man within us who is changing. Coming generations will have to take account of this momentous transformation if humanity is not to destroy itself through the might of its own technology and science.[15]

Hysteria, I believe, must be understood in the light of the momentous transformation discussed by Jung in this passage. Though suffered by individuals, it is a cultural phenomenon. Heir to a collective symbolism that has become effete and meaningless, the individual psyche is riddled with symptoms. Antiquity represented this situation as one in which the gods become malevolent and persecutory in response to not being given proper ritual honour. This way of expressing the problem is as apt today as ever. The fundamental principles and symbols, denied new vestments suitable to their place in contemporary consciousness, compel us to pay them their sacrificial due in the unconscious currency of symptomatic suffering. In doing so, however, they also compel us to grapple once again in contemporary terms with the themes of life that they in their eternalness perennially bring to bear.

The usual view with respect to hysteria's immediate cultural background in Western society associates it with the prudish sexual mores that constricted human relations in the Victorian household of Freud's day. While there is, no doubt, some truth in this account, the ubiquity of hysteria and the hysterical character throughout history and into our own times suggests that this was never the heart of the matter. To get at this we must recognize that the content of neurosis changes according to its *mise-en-scène*. The individual psyche, zealotized to the hysterical service of whatever deity has most recently been cheated by its priests, presents a wide array of afflictions, these varying in accordance with the geographical and temporal particulars. Cultural inadequacy alone is the common thread.

Taking on the features of different maladies in different times and places, hysteria, then, is the darkly compensatory anima or *femme fatale* of the prevailing spirit and the inspiratrix, as it were, of new cultural values during periods of decline. In this regard, the syndrome may be compared to Aphrodite, the goddess of beauty and mother of Eros in Greek mythology. For just as this goddess was born from the froth that was produced when the severed genitals of the Sky-father, Uranus, fell into the sea, so hysteria (the alluring goddess of analysis and mother of its eros) is called into being by the demise and fall of the symbolic forms of a decrepit, corrupt, or irrelevant paternal order.

"The gods have becomes diseases," writes Jung, "Zeus no longer rules Olympus but rather the solar plexus, and produces curious specimens for the doctor's consulting room, or disorders the brains of politicians and journalists who unwittingly let loose psychic epidemics on the world."[16] The same assertion can be made with regard to the Christian God. For the shadow of this object has fallen heavily upon the ego during the millennium of its reign, producing that fatal confusion of phallus and penis that Lacan and Jung, among others, have warned against.

Perhaps this is why the personal mother (if Bollas is to be believed) is so loath to touch her child's genitals; this the reason her child (as Bollas further suggests) experiences the absence of her touch as a kind of presence in which awed withdrawal and inhibited attraction figure. In a *fin de siècle* culture, and even more so in an end-of-the-millennium culture, the child and the phallus really are one.

As Jung expresses this with respect to his own childhood in his memoirs, "Children react much less to what grown-ups say than to the imponderables in the surrounding atmosphere. The child unconsciously adapts himself to them, and this produces in him correlations of a compensatory nature. The peculiar 'religious' ideas that came to me even in my earliest childhood were spontaneous products which can be understood only as reactions to my parental environment [he refers specifically to his minister father's spiritual malaise – GM] *and to the spirit of the age*."[17]

Phallic mother – phallic child

Winnicott, confining his vision of the psyche to the vicissitudes of child development within the family context, has discussed the catastrophic anxieties that the
dependent infant is subject to when its mother is late by those few excruciatingly
long seconds that are in excess of what the child is able to bear. Sensitive to the
same problem, but conceiving of the psyche in broader terms than Winnicott's, we
are compelled to take up the related question of how mother's lateness is to be
interpreted. Does the failure of her instinct have anything to do with the upheaval
of the religious and cultural forms that had served and facilitated her?

In his poem "On the Morning of Christ's Nativity," John Milton writes of the
metamorphosis of the gods with which the millennium that has just ended began.
Referring to the birth of Christ, he observes that with this event the oracles of
paganism were stilled. "Apollo from his shrine/Can no more divine,/With hollow
shriek the steep of Delphos leaving."[18] Revisiting this remark, at a time when
Christ is no longer a vital enough symbol to hold back the "black tide of mud . . .
of occultism" from a mother's reveries, we may better appreciate the plight of the
contemporary mother and family. Arrested by the numinosity and phallic grandeur
that has become attached to her child during a period of unprecedented social and
cultural change, a mother may slip into post-partum psychosis, feeling wholly
unequal to her task. How could the Holy Spirit have given her such a child (she
unconsciously thinks to herself), when she, far from having the necessary creden-
tials as a virgin, remembers only too clearly the night she did it with hubby?
Failure to thrive as mother (or to be there as dad) are the hieroglyphs of a religious
problem writ so small it can barely be read as such.

In this connection, we may recall Jung's childhood dream of an enormous
phallus – the size of a large tree trunk, but fashioned of naked flesh – which
stood erect upon a king's throne in an underground vault.[19] "Yes, just look at him,"
declared the voice of Jung's mother as Jung, "paralysed with terror," gazed upon
the phallus, "That is the maneater!" Though recollected by Jung during his famous
"confrontation with the unconscious" in midlife, the dream was dreamt when Jung
was "between three and four years old," that is, at the precise time Bollas associates with the "sexual epiphany" that traumatizes all children. During this time, as
Jung also notes in his memoirs, his parents' marriage was troubled and his mother
was hospitalized for depression.

Commenting on this dream, Winnicott explains the immense phallus as "a
projection of [Jung's] own phallic excitements," relating this to Jung's not having
had sufficient help from his parents in relating to his budding instinctual life.[20]
While this personalistic interpretation is correct in a limited and obvious way,
it iatrogenically promotes identification of phallus with penis by using these
terms (as Bollas does) as if they were synonymous and by leaving the archetypal
dimension of the dream's symbolism unexplored.

To get at the archetypal significance of Jung's dream, one need only consider its
images in the light of the themes from his life's work that are prefigured in them.

The notion of the archetype and the objective psyche, of consciousness and the transformation of the God-image: just as the task of the poet, according to Coleridge, is to "carry on the feelings of childhood into the powers of manhood,"[21] so Jung gave mature expression to the affect-imagery of this early dream in these later concepts and theoretical formulations. Making this same point in a work in which the archetypal symbolism of Jung's dream is thoroughly examined, von Franz summarizes:

> Jung's first dream of the royal phallus in the grave, and his fear that it might crawl over him like a worm, is to be understood in the light of [the] myth of the king's renewal. The "old king," the Christian outlook or the Christian God-image, is dead and buried; that is, he has fallen into the depths of the collective unconscious, into matter, and into everything that would be attributed to his adversary. There it has been transformed into the worm-like phallus which raises itself up toward the light. The worm or serpent in alchemical symbolism is the first form taken by the phoenix and by the old king. After his death they are the beginning of his rebirth; it is an initial, primitive archaic life-form, out of which the new image of the king develops. The orientation of the phallus toward the light, in Jung's dream, shows that this new content is striving toward the region of consciousness. One could in fact understand Jung's whole life as a struggle to free the "new king" from the depths of the collective unconscious.[22]

Elephantiasis

A popular adage speaks of the salutary effect of naming the "elephant in the room." In the psychoanalytic consulting room, perhaps in any room, the largest of what is in all likelihood a herd of elephants, is that fallen, and yet resurgent, deity of deities, the phallus. Emblem of the paternal order, as long as an adequate interpretation of life issues from it, the phallus switches allegiances, when such is not the case, becoming the majestically powerful "thing-presentation" of the Great Mother (or collective unconscious), her phallus, her poet, her visionary son.

Personalistic psychology, unable to discern those powers and principalities of collective consciousness and the collective unconscious that transcend the human subject, reinforces the identification of ego and (unnamed) elephant, penis and phallus. Drawing upon theories that are little more than *ad hominem* arguments couched in clinical language, it speaks, not of the symbols, symptoms, and signs of the times (the gods that have become diseases), but of *patients* and *their* grandiosity, *their* narcissism, *their* use of projective identification, etc. It is said (to take up only the last of these) that the disturbed patient (or analyst) omnipotently imagines that he or she can put repudiated parts of himself (or unwieldy valued ones) into another person who, in turn, feels strongly compelled to behave in a manner that confirms the projection. Bollas, as we have already mentioned, draws heavily on this notion in his discussion of the role that recognition of typical countertransference reactions can play in the differential diagnosis of hysteria.

Analytical psychology, by contrast, taking a more transpersonal or archetypal view of these simultaneously intrapsychic and interpersonal processes, speaks, not of the *patient* putting parts of him or herself into the person of the analyst, but of an archetype or divine hypostasis having its way with them both.

There are many precedents for this conception. Traditional wisdom routinely utilizes the motif of gods intervening in human affairs. By personifying typical situations of life, it draws a distinction between the personal and transpersonal, the human and divine. Love, War, Motherhood, Business, Old Age, Death, etc., each of these has a rich and elaborate psychology of its own over and above the personal psychology of the human beings who are compelled to play them out. Places have a spirit in them, as the ancients imagined, a *spiritus loci*. Typical moments in the soul's life may be recognized as such by their determinate quality. Transcending the particular psychology of this or that person, the psychology given by the situations in which we find ourselves (the spirit, for instance, of a time or place) is readily conceived as coming upon us as a god.

Examples are legion. We have already mentioned the ravishment of Leda by Zeus and Mary's becoming pregnant by the Holy Spirit. In the Book of Enoch we read of angels becoming enamoured with the daughters of the sons of men and coupling with them to create a race of giants.[23] There is a similar reference in the Old Testament as well.[24] Apropos of these stories, women, it is said, must cover their heads in church, lest the angels become attracted to their hair and repeat with them the escapades of earlier times. Especially important for the perspective it offers on psychotherapy's central mystery, the transference/countertransference process, is the New Testament passage in which Jesus says to his disciples, "where two or three have gathered together in my name, there I am in their midst."[25] Turning this around, we could say that it is the incarnating god (or constellated archetype) that brings us together – be it in twos and threes or greater numbers still.

Further to these examples, we may recall the aforementioned illustration from the *Rosarium Philosophorum*, elucidated by Jung in *The Psychology of the Transference*, wherein the Holy Spirit, in the traditional guise of a dove, descends from above to cross the branch in its beak with those of the anima and animus figures, Diana and Apollo. Our projections upon each other, this picture seems to say, come upon us from above, i.e., from a transpersonal, archetypal source.

A symbol, according to Jung, is an imaginative representation, or registration even, of that most potent force in our lives, the unknown. Being finite, however, no single symbolic image can be divided into the vastness of the unknown without remainder. On the contrary, one symbolic form leads to another and to another still.

These reflections are especially true with regard to the symbolism we have drawn upon in these pages. The star fallen from heaven and the phallus in the nursery, the dove above the royal couple and the elephant in the room, the king in his coffin and the babe in the manger – to this list of tautegorically identical symbols many others could be added. We shall, however, have to confine ourselves to discussing just one more.

A Norse myth tells the story of Thor's visit to the castle of his traditional enemy, Utgard-Loki, King of the Giants. During his stay, Thor is challenged to a series of contests, all of which he fails. One of these is simply this: to lift a cat off the palace floor. Bending himself to this seemingly easy task, Thor finds, to his chagrin, that he is unable to lift the little creature. The most he can do is to raise one paw off the floor. For all his mightiness and renown as a powerful god, Thor becomes the laughing-stock of his adversaries. It is not until the next day that he learns the truth about his humiliating defeat. Just as he is about to leave the castle, his host, King Utgard-Loki, apprises him that trickery had been involved. The cat that Thor could not lift was not a cat at all, but a small segment of the dreaded Midgard Serpent that encircles the world! (We may think, in this connection, of the famous *arc de cercle* or arching posture which Charcot's patients displayed during major hysterical attacks.) Though the giants had seemed to laugh at him, they were in fact quite frightened. For when Thor had raised what he thought to be the cat's paw, he had almost torn the Great Serpent loose from its firmament, an event that, had it happened, would have unleashed terrible consequences upon the world.

While holding our mercurial list of synonymous symbols in mind, we may read this additional one analogically in relation to the psychoanalytic situation. The crux of such a reading, as Wolfgang Giegerich has shown,[26] is the value that the story ascribes to defeat. Thor's failure to lift the cat is a way of expressing that it is not a cat, but something greater, that he has had in his grasp. Relating this to analysis, we are compelled to ask, do our patients also grapple with something greater than they seem to? Are the symptoms they suffer, the problems they present, and the transferences they develop, like the unliftable cat in our myth, portions of the great Midgard Serpent? And the impossibility of "the impossible profession" – does this have a similar meaning?

It was in not being able to paint that Marion Milner, the psychoanalyst and Sunday painter, found that life was able to enter her paintings. Setting out to paint a vase of flowers or a simple landscape, Milner found that she could no more do so than Thor could raise up Utgard-Loki's cat. But then one day, lo and behold, there on the page before her was something most extraordinary: a picture with an entirely different subject matter than she had intended, but marvellously alive for all that.[27]

Can this lesson from painting be applied to analysis? Is it in not being able to analyze that we analyze? In not being able to listen that we listen? In our not being able to help that healing comes?

"Thor's failing," writes Giegerich, "is conversely his mark of distinction over against Everyman.

> The fact that Thor failed in lifting the "cat" shows that he had a *real* access to the archetypal level; he was *in fact* (even if not *in mente*) in touch with the Midgard Serpent. Had he been able to explicitly "see through" right from the

beginning, he would probably not have tried to lift the cat in the first place, thereby foregoing the possibility of a genuine contact with the archetypal level. His seeing through would have been an easy, merely intellectual ("academic"), substitute for a committed relation to the archetypal dimension. But as it was, he did not realize beforehand what he was dealing with, and thus he exerted all his strength. It was only his failure that forced him to realize that what he had been struggling with must have been more than an empirical cat.[28]

But what is this more-than-empirical reality that Thor, in not being able to raise up the cat, grapples with? Giegerich continues:

> In Midgard [the human world of ordinary reality and social realism – GM], things are confined to their positivity (to what they positively or literally are). . . . In Utgard [the realm of the gods and giants], a cat is more than a cat. It comprises also what it is not, its own logical negativity. The cat is rooted in what is below the ground, its head and tail continuing far beyond that little stretch that is visible above the ground: it is also that which encircles the entire world. . . . Thus, it is not just one more thing in the world, only much larger than other things, but it is the absolute, the uroboros, the ontological and *logical horizon* for every thing in the world and for the world as such. It is the whole status of consciousness, the whole mode of being-in-the-world, the entire ontology or *logic* within which not only the ontic and empirical cat, but every ontic or empirical entity is being apperceived and which constitutes its significance.[29]

As helpful as it can be to name the elephant in the room, perhaps it is in not being able to do so, even as Thor was unable to lift the cat off the floor, that the "*logical horizon* for every thing in the world and for the world as such" impresses itself upon us and a new status of consciousness is sighted, if not yet achieved. Though we must not be too hasty in naming the god, let us remember the adage of the Delphic oracle (which Jung had carved above the door of his home in Küsnacht): "Invoked and not invoked, the god will be there."

Thor in the nursery

This supplement of reading is fast becoming the castle of King Utgard-Loki! The "grand symbolical images" which are its giants, however, do not laugh at a Thor who is unable to lift the cat off the floor, but weep for a theory that lifts hysteria so easily! In Bollas's *Hysteria*, the cat that is not a cat is shown to be nothing but a cat after all. For as we have already discussed in previous sections, those segments of the world-encircling Serpent known in Christendom as Mary, Joseph, and the Christ-child are treated by Bollas as though they were nothing more than mom, dad, and their unfortunate progeny. The Holy Spirit, likewise, is spoken of satirically, as if it were nothing more than the hysteric's attempt to escape from sexuality by vacating the body-self. Reduced from the realm of cultural objects (a higher organizational level) to that of the personal complexes, all these figures, and sexuality too, are lifted in a snap.

The reader observing this feat feels none of the danger that the giants in the Norse myth felt when Thor managed to raise the cat's paw off the ground. The "*logical horizon* for every thing in the world and for the world as such," or, in the terms of the myth, the mighty Midgard Serpent, is not threatened by this theory, although in a lesser sense the world does seem to have come to an end, as Eliot put it in "The Hollow Men," "not with a bang but a whimper."[30]

Confusing the grief felt for the death of the gods (more recently, for the death of God) with the grief it would facilitate for the losses of childhood, psychoanalysis forfeits its role as the new myth of interpretation to become little more than a branch of social work or paediatrics. "I often scratch my head at a meeting," exclaimed Jung while lecturing at the Tavistock Clinic in 1935, "and say: 'Are they all midwives and nurses?' Does not the world consist chiefly of parents and grandparents? The adults have the problems. Leave the poor children alone."[31]

Bollas's term for cat-lifting and elephant-naming is the "psychoanalysis of the unthought known." In a glossary definition, he relates the unthought known "to any form of knowledge that as yet is not thought." This unthought knowledge, he goes on to say, is transferred to the analyst via "patient projective identifications." Sitting in the atmosphere of their patients' presence, "psychoanalysts . . . come to know something, and psychoanalysis of the countertransference becomes the effort to think this knowledge."[32]

While Bollas's definition, as excerpted here, is broadly enough conceived to include the cultural and religious atmosphere that our supplement of reading is attempting to think, he, like Freud before him, looks at the psyche from only one room, the nursery.[33] Encapsulated within this theoretical space, confined within the empathic and interpretive possibilities of this room, the elephant is domesticated, the cat tamed, and the Midgard Serpent never even sighted.

The objects whose shadows have fallen upon the patient's ego are assumed by Bollas to be familial ones. Constrained in this way, psychoanalysis of the *patient's* unthought known amounts to little more than psychoanalysis thinking yet again what it already knows about infantile sexuality, child development, family life, and the primitive mental mechanisms in terms of which these are internalized. Subjected to the same fate, the Cultural Phallus, or more broadly speaking, the effective (if sunken) God-image, is projected upon literal children and touched upon – *horribile dictu* – even less than our children's actual genitals are.

"Who gave us the sponge to wipe away the whole horizon?,"[34] cries the madman in Nietzsche's *Joyful Wisdom*. Not the mother, surely, who, while bathing junior, failed to scrub his widdler. But the *idea* of there being such a mother; the *theory* that would make such a monument of her omission. When the hand that rocks the cradle must be as careful as the last hundred years of psychoanalysis have led us to believe it must be, then God really is dead.

How could something so small and something so big be mistaken for each other? Without knowing it, has the nursery view of psychology been holding its candle in the sunlight? We have already suggested that in those moments of history that are "the right moment[s] for 'a metamorphosis of the gods'," cradles actually do get invested with huge, archetypal loads.

The sentiment that identifies children as the hope of the future is never more true than when it is most odious to declare. Children in our time have obtained the status of the gods for whom they once were given in sacrifice. Now *they* are the gods of a myth called therapy. This change, however, is just an enantiodromia. Children are still the sacrifice (if no longer literally, then logically) to the gods that our ideas concerning children now claim them to be. Will psychology never understand that just as the cat is not a cat, the child is not a child?

The erotics of absence

Elephant heads on cat bodies. Cat heads with elephant bodies. Babies with gargantuan phalluses. Phalluses with babies attached. In attempting to think the unthought knowledge that Bollas's *Hysteria* conveys, we may be reminded of Yeats's question: "And what rough beast, its hour come round at last,/Slouches toward Bethlehem to be born?"[35]

But for Bollas (as for much of the tradition he represents) it is a simple matter. The pram of modernity is not hitched to a a newly rising star; it is fixed to an illusion. And the religious contents that the hysteric presents are really nothing of the kind. Far from being the potent, compensatory response of the collective unconscious to the spirit of the age, as Jung conceived it to be, the Divine Child is but the conceit of an infantile neurosis.

In *Hysteria*, the pathological process responsible for the manufacture of such sham spiritual contents is explored by Bollas under the heading "erotising absence." "The mother's comings and goings create an absence," he writes,

> which becomes an important form of presence in anyone's life, but the hysteric feels that her absence is driven by an intense withdrawal from her child's sexuality, a rift that presents and represents itself as an erotic question between child and mother.
> . . . Whilst ignoring the child's body self as her erotic object, [the mother] objectifies before his or her eyes, through performance and narrative, a spectral child who she engages in highly sensuous ways. It is as if she were reading a book held out in front of her, that is the story of her love of this child, to which she directs the child's attention, riveting him or her to the story through gaze and voice.[36]

Bollas goes on to explain how the young hysteric-to-be identifies with the "spectral child," recognizing it to be the "mother's secret object of desire and then, through self-stimulation, erotise[s] this object, which is either narrated back to the mother or performed in her presence."[37] A catalyzing agent in this deleterious process is the mother's ambivalence with regard to touching her child's genitals. For this, Bollas surmises, adds an inordinate vividness and intensity to the masturbatory theatre in which the child omnipotently seeks to merge with the mother by becoming her fantasy child, "absence of [the mother's] touch suggest[ing] its own sexuality."[38]

> Perhaps, the child wonders, the mother's erotic life is too powerful to be released upon the self. In the absence of such stimulation, however, the child caresses himself or herself, increasing the quantity of sexual mental contents, those not shared with the other. During such self-stimulations the child is momentarily absent from his or her world, caught up in a reverie, evident to others by the child's distracted look. In time he or she will see such a look upon the mother's face – perhaps like the smile of the Mona Lisa – reflecting the pleasure of unseen desires. This look becomes an erotic object shared between the two. At the same time, the body is almost continuously excited by life, on the verge of being overwhelmed by the phantom touch of experience.[39]

How might our supplement of reading think the unthought knowledge that Bollas's account of the child's distracted look, momentary absence from the world, and Mona Lisa smile conveys? Is the mind of the (hysterical) child really only a *tabula rasa*, which masturbation, taking dictation from the mother's narrative, inscribes with a false self? Or does such a view leave the implicit knowledge of a greater mind unthought? Is there an authentic spiritual aspect of the unconscious that Bollas's dialectical materialist account of the erotizing of mother's absence leaves unacknowledged, unthought?

While meditating on these questions, Wordsworth's poem, "Ode: Intimations of Immortality From Recollections of Early Childhood," enters my associative stream along with Jesus' depiction of heaven as the house of his Father, in which there are many dwelling places – not just a nursery.[40] At the same time, Bollas's depreciatory view of absence brings to mind the unseen factors in life that must be imaginatively perceived, intuited, or thought – the whole order of invisible things. And following on this, a quotation from the work of James Hillman: "If a culture's philosophy does not . . . give credit to the invisible, then . . . [the invisible] . . . must squeeze itself into our psychic system in distorted form."[41] My reverie continues. I find myself thinking of Eros, the child-god who in antiquity cathected the whole of existence at the bidding of a pantheon of invisible deities. Is it he that has had to squeeze himself into that mode of appearing that Bollas has described in his theory of hysteria? Erotizing absence? Is that really something the hysteric does? Or does this only appear to be the case to the extent that psychoanalysis has itself denied Eros?

In Wordsworth's poem, what Bollas describes as the child's "distracted look," "momentary absence from the world," and "Mona Lisa smile" is conceived along Platonic lines as a visionary power grounded in a knowledge of eternal ideas. Plato, we may recall, maintained that prior to birth our souls are immersed in the realm of the eternal forms or ideas. At the instant of birth, however, this knowledge is lost and it is only through philosophical discipline that we recover or "recollect" it during the course of our lives. In his adaptation of this view, Wordsworth imagines that the child does not lose its original knowledge immediately with birth, but retains it for a time, "the glory of the unborn soul . . . [being only] gradually quenched by its descent into the darkness of matter."[42]

Referring to the child as "Thou, whose exterior semblance doth belie/Thy Soul's immensity," Wordsworth celebrates it as the "best Philosopher,"

> who yet dost keep
> Thy heritage, thou Eye among the blind,
> That, deaf and silent, read'st the eternal deep,
> Haunted forever by the eternal mind –
>   Mighty Prophet! Seer Blest![43]

Like Bollas, Wordsworth, in these lines, also reflects upon the child's other-worldly, distracted look. But in contrast to the analyst's account of this in terms of the child's erotizing maternal absence via masturbatory fantasy, Wordsworth links it to a *real* spiritual presence, the archetypal "vision splendid," which "fade[s] into the light of common day."

> And the Babe leaps up on his Mother's arm –
> I hear, I hear, with joy I hear!
> – But there's a Tree, of many, one,
> A single Field which I have looked upon,
> Both of them speak of something that is gone:
> The Pansy at my feet
> Doth the same tale repeat:
> Whither is fled the visionary gleam?
> Where is it now, the glory and the dream?[44]

If "the Child is father of the Man," as Wordsworth declares at the outset of his poem, perhaps it is because that look that Bollas characterizes as distracted or other-worldly is the sign and insignia of a visionary power, which, when retained into adulthood, or recovered then through philosophic discipline, is that by means of which we are able to name the elephant in the room and know when a cat is not a cat.

In his "Introduction to Wickes's *Analyse Der Kinderseele*," Jung also celebrates the immensity of the child's soul. Writing as the psychologist of the collective unconscious, however, he presents a less idealized account of the child than Wordsworth does. In Jung's view, the child's access to what the poet calls the "eternal deep," impressive as this may be, is seen as being indicative of its lack of differentiation from the collective unconscious. And that fading of the "visionary gleam" or "vision splendid" into "the light of common day" that Wordsworth laments is regarded, likewise, as the all-important emergence of the child into consciousness. As a psychiatrist, Jung was too familiar with children who never make the passage out of the embrace of the Great Mother to regret the disenchantment experienced by the majority of children who do. As a psychological investigator, however, he was very much interested in the dreams and fantasies produced by children during their early, undifferentiated crepuscular period, not so much for their relevance with respect to child psychology, but for the data they provided in support of his hypothesis of a collective unconscious.

> Because of its universal distribution the collective psyche, which is still so close to the small child, perceives not only the background of the parents, but, ranging further afield, the depths of good and evil in the human soul. The unconscious psyche of the child is truly limitless in extent and of incalculable age. Behind the longing to be a child again, or behind the anxiety dreams of children, there is, with all due respect to the parents, more than the joys of the cradle or a bad upbringing.[45]

Two paragraphs later, Jung goes on to identify "[t]he infinity of the child's preconscious soul . . . [to be] . . . the mysterious *spiritus rector* of our weightiest deeds and of our individual destinies . . ." It is this, he says, "which make[s] kings or pawns of the insignificant figures who move about on the checker-board of life, turning some poor devil of a casual father into a ferocious tyrant, or a silly goose of an unwilling mother into a goddess of fate."

> . . . behind every individual father there stands the primordial image of the Father, and behind the fleeting personal mother the magical figure of the Magna Mater. These archetypes of the collective psyche, whose power is magnified in immortal works of art and in the fiery tenets of religion, are the dominants that rule the preconscious soul of the child and, when projected upon the human parents, lend them a fascination which often assumes monstrous proportions.[46]

In the same way that the cat in our Norse myth turned out to be the Midgard Serpent, the child, as grasped by Jung, turns out to be the Ancient of Days. In other writings, Jung moves even further in this direction, that is, further away from the psychology of actual childhood to the idea "child" as a motif of the collective psyche. While he did, to be sure, recognize that the many different phases and experiences that individuals go through during childhood live on in the unconscious in imaginal form, he also maintained that such personal psychic contents were only partly, or apparently, personal, apperception being underpinned from the beginning of life by what he called the 2-million-year-old man, or collective unconscious.

In this connection we may recall Winnicott's adage, "there is no such thing as a baby."[47] This statement aptly sums up Jung's view as well. In contrast to Winnicott, however, who would stress the nursing couple, mamma and baby, as being the more essential unit (the baby being unable to exist alone), Jung, additionally, would pair the child with the collective unconscious or Great Mother. It is this pairing that lends the child the divine countenance that Bollas tries to account for with his theory of erotizing absence. And by the same token, this is why the images of the child can be regarded as symbolizing the archetypal psyche, or as Jung, expressing this more exactly, puts it, "the preconscious, childhood aspect of the collective psyche."[48]

> [L]ay prejudice is always inclined to identify the child motif with the concrete experience "child," as though the real child were the cause and pre-condition of the existence of the child motif. In psychological reality, however, the empirical idea "child" is only the means (and not the only one) by which to express a psychic fact that cannot be formulated more exactly. Hence by the same token the mythological idea of the child is emphatically not a copy of the empirical child but a *symbol* clearly recognizable as such: it is a wonder-child, a divine child, begotten, born, and brought up in quite extraordinary circumstances, and not – this is the point – a human child. . . . The same is true of the "father" and "mother" archetypes which, mythologically speaking, are equally irrational symbols.[49]

Chapter 4

The Dove in the Consulting Room

Hysterics enter the other (the analyst in the countertransference) as a charming child in adult form, seducing the other to be swayed by the image, seducing the other into abandonment of carnality and acceptance of transcendence to the higher orders of some divine presence, trying to destroy the other's participation in the maturational order that engages the self in the secular world.[1]

Christopher Bollas

The gulf that Christianity opened out between nature and spirit enabled the human mind to think not only beyond nature but in opposition to it, thus demonstrating its divine freedom, so to speak.[2]

C. G. Jung

Annunciation

In a seminar given in 1925, Jung described the psychotherapeutic experience as a regenerative encounter with the numinous energies of the collective unconscious. This idea, of course, was by no means new. As early as his *Wandlungen und Symbole der Libido*, Jung had discussed the prospective meaning and rejuvenating impact of the incest fantasy. Regression, he had argued in that early work, if followed back far enough, immersed the subject in deeper, mythological layers of the unconscious. Like the re-orienting descent into the underworld braved by the hero in numerous myths, the patient's regression could be understood as potentiating a rebirth, or renewal, of his or her conscious attitude. On this occasion, however, Jung drew upon another analogy in connection with the same dynamic, that of the miraculous conception of Christ, via the power of the Holy Ghost. "Analysis," he told his audience,

> should release an experience that grips us or falls upon us as from above, an experience that has substance and body such as those things [that] occurred to the ancients. If I were going to symbolize it I would choose the Annunciation.[3]

Our task in this section is to square Jung's comparison of analysis to the

Annunciation with Bollas's consulting-room account of the hysteric's characteristic style of erotisizing the transference and sexualizing therapy. At first glance, this might seem an unlikely enterprise. After all, how can the non-sexual impregnation of the Virgin Mary be compared to something as sexual as erotic transference? And by the same token, how can the implicit, and at times explicit, sexuality of the consulting room be seen, on the model of the Annunciation, as "fall[ing] upon us as from above"? These questions will settle themselves in the course of our considering them. Here let us merely recall that the analogy between the hysteric and the Holy Family is Bollas's own and that in his view the eros of even the most promiscuous hysteric is underpinned by anti-sexual, counter-genital fantasies. For all his or her show of sexuality, the hysteric, as we have already heard from Bollas, clings to virginity and childish innocence. While seeming to enter into erotic connection and even intercourse with the other, the hysteric unconsciously intends to subvert the embodied existentiality that a mature sexual life would require and to virginally conceive, or recapture, through the spoiling of sexual relations (and much talk of "spirituality") the infant or child he or she once was.

The Jungian question in the face of any psychological phenomenon is the question of purpose. What is the psyche aiming at? What does the soul want? With respect to the case at hand we are led to ask after the purpose and possible spiritual validity of precisely those kinds of transference/countertransference enactments that Bollas, consistent with his theory, has so convincingly shown to be nothing more than the unregenerately infantile derivatives of hysteria's anti-sexual aetiological background. Our aim here, as it has been throughout these pages, is not to refute Bollas's theory (which contains many important insights), but to provide a supplement of reading that brings a more archetypal perspective to bear on the issue. The psyche, as Jung repeatedly emphasized, is not an exclusively personal affair. In addition to formative experiences of the object-relations variety, it is pre-possessed or overdetermined by an *a priori* creative power that may be conceived of as being rooted in the archetypes of a collective unconscious. It is this power, welling up from within the patient in the form of compelling dreams even as it reaches him or her interpersonally via archetypal transferences, that Jung had in mind when he compared the analytic experience to the Annunciation.

Bollas, writing with the voice of a responsible critic of the "psychoanalytic romance"[4] that analysis can become for the hysterical patient, fills the pages of *Hysteria* with a number of blue case vignettes drawn from his practice as a supervisor and consultant. The analytical psychologist reading these accounts may be reminded of the "frank eroticism"[5] of the *Rosarium Philosophorum* woodcuts, which Jung elucidates in *The Psychology of the Transference*.

Let us briefly review several of the cases that Bollas discusses, assuming as we do so that Jung had similar cases in mind when he compared the analytic experience to the Annunciation.

In a chapter titled "Seduction of the Therapist," Bollas tells the story of a patient, Gerald, who would routinely tell his female analyst about his consuming interest in her breasts, bottom, and thighs. "'I'm going to throw you down on the desk, spread your legs, and come into you like a wild stallion,'" Gerald would exclaim from the couch while in the throes of hysterical passion.[6] The analyst, interpreting this material in the light of Bollas's theories (I assume him to have been the consultant in the case), was able to facilitate a lessening of the intensity of the patient's defensively sexualized reveries. "From near-orgasmic masturbations" the patient's utterances changed to "mnemic events saturated with grief over losing the mother."

> The analyst's breasts, or bottom, or thighs were now like signs of lost objects, but increasingly he talked about work and different women whom he found interesting. When he realised that all his life he had been choosing auto-erotic sex objects rather than sex objects from the real, and when he could see that this was linked up with his wish to be a good boy rather than a sexual man, a strategy which imposed limits on his maturation and the realisation of adult ambitions, he found himself in a period of intensely meaningful struggle between these two vectors. In the end, he gave up the predominance of the auto-erotic universe and the mnemic erotics of the mother's body and found a real sex object in the world with whom he got on with his life."[7]

The other cases Bollas discusses with respect to the erotic transference and sexualization of therapy all had a less fortunate outcome. Though he does not explicitly diagnose the analysts and therapists involved, he leaves us with little doubt that they, too, had hysterical characters, or, short of that, had entered into collusive, anti-therapeutic alliances with their hysterical patients through hysterical sectors of their own personalities.

Quentin, a psychologist who had read widely in the analytic literature, but who nevertheless harboured a sentimental belief that "most of his patients had been traumatized by faulty parenting in their childhoods and . . . needed some form of transformation through a new type of empathy in the clinical environment," met his *bête noire* in the figure of Susie, an emotionally distraught woman whose recent romantic rejection had confirmed an image of herself, stemming from childhood, as a "loser."[8] Consistent with his practice with many other patients, Quentin offered to sit with Susie on the couch one day when she seemed to be suffering acutely, and to provide her the solace of holding his hand. While this seemed to be appreciated by Susie, the next day Quentin was surprised to find a strange man in his waiting room serving him with a subpoena. Though Bollas does not say so in so many words, I think it is consistent with his theory to see in this traumatic turn of events the sexuality that Quentin, on the model of the hysteric's mother, had been as unwilling to allow into his awareness returning in the Name-of-the-Father.

Jerome and Heather, another analytic couple discussed by Bollas, acted out a very similar hysterical dynamic, one that also conducted them to a violent rupture involving charges of malpractice.[9] An inadequately trained analyst, Jerome "did not appreciate that he was colluding with an hysterical analysand's erotisation of the transference" when he gave her "encouragement to read papers, attend conferences and . . . to collaborate with him on book reviews."[10] To him, it seemed, Susie – herself a mental-health worker – had "blossomed" during the analysis largely due to his provision of such "auxiliary ego work."[11] Thinking about this couple in terms of the Holy Family image, we may suggest that like Joseph standing by Mary after she had become pregnant by the Holy Ghost, Jerome stood by Heather, a celibate husband to her fruitful chastity, in honour of her having become pregnant by the psychoanalytic spirit. When Heather, by now deeply in love with her analyst, became despondent over the fact that she could not marry him, Jerome consoled her with the thought that when the analysis ended they would continue to be colleagues. The innocence in which this shared fantasy of togetherness in eternity allowed them to commune was soon shattered, however, during an eight-hour car ride that the two took together on the way back from a conference at which they had both presented papers. Heather, who was wearing a sexy outfit, "blurted out to him that she wanted him to make mad passionate love to her."[12] Enraged by her analyst's rebuff, Heather responded by breaking off the analysis and reporting him to his professional association. Jerome, doubtless, was shocked by how quickly the divine child of his Joseph-and-Mary therapeutic alliance gave way to the merciless Herod in the archetypal foreground of his life. He had forgotten, evidently, if he was ever aware, that these figures, whatever the names we now affix to them (e.g., libidinal ego, anti-libidinal ego, etc.), are tautegorically identical moments within the Annunciation-like experience that psychotherapy, for weal or woe, can be. The Christ-child is, in another sense, Herod; Herod, Christ. To identify with any one element of an archetypal field is to fall prey to the entire pattern.

Keeping the Sabbath

When Jesus came upon a man working on the Sabbath day, the Pharisees, wishing to test him, asked for his opinion on the matter. In reply Jesus is said to have declared, "Man, if indeed thou knowest what thou doest, thou art blessed; but if thou knowest not, thou art cursed, and a transgressor of the law."[13] I do not think it is only the fact of a particular analytic couple failing to keep the Sabbath that puts me in mind of this logion, or saying, of Jesus from the Codex Bezae. Jerome's sin in the case just discussed (I imagine him and his patient to have been driving home from the conference together on a Sunday) is obvious enough to the rule-conscious Pharisee in us all. Condemning him is a simple matter. Jesus' statement, however, adds something more. It emphasizes a kind of awareness, consciousness, or knowing. It moves us from the specifics of the case at hand to a consideration of the universal principle involved. The Pharisees in the story were not really interested in the fact of the man's working on the Sabbath, but rather in Jesus' attitude toward this fact. Likewise, our attention should focus not on Jerome's (mal)practice so much as on our own (mal)theory. As with many of Jesus' revisionary dictums, this one, I believe, has to do with moving from the empirical or literal level to the metaphorical or logical, or, as St Paul might put it, from the letter of the law to its spirit. We do not know whether Jerome thought of himself as a working analyst when he drove home with his patient from the conference or whether he thought of himself and his patient as having the day off. This question, however, already falls well behind the kind of consciousness that Christ's logion requires. Applied to analysis, the logion implies that for the analyst the Sabbath must be kept every day. We know this, I believe, when we bump into our patients at the theatre or in other such places. Transferences do not take days off; on the contrary, they usually intensify on weekends and holidays. For this reason, if for no other, as analysts we are never off, even when in other respects we are. On the heels of this pious statement, however, we must ask ourselves if we are ever truly on duty. Ironically enough, it is in actual analytic hours that we may find it more difficult to "keep the Sabbath." For even the most impeccably conducted analysis from the ethical and technical points of view can fail to be an analysis by being either too much like Jerome and Heather's trip to the conference together or by not being enough like it. As in the saying of Jesus, it all depends on the consciousness, the knowing involved.

Ave Maria

What, we must now ask, is this consciousness, this knowing, that resolves, or better, absolves clinical practice from the conflict between the Sabbath day and every day that runs through our concerns about dual relationships and other ethical issues? The usual answers – "remediation for the wayward analyst, more personal analysis, more supervision" – will not do. To say that so-and-so is a bad analyst and leave it at that is no more helpful than to say that some other so-and-so is not a good Jew, Christian, Muslim or whatever. In each of these cases, an individual is singled out as the scapegoat on the basis of a model that goes unquestioned. For an answer to be satisfactory it must be made at the level of the theory. It must address psychoanalysis itself as an approach inclusive of and responsible for the practice of those who seem to let it down. Revised in the light of these considerations, our question then becomes: by what unconsciousness has psychoanalysis (here in a sense inclusive of analytical psychology) become accursed, the transgressor of its own laws?

In "The psychology of the child archetype," Jung declares that "psychology, as one of the many expressions of psychic life, operates with ideas which in their turn are derived from archetypal structures and thus generate a somewhat more abstract kind of myth." Underscoring his point, he goes on to say that "psychology . . . translates the archaic speech of myth into a modern mythologem – not yet, of course recognized as such – which constitutes one element of the myth 'science'."[14]

Our question as to the unconsciousness with which psychoanalysis, the science of the unconscious, is itself accursed may be clarified in the light of this statement. Guided by its logic, we are led to ask: what archetypal structures have been lost in the translation of the archaic speech of myth into that more abstractly conceived myth that psychoanalysis may be considered to be? Earlier we followed this method in our discussion of Bollas's omission of Herod and the Magi from his Holy Family analogy. Here we draw upon this method once again, considering psychoanalysis in the light of two further omissions in Bollas's analogical use of this mythologem.

The omissions I refer to here are the Holy Ghost, by whom Mary was made pregnant with Jesus, and the Angel Gabriel, who appeared to Mary in a vision and to Joseph in a dream, to inform them that it was by the will of God and the power of the Holy Ghost that Mary had conceived. While finding in Jesus' parents a metaphor for the parents of the hysteric, Bollas neglects to consider the salvific significance of these other figures. This, I submit, is more than a mere oversight on his part. Given the seminal role that Gabriel and the Holy Ghost play in the mythology to which he alludes, leaving them out has something of the character of a negative hallucination. Hysterically blind to the phenomenology of the spirit in our lives, the psychoanalytic perspective that Bollas utilizes sees at best only one half of its patient's psychology – the personal half. Is this why the patients and analysts with whom Bollas is concerned in *Hysteria* behave (or seem to behave) in the ways he purports them to? If hysteria, like beauty, is in the eye of the beholder, is it the analytic theorist's lack of vision with respect to the role played by the spiritual dimension of the unconscious that leads him or her to render such an ugly portrait of it?

Joseph and Mary, we may easily imagine, would have behaved quite hysterically had they, for lack of the knowledge brought them by the angel, taken Mary's pregnancy as a sign of infidelity on her part and assumed themselves to be disgraced on this account. Like the couples in Bollas's case studies, they would have had no immunity against the charges of impropriety that their society would have brought against them and that they would have brought against themselves. The Holy Ghost, unrecognized as such, would have been experienced as a malevolent force, even as today, within the ontology of Western Enlightenment consciousness, its manifestations are often regarded as symptoms requiring psychiatric help.[15]

On the last page of *Hysteria*, Bollas, summarizing his theory of that disorder, makes explicit reference to the "holy ghost." The Holy Ghost to which he refers, however, bears no relation to the actual spirit that bears that name in the religious thought to which psychoanalysis is heir. Blind to the significance of that spirit's force or power, even when it appears within the associative stream of his own writing, Bollas depotentiates it with lowercase script and twists it to the service of his theory, where is becomes – *horribile dictu* – just another name for Oedipus and the false self!

"The internal father," Bollas reminds us, "is a shaky structure" for the hysteric.

> Needing to adapt to reality – in order to fulfil the other's desire for socialisation – the hysteric hates a psychic structure that progressively separates the child from the open arms of the virgin mother. The maturational logic of the self – its destiny drive – is ambivalently regarded and true self realisations,

through use of the object world, are retarded in order to signify loyalty to a past meant always to repudiate the future. Mother-past and father-future are a couple, the primal scene of which is intended to create a holy ghost in the present, who can magically move back and forth between maternal and paternal orders.[16]

The Holy Ghost, as Bollas presents this figure, is no longer the heavenly seed by which Mary was made Mother of God, no longer the divine numen poured out upon the apostles at Pentecost, no longer the Third Person of the Trinity. These references are forgotten by Bollas, repressed, as is the link that identifies the Holy Ghost as the Paraclete or interior Christ, the helper/counsellor/advocate whom tradition conceives to have resurrected himself within our souls – absence of the outer historical figure being the most compelling form of his inner, psychological presence. Appropriated to serve Bollas's reductive analytic agenda, the Holy Ghost is treated as a mere alias of that triangulated "'child within' who," as we have already heard from Bollas, "castrates the self's achievements in the real by periodic uprisings that shed the self of the accoutrements of [adult] accomplishment."[17] Once again, psychoanalysis, as Jung noted of Freud, proves itself unable to credit what religion and philosophy have learned about the psyche.

In analytical psychology, by contrast, the psychological significance of religion and philosophy *is* valued, and the Holy Ghost (i.e., the autonomous psyche), as Jung's comparison of analysis to the Annunciation attests, especially so. In his autobiography, Jung goes so far as to suggest that "a further development of myth [which, as we have already heard, is what he conceived modern psychology to be] might well begin with the outpouring of the Holy Spirit upon the apostles . . ." at Pentecost. For by this the apostles "were made into sons of God, and not only they, but all others who through them and after them received the *filatio* – sonship of God – and thus partook of the certainty that they were more than autochthonous *animalia* sprung from the earth, that as the twice-born they had their roots in the divinity itself."[18]

The outpouring of the Spirit of God upon the apostles at Pentecost has been called a "second annunciation" because as a result of it the Church was born. In the above passage, Jung follows this divine process a step further. In the last centuries of the Christian aeon, the period that has culminated in what we now call modernity and postmodernity, the Holy Ghost has descended upon the individual. With this development the imperative to establish the Christian collective, i.e., the Church, has given way, or been interiorized, into what Jung has called the individuation process, in fulfilment of Christ's statement: "Ye are gods."[19] Outside the empirical Church there is still salvation, the individuation process itself being the *ecclesia spiritualis*, or church of the spirit, the building stones of which reside in each individual person's unique relationship to the autonomous psyche, or, as this was once called, the Holy Ghost.

It is important to understand that Jung is not writing as a theologian when he expresses these ideas, but as a psychological theorist and practitioner summing up over sixty years of scholarship and clinical practice. When he worked with the symbolism of Christianity and the other religions he did so as the psychologist of the *collective* unconscious. His aim was to look at culture as if it were a Rorschach inkblot to catch glimpses of the objective psyche as it is reflected in the fantasies, opinions, and debates of the *consensus gentium*. The implication of this research for clinical psychoanalysis (and I again suggest we assume Jung had in mind patients and analysts such as those we have discussed above) is that the analytic hour is the primal scene, as it were, of a *third* annunciation (or second Pentecost). This third, individuation-engendering annunciation, we must hasten to emphasize, is not produced, autochthonously, by the drive-reducing or even object-seeking libidinal urges and intercourses of mom and dad, infant and mother, analyst and analysand any more than the Holy Ghost is merely the hysterical offspring of a *mother*-past and a *father*-future as Bollas strangely implies. On the contrary, the process works the other way around (the Holy Ghost being the effective power of an *increatum*): a Self-incarnating cathexis of spiritual libido comes upon the afore-mentioned couples from above on the model of the Annunciation.

While it is true that the vertical dimension, given no recognition in the secular metapsychology of psychoanalysis, must appear horizontally (as sexualized transference, for instance, and the urge to act this out), the many "intercourses" of psychotherapy, if they are indeed to be therapeutic, are of a symbolic nature, happenings in the spirit, the so-called third area or place of illusion. *We* do not have to make these happen, tempting though it may be to ward off the numinosity of their already having happened by continuing to behave as if we had to. All that is required of us is awareness that the spirit, psyche, analysis, "interpenetrating mix-up," analytic third, or what have you, is making us.

Psychoanalysis, as Emily Dickinson said of Art, is indeed "a house that tries to be haunted."[20] With this poet as our Gabriel, we can recognize the love-in-the-room, the colleague-in-the-room, the sex, the aggression, and the hate-in-the-room without making it the analyst's or the patient's in an exclusively personalistic sense. Nor must we always reduce these images and emotions analytically as if they were only replicative of our earlier relationships. We must recognize that in addition to affording insight into the patient's representational world, the spirit-in-the-room, even when it robes itself in reminiscences from personal history, is also *presentational*, an amorous, lustful, aggressive epiphany of the objective psyche, the annunciation of the archetype to our times.

"'I'm going to throw you down on the desk, spread your legs, and come into you like a wild stallion,'" exclaims Gerald, his vision of what is happening to him constrained by the horizonal perspective of the theory in which he, his analyst, and her supervisor are couched. "Batter my heart, three-personed God,"[21] declares a more conscious John Donne in the transports of a similar, if not the same, ecstasy.

The dove in the consulting room

Paul Kugler, a Jungian analyst whose theoretical work has been concerned with the interface between psychoanalysis, poststructuralist hermeneutics, and postmodernism, has contributed the important insight that an analyst's primary ontological commitment will determine what becomes real or comes true in an analysis.[22] By ontological commitment Kugler means the analyst's fundamental assumptions about what constitutes reality. If, for example, an analyst grounds his or her clinical authority in drive theory, he or she will be led by this commitment to make very different decisions with respect to what will be taken literally and what metaphorically from those made by a second analyst, who regards the infant's relation to the breast as ontologically primary. The way each analyst listens and the interpretations each gives would vary accordingly, even if they were analyzing the same patient.

In an earlier section, mention was made of the Winnicottian adage, "there is no such thing as a baby [but rather] a 'nursing couple'." This idea (I think it is obvious) is indicative of an ontological commitment that privileges the relation of the infant to the breast. Recognizing with Kugler that other analysts or schools of analysis can be shown to work in terms of very different assumptions as to what constitutes reality, we may adapt Winnicott's adage to say: there is no such thing as a patient, but rather an analytic or epistemological couple.

Does knowing this help analysts and their patients to keep the Sabbath? Is *this* the knowledge that absolves psychoanalysis from the unconsciousness that led the couples in Bollas's case studies to become transgressors of its law?

We return to these questions indirectly by means of another question. On what *grounds* does one interpret, not reductively, but from *above*? The influx of archetypal libido that the Annunciation and Pentecost metaphors valorize was regarded in antiquity to be of divine origin. The Spirit of God, which came upon Mary in the form of a dove, was dispatched from the height of heaven. To the proselytizing apostles the Spirit took the form of inspired flights of ideas spoken in many languages, tongues of fire. In the woodcut from the *Rosarium Philosophorum*, which was discussed in some detail in an earlier section, the same movement occurs. Hurtling downward, the Holy Ghost (once again as a dove) is depicted as coming upon Apollo (representative of the *artifex*/doctor's anima) and Diana (the image of the *soror mystica*/patient's animus) from a star.

If, as Jung says, "analysis should release an experience that grips us or falls upon us as from above . . ." an experience, moreover, that is comparable to the Annunciation, interpretation, too, must come upon us from on high. This point we may underscore by recalling Jung's statement in *Mysterium Coniunctionis* that doves appearing in the symbolic material would usually "be capable of an 'interpretation from above downwards'."[23]

But again we must ask (with the image of the dove in mind): on what *grounds* are interpretations from above made? No sooner is this question posed than the dynamic instability of its imagery impresses itself upon us. The dove, being a bird, is of the airy element. Far from being "grounded," it lives in the sky. Likewise, the kind of inspired comments we refer to with the phrase, "interpretation from above," seem to come "out of the blue," from divinity itself, perhaps, not – and this is the point – autochthonously, from any (extra-psychic) ground of certainty.

Kugler's views with respect to the role played by the analyst's ontological commitment pull the rug out from under psychology's feet. For with the recognition that there are many different standpoints, the ground which we had previously taken for granted becomes relative, unstable, not ground at all any more, but a floating, dust-filled cloud. Unhinged, cast adrift, floating in infinity; terror seizes us, "poetic fright."[24] The autonomy of the psyche was just a facile idea of our own until the spirit that "bloweth where it listeth" whisked us up. Like Nietzsche we feel a loss of orientation with the relativization or death of our principal god-term. Where, we declare with him, is up and down, where sideways? Casting around for another amplification, we say with the Satan of Milton's *Paradise Lost*: "Which[ever] way I fly is Hell: myself am Hell."[25]

If, however, we are able to tolerate the dreadful uncertainty with which this loss of ground afflicts us, our airy, suspended state may take into itself, as so many swirls of dust, all that has been voided. With this change of attitude, if not to say development, the extensivity of matter gives way to the intensivity of spirit and a dove of infinite density (having taken so much of our former earth up into itself) appears in the consulting room. Glossolalia, we speak in tongues of fire (or listen as if we were speaking in tongues), not *our* spirit's lust, but *the* Spirit's lust, the language of Desire, the discourse with the Other. But what, more precisely, is the *tertium comparationis* between psychology and the Mother of God? How is it that the dove that came to Mary comes also to analysis?

Like Mary, who knew not Joseph or any other man, psychology, as we have learned from Jung and Kugler, is without an authorizing ground of certainty outside itself. In this sense it, too, can be said to be both immaculately conceived and virginal. This statement, however, must be immediately qualified in light of the fact that psychology everywhere exists in a fallen state. Lacking the theoretical analogue of the virginal pride of the immaculate Mary, psychology has repeatedly sought for itself a husband and father in adjacent fields, only to become, thereby, the illegitimate offspring of some other discipline, a bastard science. Countering this trend, Jung repeatedly reminds us of psychology's lack of an Archimedean point outside itself. "[N]o explanation of the psychic," he writes,

> can be anything other than the living process of the psyche itself. Psychology is doomed to cancel itself out as a science and therein precisely it reaches its scientific goal. Every other science has so to speak an outside; not so psychology, whose object is the inside subject of all science.[26]

A corollary of Jung's statement about psychology's lack of an Archimedean point of perspective outside itself is the recognition, which follows from this, that all knowledge is mediated psychically such that we cannot penetrate to the essence of things. Now, it is precisely this awareness of the epistemological restraints that our envelopment in psyche imposes upon the quest for knowledge that may be regarded as being continuous with the ideas of Mary's own Immaculate Conception and the Virgin Birth of Christ. Psychology, too (when not sullied by that contemporary form of Original Sin known as dialectical materialism), is the immaculately conceived virgin mother of the divine new god-term, which it, at the same time, itself is. Succinctly put, its version of Mary's paradox is this: the epistemological critique that psychology, in its virginal intactness, necessitates, looses the firmament of all other interpretive perspectives. The stars fall from their heavens; the mightiest symbols pale. And the psyche is penetrated by its own immunity to penetration, becoming pregnant, as it were, by the unseated logo-centrism of traditional metaphysics, with its own logos, psychology. As Jung put this, "only an unparalleled impoverishment of symbolism could enable us to rediscover the gods as psychic factors, that is, as archetypes of the unconscious."[27]

It is not object-relations, but *abject*-relations, that has given birth to psychology. Just as Jesus left earthly existence behind that humankind might have his Spirit within themselves, that is, the Holy Ghost as Paraclete, so psychology arises as the inward realization of the religious tradition that preceded it.

In the previous section we reflected upon the question of our ethical consciousness as analysts in connection with the idea of there being the kind of knowledge that in itself might constitute the keeping of the Sabbath, even when it may seem that the sacrosanct requirements of this day were being broken by the analyst and patient. This, in turn, led us to a discussion of the Holy Ghost. In terms of the Gospels, this movement makes sense. Sins are forgiven by the power of the Holy Ghost, their forgiveness being a main way in which the power of divine grace manifests itself through our lives. This being so, however, it is little wonder that the blasphemy against the Holy Ghost was declared by Jesus to be the one unpardonable sin. Dreaming this mythological formulation onwards, translating it into the language of psychology, what, we may now ask, is the contemporary form of the unpardonable sin?

The answer, I believe, is denial of the autonomy of the psyche, denial of the psyche's transpersonal creative life and power. In contemporary psychoanalysis we sometimes speak of *patients* as being pre-symbolic. In the same vein, we speak of *their* diabolical "attacks on linking." Here, I think, psychology sees its own crime in projection. We have many ideas regarding how analysis works. Yet, when it does work, we know it to have been the place of a mystery. When sins are forgiven, transferences resolved, and complexes healed, it is in large measure owing to the operations of the transcendent, spiritual dimension of the psyche, that age-old archetypal level of our subjectivity, which has been represented traditionally in the symbolism of the gods and now, inwardly, in the more idiosyncratic imagery of the individuation process and the transference.

In "The psychology of the child archetype," Jung sounds a contemporary version of the warning that Jesus voiced in the Gospels when he (Jesus) warned his disciples about the sin against the Holy Ghost. "Not for a moment," Jung cautions,

> dare we succumb to the illusion that an archetype can be finally explained and disposed of. Even the best attempts at explanation are only more or less successful translations into another metaphorical language. . . . The most we can do is to *dream the myth onwards* and give it a modern dress. And whatever explanation or interpretation does to it, we do to our own souls as well, with corresponding results for our own well-being. The archetype – let us never forget this – is a psychic organ present in all of us. A bad explanation means a correspondingly bad attitude to this organ, which may thus be injured. But the ultimate sufferer is the bad interpreter himself. Hence the "explanation" should always be such that the functional significance of the archetype remains unimpaired, so that an adequate and meaningful connection between the conscious mind and the archetype is assured. [28]

Chapter 5

Listening Cure

Nowhere are we closer to the sublime secret of all origination than in the recognition of our own selves, whom we always think we know already. Yet we know the immensities of space better than we know our own depths, where – even though we do not understand it – we can listen directly to the throb of creation itself.[1]

C. G. Jung

The analyst will give way to his own associations during the silences between concentrated and focused listening. He is also aware of a paradox: that his own interpretations call upon the patient's more focused consciousness and interrupt the patient's inner associative process; they might be, then, strangely antithetical to the creativity of unconscious processes. But the patient's associations to an interpretation break it up, and many analysts practicing today see this not as resistance to the hidden truth of the comment, but as an immediate unconscious use of the truth of the interpretation.[2]

Christopher Bollas

Listening with Mary's ear

"Why is psychology the youngest of the empirical sciences?" asks Jung in the early pages of his ground-breaking paper, "The archetypes of the collective unconscious." "Why have we not long since discovered the unconscious and raised up its treasure-house of eternal images?" His answer: "Simply because we [formerly] had a religious formulation for everything psychic – and one that is far more beautiful and comprehensive than immediate experience."[3]

Traditional representations of Christ's conception depict the Holy Ghost, the spirit or sperm of God, entering the Virgin Mary through her ear.[4] The idea here seems to be of the annunciation to Mary being synonymous to, or simultaneous with, her impregnation.[5] As the Archangel Gabriel announces to Mary her glorious fate as the Mother of God, a dove enters the picture, penetrating her auricular canal. And so it is that the power of the Word became flesh in her womb.

Our supplement of reading recalls this symbolism in connection with Bollas's account of the eroticism of the ear in the psychoanalysis of hysteria. For us, Mary's ear is continuous with that quality of analytic listening to which Theodor Reik refers with his wonderful phrase, "listening with the third ear."[6] If analysis is a "talking cure," as its first patient, the hysteric Anna O., dubbed it, it is also a listening cure. The ear that listens, however, is not the literal ear of sense, but the subtle ear of imagination. The same, of course, can be said of the tongue that speaks, be it the patient's tongue or the analyst's. In analysis we listen and speak imaginatively.

Bollas, we may take for granted, agrees wholeheartedly that psychoanalysis is a talking cure wherein the voice of the unconscious is heard via a third ear. From his other books we can learn much from him on this subject. In *Hysteria*, however, an irritable, anima-vexed tone creeps into his account of the unwholesome gratification that hysterical patients derive from the analytic discourse itself through their tendency to eroticize absence. This animadversion, I believe (whatever merit his theory may have), is indicative of psychoanalysis being at war with its own doubts concerning the analyzability of hysteria. Though Bollas vigorously affirms hysterical character to be amenable to analytic treatment, offering authoritative advice on just how such work should proceed, the doubts of a tradition that has largely ceased to admit its existence goad him like a gadfly on nearly every page.

The problem with analyzing the hysteric, according to Bollas, does not lie in actual ears serving as an erogenous zone (as Karl Abraham argued they can in his 1913 paper on the subject[7]), but with "*third* ears" doing so. The fact that "sound – we need only think of the mother's cooing – can function as an erotic medium"[8] is a legacy of good-enough mothering. Our capacity later in life to be touched by words owes much to our having been spoken to in loving ways while being physically touched and caressed during infancy. In the case of the hysteric, however, the relationship between the voice of the mother and physical touch has been enormously complicated by the mother's ambivalence and censoriousness with respect to the latter. Loath to touch her child's sexual body, the mother of the hysteric-to-be compensates by offering an abundance of reactively formulated prattle instead. This prattle, however, these words, do not become flesh as in the religious formula "and the Word became flesh and dwelt among us."[9] On the contrary, for all their appearance of doing so, they merely substitute for it, in Bollas's view. Parallel to this (on the other side of the Cartesian divide), the object-seeking flesh, hyper-cathected by its own frustration, becomes a friendly, if not holy, ghost of itself. Riddled with conversion symptoms, and, yet, seemingly indifferent to these at the same time, the hysteric's flesh becomes a dissociated, spiritual body, hovering above itself, a floating signifier, a confusion of tongues. "All hysterics," writes Bollas,

> are biased to keep the word in the body, as such conversions 'remember' a form of maternal erotism. As the mother's words . . . *substituted* for physical touch, the hysteric also seeks in the sonic imagery of the word the self's erotic body, so the transformational sequence of the cure must be from body to

sound to signifier. The hysteric uses the word presentation as a thing presentation, transforming it into a direct impact of oneself upon the other's unconscious. The impish moves of the hysteric are meant to bring a smile to the other's face and an "oooohhhh" or "woooooowwww". Vowel love opens the mouth wide and cracks up the face; it is preferable to consonants, which bear the knowledge of reality. The hysteric does not intend to take the word for what it means or conveys (in-itself), but for what it affects. It not only shows the body to the other, it is meant to enter the other's body as a shimmering palimpsest of excitation, engaging other thing presentations in the other's world, a kind of intercourse within the system unconscious.[10]

Bollas's concern, in this and other passages, is that the psychoanalytic situation, with its rule of abstinence and emphasis upon speaking, replicates the hysteric's early relation to the mother in a manner that is extremely difficult to analyze. In contrast to other patients, who gain insight into the illusory character of their transference projections as they grapple with the frustrating limit or gap that the analytic frame imposes upon their relationship with the analyst, hysterical patients, having learned during infancy to eroticize absence, either feel no frustration at the fact of this gap, or are gratified by the frustration they do feel, it having for them the quality of a scintillating rest in the tempestuous music of analytic rapport. Occultly tactile, the sound of the analyst's voice becomes an erotic object while "the hysteric's free associations begin to serve a sexual function . . . the patient's words conjur[ing] topics of excitement which conclude in hysterical orgasm."[11] But the hysteric's "oh" of orgasm, writes Bollas, is "not the sign of 'O' which Bion gives to infinity,"[12] but a backfiring of this into the affinity of false compliance, a marriage of false minds.

Mistaking "pre-emptive orgasm,"[13] the "bliss of renunciation,"[14] for the real thing, the hysteric may truly doubt whether mere life could offer more. When this is the case, Bollas cautions, talking cure, third ear, and transference may become addictive substitutes for a sexual life with an actual other in the real.[15] Beginning analytic treatment in their early twenties, entrenched hysterics may "live within the transference for the duration of their procreative years; abandoning the search for an erotic partner until it is too late, they remain in analysis to grieve the loss of possibility."[16] For all that has been lost, however, the ecstasy of impossible love may be lauded as a higher form of love. "Embraces are Comminglings from the Head even to the Feet, and not a pompous high priest entering by a Secret Place,"[17] the die-hard hysteric may declare with Blake at the climax of the *Liebestod* that analysis has become.

It is noteworthy that in the course of his discussion of the hysterical patient's proneness to transference addiction, Bollas once again makes irreverent use of religious metaphor, comparing the sterility of interminable analysis to an "immaculate conception"[18] occurring by way of the ear. "Certain hysterics," he writes, become transference junkies. They find in the cosy erotism of psychoanalysis a state suited to a form of hysterical life: as the self lies alongside the erotic other, the absence of physical intimacy is itself continually exciting. Talking and talking the self to the analyst, the hysteric finds in speech not simply discharge; the analyst's voice becomes an erotic object for voice intercourse, each entering the other through the ear. This immaculate conception gives birth to many analytical children – the many turning points and insights, offspring of the intercourse.[19]

Bollas's concerns are clear. When the analyst fails to recognize that "psycho-analysis itself has become the patient's symptom,"[20] a false life may be set up in the consulting room in which "'mind-fucking'" and "insight orgasms"[21] substitute for sexuality in the real, interminable analysis for marriage. For all the apparent fecundity of the enterprise in terms of the turning points and insights that are its progeny, life itself has been aborted. Linking this scenario up with another formulation of Bollas's, which we have already discussed, it would seem that "the 'child within' who castrates the self's achievements in the real"[22] has struck again, this time as a resistance to the talking cure itself, a cutting off of the third ear.

In this connection, I am reminded of the following passage on the ear from a dictionary of symbolism:

> In ancient times severed ears were offered to the Mother Goddess as a substitute for the male organs. In Egypt devotees offered their ears to the goddess Isis, and till the early decades of the Christian era, sculptured ears were offered at the shrine of the Great Mother in other parts of the middle east.[23]

Out of the mouths of babes

"Talking it," rather than "talking about it."[24] Sex talk redolent of baby talk. The Name-of-the-Father drowned out by mother's cooing and the googoo-ga-ga of baby. "Vowel love opening the mouth wide and crack[[ing] up the face."[25] The "'oooohhhh' or 'woooooowwww'"[26] of "voice intercourse."[27] The sexual body, untouched, become a subtle body. Reversing John 1:14, the flesh vaporized to become word(s), a word, moreover, that is not intended to be taken "for what it means or conveys . . . but for what it affects."[28] Each association a "spiritual body," "a shimmering palimpsest of excitation . . ." which can enter the analyst's body through the ear "[for] a kind of intercourse within the system unconscious."[29] Patient and analyst commingling like angels. Patient and the analyst "mind-fucking."[30] "Immaculate conception giv[ing] birth to many analytic children – the many turning points and insights, offspring of the intercourse."[31]

Addicted to the transference, the analytic couple talk "psychoanalese" while their brain-children cling to the analytic frame much as Harlow's orphaned monkeys clung to their wire mothers. Provoked by this atavistic return to calf worship, the "archaic structure of the father"[32] waxes hot, if only in the form of a diatribe from the analyst's inner supervisor. But the basso of his morality-imposing voice cannot be heard. Tuned exclusively to pre-Oedipal frequencies, the third ear – no longer a third ear at all – becomes a substitute for the male organs, a sacrifice to the Mother Goddess, the "talking cure" a sort of Brigadoon world of soft sensual delusions, which the hysteric will not leave. Complete dependency; interminable analysis; "a most dangerous method," indeed.

Bollas's object-relations account of the unregeneratively infantile nonsense in which a patient and analyst may unwittingly trade during the throes of an hysterical collusion is a sobering reminder of how easily psychoanalysis, like any other enterprise, can lapse into self-parody. As a Jungian analyst, I value his insights here for the counterweight they provide with respect to analytical psychology's emphasis upon meaning. Jungian psychoanalysis is deeply invested in the meaningfulness of the psyche's productions. A shadow side of this, however, may be a certain naivety when it comes to the ludicrous dimension of the soul. Just as all that glitters isn't gold, so an inane complex may appropriate the register of archetypal symbolism in the name of nonsense. Like a "virus" downloaded from cyberspace, such a complex may even have a diabolical effect, attacking the links which the ego has made, trashing one's files. Alternatively, the volatile spiritual contents that such a complex may bring in its train may take hold of the subject in the form of a manic or depressive episode. Talking archetypes and symbols, a Jungian analysis may degenerate into its own self-parodying version of the analytic romance Bollas has described – quite unaware, until the diaper hits the fan, that "it is a terrible thing to fall into the hands of the living God."[33] In this connection I think of the penchant within what has been called "vulgar Jungianism" to make everything meaningful – just like that! – by plugging the word "sacred" into a book title, a lecture title, or, God forbid, an interpretation. Against this hysterical tendency, I cite Jung's own more modest view that life is meaningful and meaningless in roughly equal measure, and that while we may work in the hope that meaning will predominate, too great a claim in either direction usually indicates that we have succumbed to illusion. Relating this to spirit, we may remind ourselves of Jung's many warnings concerning the frightful capacity of overvalued ideas and ideals (i.e., the spirit) to take possession of the personality, producing megalomaniacal inflations. "I believe that the spirit is a dangerous thing," writes Jung, "and . . . do not believe in its paramountcy. I believe only in the Word become flesh, in the spirit-filled body. . . ."[34]

Having acknowledged Bollas's contribution (and even imbibed a big spoonful of its bitter medicine ourselves), we may now proceed with our supplement of reading. Our assumption in doing so is that Bollas's theory, for all its merit in the respect I have just mentioned, may have also gotten off the track. For no sooner has one set of illusions been dispelled with his recognition of the extent to which the hysteric is in love with the *sound* of the talking cure itself, than another is instituted insofar as the hysteric's participation in the analytic dialogue is depicted as being dumb to meaning. If this is so (and Bollas's theory is too pessimistic on this account), a spoonful of our sweet syrup may be just the right medicine.

The Jungian approach to the language question that Bollas's account of hysteria has raised is an archetypal approach, not a developmental one. Now, in making this distinction, I do not wish to add fresh fuel to the debate that has raged within analytical psychology over the compatibility or incompatibility of these two perspectives. My aim, rather, is to point out that Bollas's theory, punctuated as it is with maturational stages (which are then written across Lacan's triptych of registers), holds certain forms of communication to be meaningful and others to be nonsense – at least insofar as the hysteric is concerned.

The privileging of one form of expression over another is given with the schedulistic logic of developmental thinking itself. When, for example, something is said to be more developed or fully articulated than something else, its superiority is also implied. The archetypal approach, by contrast, is more *laissez-faire*. This is particularly so in the case of the archetypal school of analytical psychology. In contrast to the classical school, which privileges certain especially symbolical images as being representative of an archetype, the archetypal school conceives the archetype to be immanent, and wholly so, to any image whatsoever.[35] Where the former approach treats archetypes as nouns, the later approach sees them as more adjectival.[36]

Simply put, the problem is this: in Bollas's account of hysteria, the *sound* of words and the *sense* of words are divided from each other by the same demarcation line which divides pre-Oedipal and (post-)Oedipal development into the stages known by these names. Following from this, meaning is then associated with the "father" as representative of the symbolic order and mediator of the reality-principle. On the other side of the developmental divide, the sonorousness of words (i.e., words used not for what they mean but for what they affect) is identified with the nonsensical register of the maternal imaginary. Turning away from the realities of life that could be "talked about" in analysis, the hysteric is envisioned as languishing with the pre-Oedipal mother in an oceanic bliss of meaningless sounds. When such is the case, interpretation (Bollas fears) is emasculated, its seminal power depotentiated as the patient's nursing ear slurps up the analyst's words as if they were nothing more than a soothing draught of mother's milk in a time that is long past weaning. Against this perversely gratifying use of analysis, and consistent with the one-way ticket that development issues, Bollas, as we have already discussed, sees the cure as moving from body to sound to signifier, which is also to say, from autoeroticism through maternal eroticism to paternal meaning. Hoping to facilitate this transformative process, the analyst makes interpretative statements that give words to the patient's repressed desires, while simultaneously addressing the "maternal refusal of the self's sexuality."[37] But the issue of whether the patient actually hears these words as words remains.

The archetypal approach, by contrast, does not locate meaning one-sidedly in the symbolic order over which the father presides. While that realm, being identical in Lacan's thought with language, societal law, and civilization, certainly does possess an abundance of meaning, this meaning can also succumb to hypertrophy

(as Lacan well knew) even as the king in a fairy tale, or an actual ruling government, can become tyrannical, corrupt, redundant, or enfeebled. When this is the
case, the meaningfulness of what before had seemed absurd becomes evident.
Compensating the effeteness of the "father-world" or paternal order, the maternal
realm of the unconscious rises to the fore. Monotheism gives way to polytheism;
the hegemony of one voice to a cacophony of many; the repressed returns in a
Babel of confused tongues.

In earlier sections we spoke of the *fin de siècle* and quoted Jung's comment
about our living at the "right moment" for a "metamorphosis of the gods." During
transitional periods such as these (when the dominants of the symbolic order are in
the descendant), the psychoanalytic cure may be conceived of as moving in the
opposite direction from that proposed by Bollas – from signifier to sound to body!
Or, leaving the developmental logic of schedules altogether, signifier, sound, and
body may be regarded as manifesting themselves simultaneously as aspects of a
single moment or whole at every "stage" of life.

Winnicott, it may be recalled in this connection, made it a point of technique for
analysts to ask themselves with regard to a fantasy that has been represented in the
transference, "what and where is the accompanying orgastic bodily functioning?"[38]

Sometimes, in the midst of an analysis, a breakdown occurs. Looking beyond
the consulting room we may see breakdown as well in our institutions and in
society at large. Symptoms appear – in the body of the individual and in the body
politic alike. Or, when it is a case of conversion symptoms that have long been
present, these may suddenly become the focus of new concern as the famous *belle
indifférence* of the hysteric gives way.

Outwardly perceived, the movement from the fully articulate to apparently less
articulate and more obviously troubled presentations of self may suggest that a
negative transference, or perhaps even a negative therapeutic reaction, has been
triggered. Inwardly perceived, however, it is as if the stars had fallen from their
heavens and our mightiest symbols had paled. No longer exerting a hegemony or
Herod-like hold upon meaning, words "crack up," as Bollas has described it in an
earlier book.[39] Sprouting the dove's wings of a second sense, they fall upon the
body like an Ave Maria. Rebaptizing itself in the body's symptoms, the dead letter
that the Word had become in our lives becomes existentially relevant again –
living word, flesh. Or, to say the same thing in a more up-to-date way, the entire
symbolic order in which we are culturally and linguistically encapsulated falls into
the inner infinity of this couple, this transference, this symptom, this wound and
body that we are – to "die and rise the same, and prove mysterious by this love."[40]

When heard through the Christian window of that monad of archetypes which
Jung called the collective unconscious, the psychoanalytic cure moves from star,
angel, and dove to virgin, Bethlehem, and stable. Through other windows, the
"discourse of the Other" sounds in countless variations. Told in the terms of
another story, which the visiting Kings might have collected in their travels, an
analysis may seem more like the downward reach of the all-Father, Odin, who,
when hung on the windy tree ("sacrificed/myself to myself") picked up the runes

of his wisdom shrieking.[41] Through another window, the heaven-afflicted Job, his body covered with painful boils, cries out in a similar vein, "Even after my skin is destroyed, Yet from my flesh I shall see God."[42] Plagued by migraines and coughing up phlegm, Nietzsche, "the physiologist" and "first psychologist of Christianity" exclaims, "'Reason' in language: oh what a deceitful old woman! I fear we are not getting rid of God because we still believe in grammar. . . ."[43] And, then, this from the mouth of Lear (to limit ourselves to just one more example): "O! how this mother swells up toward my heart. Hysterica passio! down, thou climbing sorrow. Thy element's below!"[44]

We are a far cry from Bollas's description of the hysteric in baby land! And yet not such a far cry, for we are listening to the same patient. Questions arise. Is the impressionistic précis we pulled together above merely an artifact of the theory which presented it? Is regression as literal as the developmental models suppose? The hysteric as fixated as Bollas imagines? Or is it rather the case that the unconscious – through the patient – shows us the face that we show it?

These questions, in their turn, inspire further questions. Is the pre-verbal literally so? Pre-verbal in the same way babies are? Or is the babble of a baby, far from being pre-symbolic, a language of its own?

Melanie Klein believed that one of the most bitter grievances of early childhood stems from the consternation that babies feel when the overwhelming questions contained in the sounds which they make are not understood or answered.[45] Other theorists, on the contrary, maintain that meaningful utterance is a function of language acquisition of a later period. Meanwhile, the question remains: what is the effect of these respective viewpoints upon our adult patients? Is a patient himself in the same way when the analyst's reverie is informed by the image of a nipple in the lips of the regressed hysteric as he is when the analyst envisions a pomegranate seed in the mouth of Persephone in Hades? And what of that *tertium comparationis* upon which so much psychoanalytic theorizing is fixated – the actual babies themselves? How do they, not having had the benefit of having taken an infant observation course, apperceive the breast? As a mammary gland, a pomegranate, or a star? A proverb states that the dream comes true in the way it is interpreted; surely this is the case as well with our transferences and resistances.

Regression deliteralized

Readers familiar with Jung's writings may recall, in this connection, a famous passage of his having to do with an archetypal view of regression and incest. The passage is from the chapter titled, "The sacrifice," in his voluminous *Symbols of Transformation*. In an earlier form, this is the chapter that Jung believed had cost him his relationship with Freud. With the grotesque caricature of the regressed hysteric in mind, which we gleaned from the pages of Bollas's *Hysteria*, we may read this passage for the supplement of reading it provides to that work.

Freud's incest theory describes certain fantasies that accompany the regression of libido and are especially characteristic of the personal unconscious as found in hysterical patients. Up to a point they are infantile-sexual-fantasies which show very clearly just where the hysterical attitude is defective and why it is so incongruous. They reveal the shadow. Obviously the language used by this compensation will be dramatic and exaggerated. The theory derived from it exactly matches the hysterical attitude that causes the patient to be neurotic. One should not, therefore, take this mode of expression quite as seriously as Freud himself took it. It is just as unconvincing as the ostensibly sexual traumata of hysterics. The neurotic sexual theory is further discomfited by the fact that the last act of the drama consists in a return to the mother's body. This is usually effected not through the natural channels but through the mouth, through being devoured and swallowed, thereby giving rise to an even more infantile theory which has been elaborated by Otto Rank.[46]

At the beginning of this passage, Jung, in agreement with both Freud and Bollas, accepts that the fantasies of the hysteric have an infantile-sexual content. Unlike these contributors, however, he doubts that such fantasies are merely derivatives of the literal realities their content appears to be so obviously reducible to. As a shorthand to explain his scepticism on this point, he reminds us of Freud's crucial discovery that many of the traumatic seductions that he had initially believed to be the cause of hysterical attacks were of symbolic, not literal, significance, never having in fact taken place. In Jung's view, the same discovery applies to the vicissitudes of development as well. While we all go through a developmental process, suffering misfortunes and forming complexes along the way, the fantasies through which the psyche takes its *archetypal* bearings may have an utterly different purpose and meaning. Indeed, even when utilizing the material of our early developmental history (or as Freud would put this, when suffering from reminiscences,[47]) the psyche does so metaphorically, finding in what happened in the past, or what was felt to have happened, a "language" and "mode of expression" for our present concerns that is as "dramatic" as it is "exaggerated."

"All these allegories are mere makeshifts," writes Jung, continuing from where we left off above:

The real point is that the regression goes back to the deeper layer of the nutritive function, which is anterior to sexuality, and there clothes itself in the experiences of infancy. In other words, the sexual language of regression changes, on retreating still further back, into metaphors derived from the nutritive and digestive functions, and which cannot be taken as anything more than a *façon de parler*. The so-called Oedipus complex with its famous incest tendency changes at this level into a "Jonah-and-the-Whale" complex, which has any number of variants, for instance the witch who eats children, the wolf, the ogre, the dragon, and so on. Fear of incest turns into fear of being devoured by the mother. The regressing libido apparently desexualizes itself by retreating back step by step to the presexual stage of earliest infancy. Even there it does not make a halt, but in a manner of speaking continues right back to the intra-uterine, pre-natal condition and, leaving the sphere of personal psychology altogether, irrupts into the collective psyche where Jonah saw the "mysteries" ("représentations collectives") in the whale's belly. The libido thus reaches a kind of inchoate condition in which, like Theseus and Peirithous on their journey to the underworld, it may easily stick fast. But it can also tear itself loose from the maternal embrace and return to the surface with new possibilities of life.[48]

Jung's reference to "regression go[ing] back to the deeper layer of the nutritive function, which is anterior to sexuality," calls to mind Bollas's account of the hysteric's regressive retreat from Oedipal sexuality into the baby-land of pre-Oedipal pleasure. For Jung, however, this material, as important as it certainly is, "cannot be taken as anything more than a *façon de parler*." It is metaphorical now, even if literal before. The regressive process has merely "clothed itself in the experiences of infancy" as a prelude to "leaving the sphere of personal psychology altogether." For the analyst who has the ear to hear it, the blathering of the analysand-baby is at the same time the trumpet-blast of the Ancient of Days.[49] Seconding this connection between the mythic depths of metaphor and the collective psyche, Jung writes in another place that "whoever speaks in primordial images speaks with a thousand voices."[50] This is so, paradoxically enough, even with respect to an analysand's most forlorn and pathetic cry.[51] For as Jung has put it, "the patient must be alone if he is to find out what it is that supports him when he can no longer support himself."[52]

Retaining the concept of regression, even as he deliteralizes it (regression proving itself through this process to be a mode of deliteralizing!), Jung follows the descent of the libido down and back, again and again, into the deepest reaches of its *myth* of origins. Irrupting into the collective psyche – that theatre of "thing-presentations" or archetypal images – the suffering that underpins neurosis is shown to be given with the Bardo of existence itself – and not, as Freud maintained, with that of childhood only.

Deepening an insight of Winnicott's in the light of Jung's negativizing vision of regression, we can say that the dreadful, which has already happened, had even then already happened.[53] This, in turn, may remind us of a discovery of Freud's concerning traumatic events. During his work in self-analysis Freud found that every important recollection from his early years proved to be secondary to a similar recollection from an even earlier time. Derrida, explaining memory as the laying down of written traces or "supplements" in the mind, makes much the same point. "The supplement is always the supplement of a supplement," he writes. "One wishes to go back *from the supplement to the source:* one must recognize that there is *a supplement at the source*."[54] What Freud describes as the elusiveness of a primary trauma, and Derrida as "the supplement at the source," we may regard as the threshold of the collective psyche – the whale's belly or archetypal realm.

"There are cries of the passions," writes Antonin Artaud, "and in the cry of each passion there are degrees of vibration of the passions; and the world in other times knew a harmonic of the passions. But each illness also has its cry and the form of its death-rattle . . . And the earthquake has its sound . . . And from an illness to a passion, from a passion to an earthquake, one can establish some similarities and some strange harmonies of sounds."[55] The closer we approach to the singular, even the uniquely accidentally and personally traumatic, the more the strange harmony of the universal sounds through. Words that have long since become empty abstractions, renew themselves in that abyss of idealism that we – even in our most disillusioned moments – are, just by virtue of being alive. Listening with evenly suspended attention, the analyst hears in the music of the patient's voice not only the rage and distress of the colicky baby but the "tintinnabulations, pig grunts, eagle screams, baboon howls, and silence" through which "language, thought, and civilization" are returned "to the lower Paleolithic for a fresh start."[56]

Drawing upon Darwin's view that emotions recall actions that were meaningfully and purposefully related to the imperatives of survivial that existed during earlier evolutionary epochs, Freud makes a similiar point to the one we have just made.

> [H]ysteria is right in restoring the original meaning of the words in depicting its unusually strong innervations. Indeed, it is perhaps wrong to say that hysteria creates these sensations by symbolizations. It may be that it does not take linguistic usage as its model at all, but that both hysteria and linguistic usage alike draw their material from a common source."[57]

Like its patients, psychoanalysis must also undertake the *nekyia*, or night sea journey. It, too, must immerse itself in the depths of the unconscious, descend into the inferno, and restore the original meaning to words. While there is, to be sure, the very real danger in this of malignant regression (as Freud intimated to Jung with his warning about releasing "a black tide of mud . . . of occultism"), there is also the possibility that our regressed, de-literalized theory may "also tear itself loose from the maternal embrace and return to the surface with new possibilities of life."

Freud's "self-analysis" and Jung's "confrontation with the unconscious" were each enactments of just such a descent. Returning to the surface they brought with them new sounds, new words, new songs. "Libido," "Oedipus complex," "anima/animus," "self": with each of these "tintinnabulations" our analytic forebears contributed new possibilities of life to their century. The need for new sounds continues. The century that stands before us also needs new words and songs, new terms and theories.

If psychoanalysis is to continue to have relevance, it must continue to meet this need. If it is to remain a living language, it must renew itself again and again in the infinity of each analytic couple who would talk it deeply. Pig grunts, eagle screams, baboon howls, and child's cries, these, or rather, their silent equivalents in our day, may yet prove to be the basis of the life-giving language of tomorrow.

Perhaps – who knows – if the negativizing register of the nonsensical were listened to aright, we might hear in it the speech of the New Anthropos. But then again, as both Shakespeare and Bollas rightly warn, the opposite may also be the case. The nonsensical may be just that: "a tale told by an idiot, full of sound and fury, signifying nothing."

Meaning or meaninglessness? While working in the hope that meaning will predominate, let us leave the balance even on that question. For who, after all, are we to say? Not only does illusion await us if we make too great a claim in any one direction; more chastening still is the recognition that no practitioner, from the most workaday of analysts to the most radical and revisionist, can exclude himself or herself from the society of "those who . . . turn their eyes away when faced by the as yet unnameable which is proclaiming itself and which can do so, as is necessary whenever a birth is in the offing, only under the species of the non-species, in the formless, mute, infant, and terrifying form of monstrosity."[58]

Chapter 6

Speech and Language in Analytical Psychology

The phonetic connection between G. *Mar*, F. *mère*, and the various words for 'sea' (Lat. *mare*, G. *Meer*, F. *mer*) is certainly remarkable, though etymologically accidental. May it perhaps point back to the great primordial image of the mother who was once our only world and later became the symbol of the whole world? Goethe says of the Mothers that they are "thronged round with images of all creation." Even the Christians could not refrain from reuniting their Mother of God with the water: "Ave maris stella" are the opening words of a hymn to Mary. It is probably significant that the infantile word *ma-ma* (mother's breast) is found in all languages, and that the mothers of two religious heroes were called Mary and Maya.[1]

C. G. Jung

Jung . . . embodied qualities that Freud both admired and feared. He enacted the maternal and feminine (as did Winnicott later) which Freud found faintingly fetching, but also wished to keep outside his affiliation to the father. Ridding himself of Jung also expelled consideration of other matters which he found irksome such as aesthetics, philosophy, music, which may have felt like the wish(y) wash(y) world of maternal knowledge. To this day, too many Freudian analysts marginalise Jung whom they find flaky, impressionistic, otherworldly, or lacking in rigour, apparently unaware of the contempt expressed toward the maternal order that saturates much of Jung's work.[2]

Christopher Bollas

Complex, acoustic image, Holy Ghost

Our account of analytical psychology's approach to the language question, which Bollas's theory of hysteria has raised, would not be complete without mentioning Jung's researches in word association, Kugler's archetypal psycho-linguistics, and David Miller's application of these contributions to the exegesis of the Holy Ghost concept. In this section and the next few, we shall discuss these in their turn.

In the early years of the last century, immediately prior to his becoming a colleague of Freud's, Jung achieved international renown through his researches in experimental psychopathology. While working as a resident in psychiatry at the Burghölzli Klinik in Zurich, Jung, and an associate, Franz Riklin, administered a protocol known as the association experiment to numerous subjects drawn from both clinical and non-clinical populations. In the experimental situation, test-subjects were asked to respond, with the first word that came to mind, to a standard list of simple, yet evocative, test words such as "head," "green," "water," "murder," "long," and "five," etc. In this way, chains of association were elicited, which could then be analyzed in the light of whatever hypothetical questions had been posed.

Of course, as happens with almost every human endeavour, the experiment was never able to be completed without a hitch. Again and again, test subjects failed to hear the stimulus word, took over-long to respond, laughed, coughed, or otherwise muddled the sample they had been asked to provide. Prior to Jung, such occurrences were regarded as no more than dirt in the laboratory or germs in the surgery. Their significance was overlooked. Jung, however, brought a different ear to this experimental data. Like other notable psychological investigators of that period (William James, Théodore Flournoy, Frederic Myers), Jung had attended numerous spiritualist seances, where he had witnessed young women – many of whom were regarded to be hysterics – entering trance states and speaking on behalf of the dead. This experience, combined with his knowledge of the dissociationalist tradition of French psychopathology and Freud's study of parapraxis, equipped him to recognize the importance of the seemingly bungled responses and botched results that the association experiments regularly churned out. Though these were not the voices of the dead in the literal sense of the spiritualist movement, they did point to the presence of unconscious emotional factors and inner resistances – the dead in a psychological sense.

In Jung's hands, the association experiment had become a powerful tool. Using it not only as a method of research, but as an adjunct to diagnosis and treatment, Jung, Riklin, and their Zurich colleagues were able to bring the nuts and bolts of hysteria, dementia praecox, sociopathy, and other disturbances into the ambit of their scrutiny. What psychiatrist and layman alike came to know as the complex had been discovered.

Among the many contributions that Jung was to make through his early work with the association experiment, two publications from 1906 are of particular relevance to the issues with which we are concerned in these pages. The first of these, "Association, dream, and hysterical symptom," examined the relationship between disturbances in verbal response, the imagery of dreams, and conversion symptoms.[3] It was found that material gathered across these three spheres of interest gave expression to the same complexes. The same emotionally toned ideational factors that announced their presence by interdicting the associative chain during the word-association experiments, manifested themselves somatically in the form of symptoms in the body, and imagistically in the form of dream images.

Although arrived at through work with an hysterical patient, this finding holds true across the diagnostic spectrum. Words, dream-images, and bodily symptoms are correlatives of each other in all subjects. Linguistic–imagistic–somatic complexity is given with the nature of the psyche itself.

The other early research of Jung's that is relevant to our supplement of reading is reported in "The psychopathological significance of the association experiment." In this paper, Jung presents important findings having to do with association experiment responses made on the basis of similarities of sound.

Jung's research in this area followed upon the earlier work of another investigator. In research conducted at Kraepelin's clinic in Heidelburg, Aschaffenburg had noted that subjects gave altogether different responses to the stimulus words of the association experiment when they were fatigued than when they were alert. When rested, test subjects tended to provide associations that were meaningful from a semantic point of view. To the stimulus word "head," for example, they might respond with words such as "thought," "hat," or "hang," etc. With increasing fatigue, however, this kind of response gave way to a preponderance of associations based upon resemblance of phonetic pattern. Hearing the stimulus word "head," the tired test subject might respond with words such as "red," "bed," or "lead" etc. This shift from semantically based associations to phonetically based ones was attributed by Aschaffenburg to changes in motor stimulation brought about by physical fatigue.

Reviewing this research, Jung was sceptical of the conclusion that had been drawn by his Heidelburg colleague. To his mind, it was painting with too broad a brush to put the shift in associations that had been observed down to such a gross causative factor as fatigue. Something within fatigue, but that can also exert its influence independent of that state, must have been overlooked by Aschaffenburg. Exhausted subjects are, after all, not the only ones that make sound associations.

Drawing upon Janet's observation that "each *abaissement du niveau mental* is accompanied by a flare-up of automatisms,"[4] as well as upon his experience of the communications that came from the mouths of highly alert mediums during states of trance,[5] Jung suspected simple "lack of *attention*" to be sufficient to produce the shift that had been noted from semantic to phonetic associations. Experiments of his own, conducted at the Burghölzli, confirmed this hypothesis. Summarizing the results of these investigations, Jung reported that,

> When a longish series of associations, say two hundred, is given to a subject, he will, without really becoming tired, soon find the process boring, and then he will not pay so much attention as at the beginning. For this reason we have separated the first hundred from the second in our classifications and have found that in all cases where the subject had become bored there is a clear decrease in the internal [semantic] associations and a proportionate increase in external and sound associations. This observation made us think that the cause of sound associations is not so much muscular stimulation [as Aschaffenburg had concluded], which is absent in normal boredom, but a lack of *attention*. . . . Furthermore, we found an increase in the proportion of sound associations with subjects whose ability to concentrate had been weakened by

a recent affect . . . [and] with psychotics. . . . *It can therefore be said that the more the attention of the patient decreases, the more the external and sound associations increase.*[6]

The implications of these research findings are many. In the present context, what is most striking is the overlap between the italicized statement with which Jung ends the passage quoted above and Bollas's account of the hysterical analysand's resistance to the interpretive dimension of the talking cure. In the first part of Jung's italicized sentence, reference is made to the attention of the patient decreasing. It is the effects of this upon association that he is summing up.

In *Hysteria*, Bollas, too, is concerned with the decrease of the patient's attention. The hysteric, in his view, often does not attend to the substance of the analyst's interpretations. The upshot of this within the consulting room is the same as the outcome that Jung reports from his work in the laboratory. In the analytic situation, as in the experimental one, sound associations increase as the attention of the patient decreases. Where Jung observed a change from semantically determined associations to phonetically determined or sonorous ones as attention diminishes, Bollas characterizes the hysteric as withdrawing attention from the semantic, or meaning, level of the analytic dialogue in favour of its sensuous, phonetic aspects.

At first glance it would seem that we have come upon common ground. When set alongside each other, Jung's researches in association appear to presage Bollas's observations with respect to hysteria, even as Bollas's observations appear to confirm Jung's early research. To conclude that this is so, however, would be incorrect. As striking as the similarity between their respective findings seems to be, closer examination reveals that this similarity is actually the point of a more significant difference. This becomes immediately apparent when we remind ourselves that Jung's discovery is not limited to hysterics, but applies to everyone, regardless of diagnostic type. Through his studies in word association Jung had discovered, not a feature of hysterical pathology, but a law of the psyche.

The implications of Jung's early discoveries do not augur well for Bollas's theory of hysteria. When, for instance, the latter declares that "the hysteric's auto-eroticism cannot be overstated,"[7] we may wonder if this claim is not a function of an underestimation of what in Jungian thought is called the autonomy of the psyche. As a leading contributor to contemporary object relations theory, Bollas may be conflicted, if not to say torn, when it comes to thinking in terms of what revisionists of that school, with a nod to Jung, have recently called "subject relations."[8] Though in other books Bollas has himself used this term and made important contributions in this direction through his call for a return to Freud's account of the functioning of the unconscious, in *Hysteria* he is less a student of the psychic processes that underpin the destiny drive than he is a psychoanalytic alienist diagnosing the pathological structures that fatefully foreclose upon it.

While Bollas has much that is valuable to say about the pathological structures that ruin lives, reading *Hysteria* we are left to wonder: is the hysteric really as dissociated from the unconscious workings of the destiny drive as he suggests? Or has he merely characterized the hysteric as such in order to retain the object relations theory, which he, as clinician and theorist, is moving beyond? Loath to relinquish the satisfaction that the object relations approach has given him, has Bollas, like the Moses of Freud's Michelangelo essay, thrown the book at the hysteric so as not to have to throw out object relations theory altogether? To these questions we shall return in a later section.

The entirely depreciatory view of hysteria that emerges as a result of Bollas's approach is all the more curious when we consider that in Jung's thought the anima and animus are regarded as psychopomps of the individuation process itself. The rub here, I believe, is lack of familiarity with Jung's discovery that sound associations increase as a function of distraction and diminishing attention. Had this 1905 discovery been recognized for the law of the psyche that it is, it would not have had to appear again, almost one hundred years later, diagnostically, in projected form, as Bollas's year 2000 "discovery" of the ubiquity of hysterical character.

The siren song of the sonorous psyche is not exclusive to a particular group of people diagnosed as being hysterical; it is a dimension of the psyche itself. Though *klang* (sound) associations do point to the presence of complexes (the interior, but still positivized, objects of object relations theory), the music they make together also expresses, in a way that mediates the compensatory potential of the collective unconscious, what Jung later came to call the archetypal core of the complexes.

At the unconscious level we are all hysterical, whether diagnosably so or not. Recognizing this, Jung, in his later theory, personified the psychic factor that underpins perception and makes the world a stage, speaking of it as an inner man or inner woman much in the same way that poets down through the ages have spoken of a muse. It is these figures, operating both above and below the semantics of the ego, that sonorously communicate to us the desire of that other within ourselves through whom those outside ourselves are fatefully cathected.

In this context we may be reminded of a question that Lacan asks in relation to his dictum that "the unconscious is structured as a language": ". . . [W]ho is this *other* to whom I am more attached than myself, since, at the heart of my assent to my own identity, it is still he who wags me?"[9]

Ignotum per ignotius, the Jungian "answer" to Lacan's question is that syzygy of contrasexual archetypes, which mediates the influence of the objective psyche through our lives, the anima/animus.

Phonetic spirit

Jung's findings with respect to the sonorous dimension of speech and language would be virtually unknown today, even within analytical psychology, if it were not for the work of Paul Kugler (whose reflections on epistemological issues were discussed in a previous section). In a book published in 1982, *The Alchemy of Discourse: An Archetypal Approach to Language*, Kugler returns to Jung's early research in word association, bringing out its full significance in the light of more recent developments in the field of postmodern linguistics. According to Kugler, the points of comparison between the (seemingly) modernist Jung and postmodern linguistics reside in Jung's empirical finding that the "subconscious association process takes place through *similarities of image and sound.*"[10] Along with the related observation that semantically determined associations give way to phonetically determined ones as attention decreases, this finding dove-tails (!), as it were, with the constituting insight of Sausserian and post-Sausserian linguistics, which holds that the meaning of words is primarily a function of their relationship to each other within the reflexive domain of language itself, while only secondarily being a function of their etymological history, conceptual signification, and objective reference.

Listening to the resonances that can be heard when the depth psychology of Jung is compared with recent developments within linguistic theory, Kugler arrives at an approach to both disciplines that he calls "archetypal psycho-linguistics." To illustrate the basis of this approach, he provides a number of examples of what he calls "invariant structures of sound-meaning."[11]

The notion of invariant structures is synonymous with Jung's concept of the archetype.[12] Called phonemes when they appear in language, these structures, according to Kugler, are an immanent source of meaning within sound itself. More poetic than prosaic, the meaning of these invariant units is usually not immediately apparent. Indeed, compared with the more obviously meaningful semantic associations that give way to sound associations as attention diminishes, such meaning may be characterized as being unconscious. This point is important to stress. Sound associations, far from being meaningless, present unconscious meanings. Or put another way, phonetic signifiers, being interconnected with one another in a vast ocean of sound, projectively invest the words we speak and the objects we refer to with a surplus of significance or meaning.

One example of invariant structure that Kugler provides is of especial interest in light of Bollas's theory of hysteria. Bollas, we may recall, understands the hysteric as turning away from the sexual father along with the burdensome realities that he, as mediator of the word, brings. This turning away, moveover, is interpreted by Bollas as a turning back to the pre-Oedipal mother. He sees it as a regressive movement from meanings, which can be talked about, to the gratifying sensuousness of sound itself, a movement from the symbolic or paternal order to baby talk and motherese.

Kugler, interestingly enough, finds something of this same story sounding through a series of phonetically similar words. Carnal, carnation, carnage and reincarnation: though as object-realities these words may have little in common, the phonetic pattern that determines their associative enchainment is evocative, as psychoanalysis has long known, of what has been called the sexual defloration fantasy. The same can be said of the words violent, violate and violet. They, too, contain within their phonetic resemblance to one another the fantasy of defloration, as Freud noted in the early days of psychoanalysis in *The Interpretation of Dreams*. In contrast to Freud, however, who attributes this to mere chance,[13]

Kugler argues for a more necessary relation. "The phonetic association among these words," writes Kugler,

> is . . . in accordance with the unconscious associations of their semantic aspects. *Violate* means "to rape"; *violent* implies a show of physical or emotional force; *violet* is a bluish-purple flower. . . . This preliminary amplification of the linguistic complex will take a more concrete shape as the German, French, and Hungarian counterparts are brought into the picture. In German *Blut* is a singular meaning "blood"; the grammatically plural form is *Blüten*, "blossom"; and the verb *bluten* means "to bleed." In French *viol* means "rape"; *violette* is a bluish-purple flower, a violet; and *violer* means "to violate." The same complex of associations also exists in non-Indo-European languages. In Hungarian, for example, *vér* means "blood," *véres* is "bloody," and *verág* denotes "bloom, flower."[14]

In this example, sonorous language is shown to have a psychology of its own – quite apart from the psychology of the people who use it. This psychology, moveover, is similar to that which Bollas describes as characteristic of a particular group of speaking subjects – patients with hysterical characters. Like the hysterical patient, language itself has a sonorous mode, which is coquettishly opposed to, and sometimes "violently innocent" of, the semantic meaning it also carries. This is not to say, however, that the sonorous mode is without meaning. On the contrary, as Kugler demonstrates with his example, the phonetic pattern that words share is "in accordance with unconscious associations of their semantic aspects."[15] We might even say that the meaning that resounds within word-sounds is projectively identified into their signified concepts and referent objects even as sexuality, according to Bollas, is projectively identified into the figure of the sexual father.

Just as defenses usually express something of the unconscious content that they defend against,[16] so the sonorous mode of speech expresses something of the meaning of the significations from which it (dis)associatively (!) takes flight. Increasing the number of phonetic associations as attention decreases, the sonorous mode may also be seen as the sirenous mode, which has drawn attention onto the rocks of de(con)struction through the lure of the acoustic image in the first place. In this connection we may think of the spiritually depleted Prufrock of Eliot's poem who, while walking on the beach in his white flannel trousers, hears "the mermaids singing, each to each."[17] Or again, we may think of Ophelia distributing flowers to the cast before she drowns. In this example, the waning hegemony of semantic meaning is figured in the image of Hamlet's father, the King, having been poisoned to death through the ear – an image that we may regard as tautegorically identical with that of the mad Ophelia.

Linking all this to our discussion of Bollas's theory, we may say that the defloration fantasy is to the language that contains it what fear of the signifying power of the sexual father is to the hysteric. Or put another way, we may say that the defloration that Bollas's hysterics unconsciously provoke and take flight from is always already deconstructively enacting itself within the reflexive domain of language. This is true, not only with respect to the mermaidic/Ophelic words of Kugler's example (violet, violate, and violent), but of all words. Defloration, in this broader sense, is synonymous with what Lacanian psychoanalysis, with reference to the fissure that exists between the signifier and the signified, calls primary (linguistic) castration.

Though Jung formulated his concept of the archetype only much later, in the context of his mythological studies, it is evident that he could have done so earlier on the basis of his word association experiments. Indeed, as Kugler demonstrates with reference to the defloration fantasy, it is possible to "see through the surface structure of phonetically associated words for the underlying deep structure, the archetypal image, which connects the disparate semantic aspects."[18] Underlining this point, Kugler subsequently relates the defloration fantasy to an actual myth. In doing so, I believe, it is as much Jung's early work in word association that he is amplifying as it is the specific words through which the defloration fantasy resounds in his example. For it is only after again summarizing Jung's early findings that he makes the link between the defloration fantasy and the Demeter–Persephone myth.

> [U]nder normal conditions a person associates words according to a consideration of meaning-concept. However, the more unconscious a person becomes, the greater the tendency to associate words phonetically. And it is this shift in the linguistic mode that opens the personality to the archetypal meaning-patterns poetically collated in language through a parity of phonetic values. We find, for example, that the Homeric poet responsible for the composition of the "Hymn to Demeter" beautifully weaves the invariant complex of associations we have been examining into the defloration fantasy of the "Rape of Persephone." Demeter's daughter, Persephone, has wandered off to the remote Nysian plain, where she is busy playing and picking roses, violets, and other flowers with the daughters of Okeanos [= mermaids! – GM]. Gaia lures Persephone on in her search for flowers by presenting a strange and wonderful flower, never before seen. Astonished by the flower's beauty, she stretches out both hands to pick the delightful narcissus when suddenly the earth violently opens and Hades drives his horses out of the gaping earth, lifts the girl into his chariot, and takes his ravished bride back to his subterranean realm to consummate their marriage.[19]

Kugler's amplification of Jung's findings concerning sound association, along with his own concerning the defloration fantasy, is all the more interesting when we realize that Bollas's theory of hysteria can be led back to the same mythic background. Hades erupting from the earth to abduct Persephone corresponds, in Bollas's theory, to the traumatic epiphany of sexuality that occurs in the life of all children at about age three. For, just as the Lord of the Underworld violently removes Persephone, daughter of the earth-goddess Demeter, from her mother, so sexuality, according to Bollas, ruptures the pre-Oedipal bond of relationship between the child and mamma, the caregiver. Resisting this development, the hysteric-to-be violently preserves his or her innocence by viewing the father (and later in life, the analyst) as the bad sexual father on the model of the raping Hades.

After the abduction of Persephone, Demeter, in the throes of her grief, brings the depressive scourge of winter upon the world. Taking on human form, she then disguises herself as a nursemaid within a royal family. In this role she looks after the family's son, Demophoon, whom she daily holds in the flames of a fire. The purpose of this procedure, it turns out, is to give Demophoon an immortal body. Mimetic to this, the mother of the hysteric, according to Bollas, also handles her child's body in a manner that results in its being transfigured into a "spiritual" one. Again, as we discussed in an earlier section, loath to touch her child's genitals, "the mother hypercathects the non-genital erotogenic zones"[20] with her own repressed excitement, "lighting [the body] up like a Christmas tree with flashing desire."[21] When Demophoon's actual mother questions what his nurse is doing to him, Demeter reveals herself as the divinity she is, giving vent to her grief and fury. To get matters in hand, the gods then petition Hades to return Persephone to her mother, which he does, on the condition that she return to him for a third of each year to reign as his queen. (The transitional pomegranate seed, mentioned in a previous section, was slipped into Persephone's mouth by Hades to ensure her return.) In this arrangement we see not only the return of Persephone to Demeter, but the inclusion or integration of the sexuality that had previously been identified with death and rejected. Perhaps we should not be surprised, given what Bollas has to say about the hysteric's mother's anathema to sex, that the aggrieved Demeter is released from her fury when the corpulent minor mother goddess, Baubo, flamboyantly lifts up her skirts and reveals her genitals. At the sight of Baubo's exposed vagina, the enraged Demeter gives way to laughter.[22]

In a seminar on dream analysis given many years after his work with the association experiment, Jung returned to the theme of the depth significance of words in the light of his notion of a collective unconscious.

> Our actual mind is the result of the work of thousands or perhaps a million years. There is a long history in every sentence, every word we speak has a tremendous history, every metaphor is full of historical symbolism; they would not carry at all if that were not true. Our words carry the totality of that history which was once so alive and still exists in every human being. With every word we touch upon a historical fibre, as it were, in our fellow-beings; and therefore every word we speak strikes that chord in every other living being whenever we speak the same language. . . . So we can't possibly understand a dream if we don't understand the atmosphere, the history of the underlying images. There are personal problems in dreams which one may think only important for that particular case, but if one goes deeply enough into the structure, the speech symbolism, one enters historical layers and discovers that what seemed to be merely a personal problem goes much deeper, it

reaches the analyst himself and everybody who hears it. One can't help bringing in the way in which our ancestors tried to express the same problem, and that leads one to historical matter. . . . It all comes out of the same unconscious mind, the irrational and eternal stock, the prefunctioning collective unconscious, which repeats itself throughout the centuries, a sort of eternal, imperishable language.[23]

Bollas's theory of hysteria, though seeming to confine itself in a personalistic manner to the vicissitudes and calamities of ontogenetic development, is redolent of the "eternal, imperishable language" of which Jung speaks. While pointing this out has been our way of contesting the division he makes between meaning and sound, it also lends support to his thesis that the epiphany of sexuality in early childhood is an age-old and culturally universal vicissitude of life.

The Demeter–Persephone myth, so obviously concerned with the same themes as Bollas is in *Hysteria*, was the myth at the centre of the Eleusinian mysteries, the dominant initiatory cult of the ancient Greek world for several thousand years. Emphasizing this connection, we can say that the Eleusinian mystery was the psychoanalysis of ancient times even as psychoanalysis is the Eleusis of our era.

Holy Ghost

In his book, *Hells and Holy Ghosts: A Theopoetics of Christian Belief*, David Miller brings Jung's early work with the association experiment and Kugler's theory of archetypal psycho-linguistics to bear upon a theological controversy concerning the appropriateness of the phrase "Holy Ghost" as a translation of *hagion pneuma* in the King James Bible. Both philologically and theologically, the phrase "Holy Spirit" would have been the more appropriate translation, or so modern theologians have argued. Paul Tillich is especially adamant on this point. "The term 'Holy Ghost,'" he declares, "must be purged from every liturgical or other use."[24]

We may be reminded by this controversy of Bollas's distinction between "talking it" and "talking about it" in the psychoanalysis of hysteria. Just as hysterics, in Bollas's account, use words in an immediately gratifying way that is at the same time subverting of meaning, so the phrase "Holy Ghost," it may be argued, is as emotionally evocative and affecting as it is semantically ill-equipped to "talk about" the spirit in the grander sense of that term's meaning. For from a modern theological perspective, "Holy Ghost" implies a lesser sense of spirit than that to which the *hagion pneuma* refers. Hearing the words "Holy Ghost," one thinks (or so the critics fear) more of the spirits of the dead and of literal ghosts and ghouls than of the spirit of the divine, more of a parapsychological spirituality of hysterical, charismatic ecstasies than of God as spiritual guarantor of illumination, truth, and clarity of mind.

To illustrate something of what contemporary theology finds so objectionable about the words "Holy Ghost," Miller translates them backwards from English into other languages:

> "Holy Ghost" could be rendered in German, *das Heilige Gespenst*, or in French, *le Saint Fantôme* or *Spectre*, or in Latin, *Sanctum Phantasma* or *Sancta Umbra*, or in Greek, *to eidôlon to hagion*. These would in fact mean "Holy Shade," "Holy Shadow," or even "Holy Idol"! Impossible![25]

From the point of view of a rigorously conscious theology, the term "Holy Ghost" is indeed "impossible," as Miller's exercise clearly shows. For the depth-psychology-informed Miller, however, the slip of the tongue (if that is what it was) that led the old translators to say "Ghost" rather than "Spirit" points to an unconscious nexus of meanings and significations. From Miller's depth-theological perspective, the wrongness of the term "Holy Ghost" as a translation of *hagion pneuma* is indicative of a hidden soul value. To simply discard it as semantically illogical or incorrect would be to fall back behind Jung's insight that it is precisely the most semantically odd responses on the association experiment that can be the most significant. Perhaps, the old translators, who very likely knew the linguistic facts that their critics now point to in exposing their error, were wise to have persisted in the folly of their ghost-talk after all.

In making his case that this might be so, Miller refers to the same work of Kugler's on archetypal psycho-linguistics that we discussed in the previous section. Suspect though the use of the phrase "Holy Ghost" admittedly may be as a response to *hagion pneuma* on that great association experiment which translating the Bible into English undoubtedly was, it may yet be supportable in the light of Kugler's finding that "on a deep [unconscious] level there is a meaning-relation between phonetically associated words. . . ."[26] As Kugler further states, in Miller's citation, this "connection is not via the literal lexical meaning or syntactic relations, or common origin, but through the underlying archetypal image. The relation between phonetic associations is imagistic, not lexical, syntactic, or etymological. They are affiliated by a complex which is an acoustic image."[27]

Where Kugler, as we have previously discussed, illustrated his thesis with the phonetically associated words that when taken together are evocative of the defloration fantasy (carnal, carnation, carnage, reincarnation; violate, violent, violet), Miller illustrates his thesis concerning the depth-theological significance of what we may call the Holy Ghost translation error with the acoustic complex God–Ghost–Ghastly–Guest–Host:

> The Anglo-Saxon *gaest* is parent . . . to the words "ghost" and "ghostly," as well as to the words "host" and "guest." Could it be that when King James' translators rendered *der Heilige Geist* and *to pneuma to hagion* with the English phrase "Holy Ghost," they were, wittingly or witlessly, implying an intimacy of meanings, a complex of theological sense, in whose perspective God is Guest as well as Host when God is a Ghost? That is, God is God when

being a Ghost, and God is a Ghost when being Ghastly, the Ghastly Anger
which haunts, being at the same time the Host of the human and its strange
Guest – wounded and torn, shade and shadow, present when absent, in life and
death, forever. The Divine Host is Ghost which is at the same time Ghastly
Guest. Is this odd sense that which is implied by an improper translation, one
which is somehow correct just the same? Can it be that "ghost" and "spirit,"
"ghost" and "host" in fact do belong together in the fantasia of the eternal
mystery sustained by the word? – the Lord of Hosts a Ghost; the Ghost our
Host![28]

In making this proposal, Miller does not dispute the theological arguments that
theologians such as Tillich have made against the Holy Ghost translation of *hagion
pneuma*. True to the tradition of depth psychology, his aim or emphasis is to make
sense of the apparent error, to understand what it points to when it is not taken
literally as mere error. The result of his efforts in this regard is that the spiritual
implication of Kugler's archetypal psycho-linguistics is thrown into relief in an
ironically postmodern manner. While it may be true that the phrase Holy Ghost is
today too semantically bizarre a translation of *hagion pneuma* to be theologically
adequate (and depth psychology's term "autonomous psyche" even more so), it is
also true that it conveys a living sense of the spirit, a living sense of the word,
as Miller's playful discussion of the God–Ghost–Ghastly–Guest–Host nexus of
associations shows.

But here we must insist (even if our reasoning be rough and our words learned
in a stable): the Holy Ghost or Holy Spirit, being radically free, is an untranslatable
notion, even by the most theologically correct words. No single example of that
gift that the Ghost or Spirit brings to the inspiration of our tongues is sufficient.
Glossolalia knows no last word or final expression, the unconscious no negation except the great one that it notionally is. Though it can hystericize wombs,
mysteriously making them pregnant, by way of the ear, with new dispensations of
itself, the spirit cannot be bound or kept in boxes – even in psychological ones,
such as those that the terms "autonomous psyche" and "the unconscious" provide.
Coming as an annunciation of sudden insight that is compensatory to those truths
that have become redundant in the no longer timely particulars of their form, it
cannot be made identical with itself even by those with the best and most erudite
of intentions. Even apparent gibberish, or obviously wrong translations (and
surely our psychological terms "autonomous psyche" and "the unconscious" are
even more theologically suspect than the phrase "Holy Ghost"), can be its sign or
manifestation for those with an ear to hear it. So here, following Miller's improvi-
sational or Pentecostal (!) lead, let us play fast and loose with all that the spirit
psycho-linguistically suggests to us in its many enactments of itself. Bearing in
mind Jung's statement that archetypes are never cleanly isolated from each other,[29]
and as a tribute to Christ's statement that the Spirit (which he links specifically
with being "born again") "bloweth where it listeth,"[30] let us entertain the idea that
the particular phonetic patterns that Kugler and Miller examine are so many

annunciations (or projective identifications) into each other. Or, to put this another way, let us recognize that when we push off from the positive specifics of the various examples of archetypal psycho-linguistic patterns, these examples shed the light of their negativity beyond themselves, illuminating the spirit of the Word in the greater sense that Tillich was rightly concerned to maintain. The Word in this greater sense is similarly all that these archetypal psycho-linguistic patterns say and more. As lions lie down with lambs in that place where, in Frye's words, "Jane Austen and the Marquis de Sade have kissed each other,"[31] so the defloration fantasy may lie down with or kiss Miller's phonetic God–Ghost–Ghastly–Guest–Host complex giving us a sense – and here let us call to mind the white Easter lily so frequently presented in paintings of the annunciation to Mary – that there is indeed a subtle and effective truth to miraculous impregnation and Virgin Birth fantasies, for all our understandable concern as analysts about "mind-fucking," "insight orgasms," and the "'oooohhhh' or 'woooooowwww'" of "voice intercourse."[32]

Chapter 7

My Fair Hysteria

Archetypes are complexes of experience that come upon us like fate, and their effects are felt in our most personal life. The anima no longer crosses our path as a goddess, but, it may be, as an intimately personal misadventure, or perhaps as our best venture. When, for instance, a highly esteemed professor in his seventies abandons his family and runs off with a young red-headed actress, we know that the gods have claimed another victim. This is how daemonic power reveals itself to us. Until not so long ago it would have been an easy matter to do away with the young woman as a witch.[1]

C. G. Jung

Although analysts of most schools are quick to point out how frustrating and painful the analytic process is, they shy away from describing its deep pleasure. . . . How uncanny that [Freud] himself would repress the sexual gratification of the very process he invented, stressing its travails and its abstinence, and thus exiling it from his theory. The pleasure of analysis is not to be found in the theories of psychoanalysis, except under the Presbyterian scowls of "actings-in" or "actings-out." . . . [I]t is left to the patients furtively to tell friends how much fun a week of analysis has been, often when it has been very distressing. Freud's analysands' accounts of their work with him hardly describe joyless occasions. They write of its pleasure in a gossipy voice. Perhaps this is a fitting place for the greatest of pleasures: the love of representation.[2]

Christopher Bollas

Why can't a woman be more like a man?

In George Bernard Shaw's play *Pygmalion*, and in the musical adaptation of the play, *My Fair Lady*, Henry Higgins, a professor of phonetics, successfully teaches the vulgar flower-seller Eliza Doolittle to speak the King's English. In *Hysteria*, Bollas, as we have shown, has something similar in mind. Indeed, like his counterpart in the play, he cannot abide the way the hysteric talks the talking cure. His way of bringing about remediation is different from that of Professor Higgins, but the motif is quite the same.

The Professor Higgins character is also reminiscent of Jung. In the film version of the musical, starring Rex Harrison and Audrey Hepburn, Higgins has Miss Doolittle speak into various instruments, the better to analyze the productions of her voice. In his laboratory at the Burghölzli, Jung did much the same thing with his research subjects. In addition to measuring reaction times with a stop-watch, he monitored skin conductivity with a galvanometer and breath volume (funnily enough, considering our previous discussion of the Holy Ghost) with a pneumograph.

In drawing these comparisons I do not wish to further emphasize the misogyny, which has long been pointed out by historians of medicine who have written about hysteria from a cultural perspective. While there is, doubtless, much to this charge, there is more to Higgins than misogyny, and more than this to psychoanalysis as well. Only by thinking the unity of itself with its own opposite does misogyny, or any other concept for that matter, become a psychological one. The same can be said for characters such as Higgins and Doolittle and theorists such as Bollas and Jung. The self being as much one's own (little) self and all other selves besides,[3] we must think the unity of all of these figures even while noticing the differences. Psychology is a *complexio oppositorum*, which we fail if our representations of it are too one-sided.

So what, then, does this "complex unity" or "more" consist of? The answer to this question, I believe, is made immediately clear to us by the irresistible quality of the play itself. Throughout the years, wherever it has been staged, *My Fair Lady* has been loved by its audiences. Even recent audiences, steeped as they are in feminist theory, are not in the least put off by the sexism in which it trades. On the contrary, they are as charmed by the play as were those who first enjoyed it at its world premiere. Much of this charm, I believe, resides in the audience sensing, almost from the outset of the story, that a change is being worked within the arrogant professor. All the while that Eliza is learning to speak and deport herself like a lady, we know that her tyrannical instructor, the dry old bachelor Higgins, is simultaneously being opened to the feminine and coming to love Eliza.

Of course, the battle of the sexes is eternal. And when viewed through its lens, Eliza's learning to speak correctly seems like nothing more than her having conformed to the professor's narcissistic expectations. This, however, is a superficial reading. For at a deeper level, the two characters are tautegorically identical, metaphors of each other, an anima/animus syzygy. In the lively, if unsophisticated, Eliza, Higgins's own effeteness is compensatorily figured, even as Higgins personifies the more fully developed voice that is latent in Eliza.

Can this reading of the play be applied to analysis as well? Do we analysts not learn from our patients even as we help them? And is the love cure (even when disparaged as such in favour of a more hard-nosed cure by analysis) not a two-way street?

Bollas, as we have shown, is as arrogant as Professor Higgins when it comes to the hysteric. Writing of this type of patient, his tone is just as all-knowing and tyrannical as the one Higgins adopts with respect to Miss Doolittle. But, for all this, is Bollas not just as charming too? Readers more familiar with Bollas's other books than with *Hysteria* would find my characterization of him as being tyrannical and all-knowing most unfair.

At the beginning of this enterprise we noted with surprise how different Bollas's voice was in *Hysteria* as compared with his other books. We spoke of the manifesto-like tone of his treatise, of its nailing-down quality and driving force. This we compared to the Zeus who ravished Leda. Quoting Yeats, we asked if the hysteric, like the maiden in that myth, would "put on his knowledge with his power."[4] Now we ask the opposite question. Has hysteria, like Eliza, all the while been working a change in Bollas? For all his warnings about the hysteric's seductive power, has his love of psychoanalysis not been deepened, perhaps above all, by this patient? It makes sense, does it not, that a theorist and writer as subtle as Bollas should have an anima-muse as mercurial as the one that he writes both of and from in *Hysteria*?

But here, as we ask these questions, let us remind ourselves that the scene of writing that concerns us in these pages is not that of a single analytic writer, but of psychoanalysis itself. Besides the Midgard Bollas (whom one might see for analysis or supervision, or ask to sign one's copy of *Hysteria* or *Cracking Up*), there is another Bollas in Utgard. Like an "*x*" in mathematics, this Bollas stands for the near side of the unknown, the "infinite set" (to use Matte-Blanco's term) of all analysts, even as hysteria – Bollas's (not so) "fair lady" – can be seen (and seen through) as standing for the infinite set of all patients.

Jung's Eliza

In his memoirs Jung recalls the difficulties he had during childhood with mathematics. Algebra, in particular, proved difficult for him.

> the thing that exasperated me most of all was the proposition: If $a=b$ and $b=c$, then $a=c$, even though by definition a meant something other than b, and, being different, could therefore not be equated with b, let alone c.[5]

At the risk of subjecting ourselves to similar anxieties, we shall here make a similar proposition. If $j=h$ and $b=h$, then $j=b$. The h in our proposition, of course, stands for Higgins, the j for Jung, and the b for Bollas. Inasmuch as Higgins is the *tertium comparationis* of Bollas and Jung, the questions we have raised with respect to "Bollas" may be answered by asking them instead of that other "*x*" (or "*j*")-man, "Jung."

In 1906, an American student studying at the University of Geneva, (Miss) Frank Miller, published a memoir she had written describing a series of powerful fantasies she had had while voyaging at sea. Entitled "Some instances of subconscious creative imagination," the memoir was published (in French) in *Archives de psychologie* along with an introduction by the psychologist who was treating her, Théodore Flournoy. Though Jung never met Miss Miller in person, the fantasies recorded in her memoir came to concern him greatly. Rich in mythologems, they provided him with a clinical referent for what he had been learning about the psyche from his study of myth and religion. Introversion of libido, the dual mother, and heroic incest – it was by amplifying the Miller fantasies with mythological parallels that Jung came to present these early signature concepts. It was also these fantasies, or rather, the analysis of them, that Jung published in his *Wandlungen und Symbole der Libido*, which, in his estimation at least, cost him his relationship with Freud.[6]

To discover what the Professor Higgins in Jung learned from Eliza Doolittle as a result of analyzing the Miller fantasies we need only consult the section of Jung's 1925 English seminar in which the "subjective aspect" of *Wandlungen* is discussed. Speaking to a sympathetic audience of devoted pupils, many of whom went on to promote and further develop his ideas, Jung reflected upon that early work as follows:

> When one writes such a book, one has the idea that one is writing about certain objective material, and in my case I thought I was merely handling the Miller fantasies with a certain point in view together with the attendant mythological material. It took me a long time to see that a painter could paint a picture and think the matter ended there and had nothing whatever to do with himself. And in the same way it took me several years to see that it, the *Psychology of the Unconscious* [the English title under which *Wandlungen und Symbole der Libido* was published], can be taken as myself and that an analysis of it leads inevitably into an analysis of my own unconscious processes.[7]

Jung's insight here is a particularly seminal one. Anticipating the emphasis that contemporary psychoanalysis has given to the importance of countertransference, Jung tells his audience that what he had first considered to be an objective analysis of Miss Miller's fantasies was in fact indicative of or transparent to unconscious processes in himself. This recognition, radical as it was for its time, remains so even today, when we realize that Jung is not referring to the dynamics of the clinical situation (Miss Miller, after all, was not his patient), *but to countertransferential aspects of theory-making within psychoanalysis itself.*

For all its sophistication in the area of the therapeutic utilization of the countertransference, contemporary psychoanalysis (both "Freudian" and "Jungian") has barely even sighted the speculative or *theoretical* significance of what might be called the *archetypal* countertransference. Working within the conceptual constraints of a particular analytic school, analysts, for the most part, use their countertransference reactions technically, as a sort of empathic and diagnostic probe. While Jung also discusses in his writings the practical importance of analysts attending to what is evoked in them by patients,[8] in this early passage he already goes much further. Recognizing (after "several years") that his psychoanalytic account of Miss Miller's fantasies could be traced back to unconscious processes in himself, Jung brought home, so to speak, into the heart of his psychological theory, a sense of the immanent life of the psyche. He recognized, that is to say, his rhetorical, as-if patient to be the anima inspiratrix of that psychological development in himself that he later universalized as analytical psychology.

Explaining all this further, Jung told the audience of his 1925 seminar that at the time he was trying to understand Miss Miller's fantasies he had felt an enormous antipathy for the "fantastic or passive automatic thinking" that she displayed in such abundance. Identified with the superiority of what he called "directed thinking," he took up his psychiatric cudgels against Miss Miller's poems and fantasies, even as Professor Higgins set out to cure Miss Doolittle of her Cockney accent. Only later was he able to see himself in Miss Miller and, like the Higgins who came to love Eliza, more fully embrace the value of fantasy thinking.

> I took Miss Miller's fantasies as . . . an autonomous form of thinking, but I did not realize that she stood for that form of thinking in myself. She took over my fantasy and became stage director to it, if one interprets the book subjectively. In other words, she became an anima figure, a carrier of an inferior function of which I was very little conscious. I was in my consciousness an active thinker accustomed to subjecting my thoughts to the most rigorous sort of direction, and therefore fantasizing was a mental process that was directly repellent to me. As a form of thinking I held it to be altogether impure, a sort of incestuous intercourse. . . . It shocked me . . . to think of the possibility of a fantasy life in my own mind; it was against all the intellectual ideals I had developed for myself, and so great was my resistance to it, that I could only admit the fact in myself through the process of projecting my material into Miss Miller's. Or, to put it even more strongly, passive thinking seemed to me such a weak and perverted thing that I could only handle it through a diseased woman.[9]

An amazing passage, this, when one considers the high esteem in which Jung later held fantasy. Throughout most of his life, and down to the present day, Jung's name has been synonymous with the importance of such unconscious processes. We are surprised to hear that there was a time when he hated fantasy. Clearly, the Higgins in Jung learned much from the Doolittle-anima that he found in his as-if patient, Miss Miller.

Incarnating herself in still other forms, Miss Doolittle continued to inspire the Professor Higgins in Jung. On at least one occasion, she even turned the tables and gave him an elocution lesson! I refer, here, to Jung's initial conversation with the anima, as this is famously recounted in his memoir, *Memories, Dreams, Reflections.*

While mulling over his doubts about the value of the work he had begun on his own fantasies after the break with Freud, Jung became aware of a feminine voice breaking through to him from within. The voice said to Jung that his work was not science (as he would have wished it to be), but art. Railing against this idea, Jung suggested an alternative possibility, nature. With this idea he won the debate, but also lost the dialogue. For the inner voice fell silent. Not wanting to lose the rapport with himself that he had established through the dialogue, and perhaps sensing the silence within himself as a loss of soul, Jung responded by giving his voice over to the anima. "I reflected," he recalls in his memoir, "that the 'woman within me' did not have the speech centers I had. And so I suggested that she use mine. She did so and came through with a long statement."[10]

That the Higgins in Jung should deign to speak in Eliza's Cockney accent marks a huge shift in Jung's attitude toward the unconscious. Jung, we sense, would not have become himself in the way that he subsequently did had he not given over his speech centers to the "woman within me."

It is important, however, that we do not sentimentalize or idealize Jung's relationship to the feminine voice of his soul. To the end of his life, Jung believed (erroneously, it would now appear[11]) that Miss Miller was a seriously diseased woman. Inwardly as well, while placing a high value upon the anima and conversing with her whenever he felt himself to be disturbed in his emotional life, he was ever wary of the things that she said.

A biblical adage states that the fear of the Lord is the beginning of wisdom. Jung's wariness of the anima, I believe, has something of this sensibility about it. Just as the Lord is to be feared, so the autonomy of the psyche, in Jung's view, is to be respected. Right up until the end of his life, Jung reiterated this point, making cautionary remarks about the anima's destructive side. Reflecting upon his earliest conversation with the woman within himself, he writes in his memoirs that what she said to him about his work being art seemed to be "full of a deep cunning."

> If I had taken these fantasies of the unconscious as art, they would have carried no more conviction than visual perceptions, as if I were watching a movie. I would have felt no moral obligation toward them. The anima might then have easily seduced me into believing that I was a misunderstood artist, and that my so-called artistic nature gave me the right to neglect reality. If I had followed her voice, she would in all probability have said to me one day, "Do you imagine the nonsense you're engaged in is really art? Not a bit." Thus the insinuations of the anima, the mouthpiece of the unconscious, can utterly destroy a man. In the final analysis the decisive factor is always consciousness, which can understand the manifestations of the unconscious and take up a position toward them.[12]

Though Jung may have overly pathologized Miss Miller, I think there is much reason to respect his counsel concerning the dangers associated with the anima. If, however, we defend her in these pages, even in her infernal, hystericized aspect, it is because, as the archetype that is turned toward the deity,[13] she is at the cutting edge of that sublation of religion, medicine, and science that psychology is for our times.[14]

Being a Higgins

The Higgins in Bollas is just as adamant as is his counterpart in Jung about the anima's destructive side. Indeed, in *Hysteria*, as we have seen, he stares down the jejune Miss Doolittle with a particularly jaundiced eye. But what about the creative anima and the fantasies she brings in her train? How do these figure in Bollas's *oeuvre*? Or to ask the same question in a less dichotomizing way, how does the creativity that the anima holds in tandem with destructiveness appear in Bollas's scheme of things?

These questions return us to Higgins in his more charming aspect. As we have already suggested, this Higgins, who is in love with Eliza, is more easily found in the pages of Bollas's other books than in the those of *Hysteria*. In these books, Bollas gives considerable attention to the work of the unconscious, the life of fantasy, and the freedom (which analysis extends to the mind of the patient and analyst alike) to associate. Equally "anima-friendly" are those theoretical contributions in which he subtly extends the Winnicottian notion of object-use to include "evocative," "aesthetic," and other "transformational objects." And then there is that marvellous passage from *Cracking Up*, quoted at the outset of this chapter, in which he discusses that "greatest of pleasures," the "love of representation," which the analytic relationship uniquely fosters in our time. This quotation, so true to the tenor of the majority of Bollas's writings, provides a welcome balance to the *Malleus Maleficarum*-like tone he adopts in *Hysteria*.

But how, without too much further ado, can we come immediately to the heart of what we have just referred to as the "anima-friendly" element in Bollas's writings?

Over the years I have heard a number of dreams that stand out in my memory as especially illustrative of what Jung meant by anima. *Similia similibus percipiuntur*, several of these dreams come to my mind at this juncture in connection with the question of conceptual analogues to this notion in Bollas's thought.

In the first of these, a man dreamt that he is explaining the phases of the moon to his sister. Frustrated that she is not persuaded by what he is saying, he becomes more and more pedantic about the astronomical facts involved. Finally, however, he seems to prevail. The sister-figure accepts his lessons as the truth. But then, lo and behold, another moon appears out of nowhere. Awakening from the dream, the dreamer was filled with the impression that this process could repeat itself again and again, giving rise to an infinite series of successive moons.

In a second example, a man who had been writing a poem each morning, often drawing upon his dreams from the night before as source material, dreamt that he and a beautiful unknown woman are swimming together in a tranquil ocean. There is no land in sight and no boat, but no anxiety on this account either. The image is simply of the woman and himself cavorting in the water together. But then, the woman is nowhere to be seen. For many minutes, he dives, this way and that, searching for her in vain. Finally, however, after many minutes have elapsed, the woman re-surfaces. Her brain, evidently, has been damaged, her mind erased. But there seems to be no harm in this. On the contrary, she is now as bubbly, efferves-cent and alive as she is mindless. The dreamer awoke with a feeling of exhilara-tion, writing yet another fine poem.

This same man had another dream worth noting here. In this dream he finds himself writing a strong, declarative sentence on a piece of rough, low-grade paper. But no sooner does he set it down, than it disappears. Over and over again, with increasing frustration, he writes down the same sentence, only to have it vanish an instant later as if he were writing with disappearing ink. But then he notices – and with this recognition the dream ends – that as he writes the paper he is writing upon becomes of finer and finer quality.

We will be reminded by these dreams of our earlier references to Shahrazad and Penelope. Just as Shahrazad tames the murderous intent of King Shahrayar by telling him an endless series of fascinating stories, and just as Penelope holds her suitors at bay by unravelling her weaving each night, so the designs of the ego in these dreams are deliteralized and a "negative capability" fostered as part of what we may regard as an initiation of the dreamers who dreamt them into a more psychological mode of awareness.

Returning now to Bollas's writings, and insighting these through the lens that these dreams and amplifications provide, we will be put in mind of his description of that systole and diastole of psychic life and analysis that he refers to with the terms "condensation" and "dissemination." "Unconscious mental life," writes Bollas in *Cracking Up*,

> operates according to an oscillation that ensures its continuous – indeed cease-less – function, as on the one hand unconscious work brings together through condensation otherwise disparate ideas, and on the other hand the process of free association then deconstructs these condensations. When Freud asked the analysand to free-associate to the dream, he frequently stressed that in so doing the patient dispersed the manifest content of the dream. What was created as an act of condensation – the dream event – is destroyed by the work of free association. Both processes, however – bringing together and cracking up – are important features of the unconscious and constitute its dialectic; each time a condensation is created, its saturation with meaning guarantees that it will break up in subsequent moments of elaboration, and each unit of meaning, compacted in the condensation, now follows its own destiny.[15]

Elaborating on these ideas in this and other works, Bollas has beautifully described how analysis heals by virtue of its being a situation especially hospitable to this process of expressing or playing out the oscillations between condensation and dissemination occurring within the patient and the analyst, and, transferentially, between them both.

Some condensations are of the order of attitudes and certainties that make life too dry. We may think in this connection of the dreamer who felt he could explain the moon. Others are present in a decidedly more pathological form as fixed ideas or determinate internal objects (in Jungian terminology, highly valanced complexes). These, unfortunately, foreclose upon what Bollas, following Winnicott's notion of the spontaneous gesture or true self, calls one's "personal idiom." When this is the case we feel our lives to be subject to an unalterable fate. The free-associative process sponsored by psychoanalysis, however, "cracks up" these overdetermined phenomena, freeing the self to disseminate its idiom.[16] Filled in this way by modernity's version of what Jesus, in his conversation with Nicodemus, called "the Spirit [that] bloweth where it listeth,"[17] we feel the hold of "fate" give way to a fulsome, "separate sense" (or optimum of analytic rapport), such that one's true self, or "personal idiom," may give a fuller sail to its "destiny."

Psychic genera and the soul of things

The dreams I have recounted help us to recognize two further analogues of analytical psychology's anima concept in Bollas's writings: his notion of "psychic genera"[18] and, related to this, his extensions of Winnicott's theory of object-use.

Like positively valanced complexes in Jungian theory, psychic genera, according to Bollas, are constituted of impressions that have been received from the world of experience and combined into attitudes, perspectives, and representations that contribute to the realization of one's idiom.[19] The generative opposite of psychical trauma,[20] genera are present within, or continuous with, the oscillating cycles of condensation and dissemination, which we learned about above. In contrast to the binding or foreclosing effect that traumas have upon the personality, genera develop through what Bollas, with object-use in mind, calls the "successional elaboration of idiom."[21] It is by playing with or otherwise engaging the persons, places, and things of the world in which we live, move, and have our being that the "inherited proto-nucleations of any child's idiom,"[22] become enriched with content and strengthened.

As might be expected, which disposition toward life predominates within a given personality – the traumative or the generative – is strongly influenced by the quality of the parenting that has been received. Children who have been traumatized by their parents are correspondingly less able to make use of the bounty of the world's objects for the purposes of their becoming than are children whose parents facilitated "the elaborative dissemination of their personal idiom."[23] If the former group may be said to be genera-poor, the latter, by comparison, are genera-rich.

To the casual reader, Bollas's proposals with respect to psychic genera might seem straightforward enough. That the unconscious is creative has long been a part of its popular definition. And we all know it is better to have parents who are competent and loving than parents who are not. It would be incorrect, however, to conclude from this that Bollas is merely reiterating what we already know. What we know, or think we know, still needs to be worked out theoretically for psychology. In line with this, Bollas writes in a strongly theoretical manner with the aim of redressing a deficiency within the psychoanalytic tradition itself.

This deficiency has to do with creativity. As a subject matter for psychological reflection, creativity, oddly enough, has met with neglect within mainstream psychoanalysis. From the very beginning, the topic has stirred up resistances. When Jung, for instance, proposed to Freud that psychoanalysis be balanced by what he referred to as "psychosynthesis," Freud shook his head unsympathetically and then launched into an account of how he, himself, had once thought certain numbers, if creatively connected, would allow him to predict the date of his own death![24] In his view, psychoanalysis had to do with routing out what was pathological about fantasy – not with the creation of new illusions about life, however heartening these might be.

Even when reflecting analytically upon the works of outstanding artists and writers, Freud kept to this policy. Standard themes of psychoanalytic interest such as the Oedipus complex could be discovered in artistic works and discussed accordingly, but creativity per se was set apart as not being a subject matter for psychoanalysis. With what appears to be an admirable sense of modesty with respect to the limits of analysis, Freud writes in his "Leonardo" essay, that "the nature of artistic achievement is . . . psychoanalytically inaccessible to us."[25] In "Dostoevsky and parricide" he says much the same thing: "Before the problem of the creative writer, analysis must lay down its arms."[26]

Freud, of course, was himself a highly creative man. In addition to the acclaim he earned as a scientist, he was awarded the Goethe Prize in recognition of his writerly accomplishments. And this is to say nothing of the seminal contribution he made to the psychology of creativity at the beginning of his analytic career with his discussion of the work of the unconscious in *The Interpretation of Dreams*. When considered in the light of these achievements, his reticence with respect to creativity as a subject matter suitable for psychoanalytic study seems somewhat strange.

In part, I believe, Freud's position on this issue was redolent of his disaffection with hypnosis. As a scientist bent on the investigation of unconscious processes, he was ever leery of hysterical compliance and suggestion. Related to this was his concern that what presented itself innocently, even grandly, as an expression of creativity might actually be, for all its artifice, something much less than that, a mere defense mechanism perhaps. Having struggled during the course of his self-analysis with that anima in himself that he called "my little hysteria,"[27] Freud was as sceptical of its creative significance as was Jung when the not-so-little (indeed, nearly psychotic) hysteria in himself, which he called "the anima," insinuated to him that the work he had undertaken on his fantasies was art.

Beyond these issues, however, Freud's resistance seems to have been based on the fact that a full recognition of the place of creativity in psychic life would have required an expansion of the notion of the unconscious beyond the limits that his theory of repression had set for it. Expressing this in terms of a similar dilemma in religion, we could say that, just as the Church as an institution has tended to tighten up against the Holy Spirit (even while claiming to believe in it), so psychoanalysis has tended to tighten up against the idea of creativity insofar as the autonomy of this spirit poses a threat to more established psychoanalytic pieties.

Cognizant of the threat that a creative unconscious poses with respect to the epistemology of (Freudian) psychoanalysis, Bollas takes especial care to re-emphasize the merits of the classical account of repression and trauma in the course of making his proposals concerning psychic genera and creativity. Succinctly put, his theory is as follows: just as condensation finds its dialectical contrary in dissemination and fate in destiny, so the *repressed* unconscious is opposed, or rather, complemented by a "receptive unconscious," in which new thoughts, intuitions, and attitudes are protected from premature conscious scrutiny during the course of their being incubated.[28] This incubation process, as Bollas goes on to explain, exists in the subject as a state of "generative chaos."[29] Drawn by the gravity of nascent unconscious ideas, feelings, and self-states, hundreds of impressions repeatedly come together in what at first can only be an unstable fashion. While this, doubtless, may be hard for the subject to bear, in the *petite* (and sometimes not so *petite*) *hystérie* of creative work "[c]haos is tolerated, indeed facilitated, as the subject knows it is essential to the process of discovering new concepts about living."[30]

It is this theme – tolerating the chaos of creative tension – that Bollas's theory, Jung's anima concept, Freud's "little hysteria," and our dream examples have in common. This is especially obvious in the first two dreams. The sister, who is reluctant to accept the dreamer's account of the phases of the moon, and the swimmer, whose mind is erased when she sinks below the surface of the ocean, obviously personify the unknowing, receptive attitude that is so crucial to the generation of new ideas and perspectives.[31] The third dream reflects the same issue. True to her deliteralizing, negativizing role, the anima in this case is not even imaged. Or, putting this another way, we could say, such is the tolerance of generative chaos reflected in this dream that the anima can now be recognized as being *absolutely* present, present, that is to say, in the sublated form of her own absence, as the *notion* of soul per se.

A statement from Jung's *Mysterium Coniunctionis* underscores the association between genera production, generative chaos, *petite hystérie*, and the anima that our dream examples have provided us the means to see. In the course of elucidating a series of alchemical symbols related to "the separation and synthesis of psychic opposites," Jung says the following about the anima: "She is the chaste bride and whore who symbolizes the prima materia, which 'nature left imperfected.' . . . She is that piece of chaos which is everywhere and yet hidden, she is that vessel of contradictions and many colours – a totality in the form of a *massa confusa*, yet a substance endowed with every quality in which the splendour of the hidden deity can be revealed."[32]

This quote, so illustrative of generative chaos and the production of psychic genera, brings us to the further comparison we had proposed to make between the anima concept and Bollas's thought. Giving Winnicott's notion of transitional objects a Bachelardian twist,[33] Bollas has written insightfully about the power of objects such as a bicycle, a Beethoven symphony, or a particular artistic medium to evoke through their intrinsic qualities (and quite apart from whatever projective identifications the subject makes into them) affluxes of genera that facilitate true self-realization.[34] Similarly, the "she" Jung refers to in the passage above is as much the stone we feel moved to pick up off the beach as she is "that girl" who turns our head on the street.

Esse in anima, being in soul: what Bollas regards as the intrinsic qualities brought by each thing for our use in producing genera, Jungian thinkers such as Robert Sardello and James Hillman, writing with reference to the antique notion of the *anima mundi*, regard as the aesthetically perceived soul of the things themselves.[35] Keats, with his notion of Soul-Making, is an obvious influence on the thought of Sardello, Hillman, and Bollas alike. Even more so Gaston Bachelard, who already in the 1960s was writing about the reveries that objects inspire:

> Suddenly an image situates itself in the center of our imagining being. It retains us; it engages us. It infuses us with being. The *cogito* is conquered through an object of the world, an object which, all by itself, represents the world. The imagined detail is a sharp point which penetrates the [waking] dreamer; it excites in him a concrete meditation. Its being is at the same time being of the image and being of adherence to the image which is astonishing. . . . A flower, a fruit, or a simple, familiar object suddenly comes to solicit us to think of it, to dream near it, to help it raise itself to the rank of companion to man.[36]

Reading Bollas on the subjects we have discussed in the last few sections, the analytical psychologist will be ready to claim him as a member of his or her own tribe. The distinction between condensation and dissemination, repression and receptivity, trauma and genera, fate and destiny: these ideas, so reminiscent of Jungian themes, are expressed by Bollas with exemplary clarity. The same can be said for the terminology he has introduced with respect to ego-development and individuation – "personal idiom," "aesthetics of one's being," the "destiny drive." Somehow, the compass points Bollas has provided with these concepts narrow, in many respects, the gap between the Jungian map and the territory modelled by it. At least this has been my experience when reading his texts.

But then there is his year-2000 offering, *Hysteria*. Reading this treatise, now in the context of his other works, one senses the presence of a humbug – "genera begone!" Though every recent writer on the subject, including Bollas himself, has recognized hysteria to have been the chaotic matrix from which psychoanalysis was generated, Bollas regards the creativity of the hysterical characters we treat today to be nothing more than a seductive sham. Far from genuinely working within analysis toward the creation of new attitudes, the hysteric, in his view, aims only to repress the trauma of sexuality's arrival during childhood and to return to mamma-the-caregiver's arms. But against this view (and notwithstanding that there may well be many patients who struggle with precisely the issues Bollas has laid bare) the fact remains: hysteria, even in its subtler, contemporary form, continues to be the generative chaos out of which that incredible nexus of psychic genera, psychoanalysis itself, is generated.

The professor's mother-complex

Does psychoanalysis have a mother-complex? Higgins certainly has one. In *My Fair Lady*, he and Eliza share a number of scenes with his mother. There is the visit to her home for tea, the day at the races together, and the ball.

Re-staging these scenes in terms of Bollas's concepts, Higgins's mother may be regarded as playing the role of Fate, Eliza that of Destiny. Much of the time, the former principle upstages the latter. In the scenes they share, Destiny, in the person of a reticent Eliza, deports herself most awkwardly. Irritated by this, Higgins, at the same time, enacts something of his own handling during childhood – the shadow of mother/object falling between himself and Eliza in the process. Watching this play out, the audience is left with a vivid impression of the professor's limited ability to make use of the intrinsic qualities of the new and potentially animating object that life has presented him with. At the same time, however, the disseminative forces of destiny occasionally steal the show. Forgetting herself, Eliza reverts to her unmannerly ways at just the right moments to crack up the hoity-toity atmosphere. These moments, as it turns out, are decisive for Higgins, making a new man of him. In the "Director's Notes" of the program we find the following:

> To be a character is to enjoy the risk of being processed by the object – indeed, to seek objects, in part, in order to be metamorphosed, as one "goes through" change by going through the processional moment provided by any object's integrity. Each entry into an experience of an object is rather like being born again, as subjectivity is newly informed by the encounter, its history altered by a radically effective present that will change its structure.[37]

The version of the musical that enacts itself in the pages of *Hysteria* is very different from the production we have just imagined drawing upon Bollas's other books. Cast plain and simply as a stock-type, hysterical character, Eliza, with her vulgar speech and drunken father, enacts the part of Higgins that will not leave mamma psychologically. Or, more straightforwardly, she is simply the hysterical patient of the analyst Higgins. For all her show of wanting to change, she is in fact bent upon repressing the call to sexual life and reality, as Bollas has described.

In this staging of the musical, the light, comedic tone that was present when the story being told was that of creativity, the work of the unconscious, and the mutative use of objects is totally replaced by a tragic and at times inquisitional one. For in Bollas's account, as we have seen, there is nothing regenerative or genera-producing about the hysteric's use of an object. Indeed, to express this in terms of Winnicott's distinction, the hysteric, unable to really "use" and be nourished by an object's otherness, is locked into the omnipotent stance of mere "object-relating."[38]

These different stagings of the musical correspond to the two main themes to which Bollas returns again and again in his writings: the work of the unconscious (especially as this is facilitated by the analytic process), and the object-relational mapping of various pathological structures (such as psychopathy, homosexual cruising, and the fascist state of mind[39]). We have briefly rehearsed something of Bollas's contribution to the first of these endeavors in our discussion of his ideas concerning the ebb and flow of condensation and dissemination, the transformative potential of the transitional objects, and psychic genera. As for his second area of interest – the analysis of pathological structures – here as well it is important to recognize the impressiveness of Bollas's contribution. When we read, for instance, about how the psychopath is driven to seek out innocent victims in order to evacuatively re-enact the murder of his or her own innocence, we feel that psychoanalysis has once again deeply comprehended the dynamics of a dark area of the human soul.[40]

But is hysteria, like psychopathy, the analyzable structure Bollas claims it to be? Is it really nothing but a nexus of complexes, cut off from genera? Or should we, rather, regard its capacity to resemble so many other conditions to be an indication of its status as the anima or muse of psychological imagining?

Jung said of Freudian psychoanalysis that it had made its theories, so suited to the nature of neurotics, too dependent upon those ideas from which precisely its patients suffered.[41] In claiming that the hysteric cannot leave mamma, is psychoanalysis, especially in those quarters in which it draws upon the findings of developmental psychology and infant observation, a pot calling the kettle black?

Mysterium hystericum

Thomas Sydenham, the noted seventeenth-century physician, anticipates the sublated, anima sense of hysteria that we are attempting to conceive in these pages when he states that "the shapes of Proteus and the colours of the Cameleon are not more numerous and inconstant than the varieties of hysteric disease." Commenting on this passage in an essay of his own on hysteria, the Jungian analyst Niel Micklem writes:

> This fascinating illness has proved itself adaptable to the situation of the moment, to the age, to the culture and even to the physician. Patients produced their symptoms, yet what comprised hysteria in one century differed considerably from that in the next. It becomes apparent throughout this changing pattern that here is an illness that has been as much in the minds of the physicians as in those who were the sufferers.[42]

Micklem continues,

> Throughout the 4000 years of recorded observations this changing pattern of hysteria has proved itself to be more than what appears on the surface to the

scientist who would deal with it. It has been an unending challenge to the heal-ing professions, *by being something more than what is usually understood by the term illness.*[43]

As "something more than what is usually understood by the term illness," hysteria is a mystery. Changing its intrinsic qualities in accordance with the spirit of the times, it, no less than the transformational objects that Bollas has described, is available to be used by the subject (and here we mean that subject of all subjects, psychology itself) for the purpose of becoming what it is.

The positivistic mind, however, has difficulty with mysteries. It is as irritable and awkward as are Higgins and Eliza when Higgins's mother is in the room. Like the dreamer who wanted to explain the moon to his sister, the positivist in psychology wants to *explain* hysteria. But here again, no sooner is that "generative chaos" or "more than" that goes by the name "hysteria" accounted for in one way, than another moon enters the picture. In the same year that Bollas's *Hysteria* was published, Juliet Mitchell's *Mad Men and Medusas: Reclaiming Hysteria* appeared. In Mitchell's book, it is sibling relationships – not the factors that Bollas emphasizes – that are presented as being decisive in the making of hysteria.

Briefly illustrating Mitchell's theory with reference to our moon dream example, we can imagine that for her the sudden addition of the second moon into the picture would correspond to the birth of a new sibling, even as it is to his sister that the irritable dreamer so righteously presents his soon to be nullified account of the first moon. Displaced by a sibling, the hysteric, in Mitchell's (Bollas-rivalling) view, seeks parental love in the powerful, yet regressive, mode of the symptomatic suffering. Taking this a step further, we might account for the hysteria over hysteria in contemporary psychoanalysis in the same way. Unable to tolerate the analytic siblings we find among those of our own generation, we regress back to an ideal parent in the form of one or another of the analytic theorists of an earlier period. But against this totalizing of Mitchell's theory, the (murdered Jungian!) sibling that I am must here object that hysteria can no more be accounted for by the trauma of the sibling than it can by the trauma of seduction. Both these theories, and Bollas's too, are, at best, generative grist for the hysterical mill in which a truly psychological vision is being parthenogenetically prepared.

Questions of truth

In placing Bollas's theory of hysteria alongside Mitchell's my intention is to suggest that each theorist's views can be read in a way that disseminates the condensations of the other's. In no way, however, do I wish to suggest that these authors have not made important contributions to their field in the course of expounding their views. On the contrary, reading what Bollas and Mitchell have written about hysteria, we learn much about sexuality, childhood, the logic of sibling relationships, and so on. But the "more than," the moon, the mystery that, time and again, presents itself as hysteria remains.

How else could it be? Hysteria inspires many aetiologies of itself, many inter-pretations of what its complexes are. But when the math is done, none of these accounts can be divided evenly into the condition they were put forward to explain. There is always a remainder. What alchemy called the *multifactio* stretches to infinity.

The multiplicity of hysteria, its dissociability into many tellings of itself, constellates the question of truth. We wonder which of our theories is valid, which is true. With further reflection, however, our focus changes. Recognizing that the theories that hysteria has inspired are as much "the cry of their occasion"[44] as are its clinical symptoms and cultural forms, we move away from empiricism, verification, and proof. What is needed, we intuit, is not positive certainty, but a *notion* of psychology large enough to contain the *embarras de richesse* which hysteria and analysis, as foils of each other, again and again have shown them-selves to be.

In this connection, Giegerich's distinction between true psychology and immediate psychology is especially pertinent. True psychology, in Giegerich's view, always begins as the sublation of immediate psychology.[45] It generates itself in those moments in which psychological phenomena are reflected into themselves, interiorized, thought.

By "immediate psychology" we here intend the stuff of observation. But also something more, for observation implies a vantage point. To observe something one takes a position with respect to it. Whatever this vantage point or position is (drives, object-seeking libido, the letter in the unconscious, family systems, the breast), logically speaking, it is in the status of external reflection.

Internal reflection, by contrast, has the distinction of not being fathered by any principle outside the psyche. It is immaculate conception (and this in precisely the sense that observation and perception never can be).

Resisting interpretation (even as Penelope held her suitors at bay), hysteria negativizes the immediate accounts of itself that external reflection provides. Or, putting this another way, by resisting the accounts of itself that it receives from without, the hystericizing psyche creates from within its own "generative chaos" the internal mode of reflection, psychology proper.

It is precisely because Breuer and Anna O. did *not* have sex with one another that the Higgins and Eliza in them did in a higher or logically negative sense. The pregnancy that resulted from this process, though labelled "false" by medicine, was, psychologically speaking, the real thing. Indeed, as each of the positive symptoms of conception and pregnancy were shown to be negative, hysteria revealed itself through Anna to be the positivistic precursor of logical negativity, the mother of true psychology.

St Bernard's prayer

> O Virgin Mother, daughter of thy Son,
> Humbler and more exalted than all others,
> Predestined object of the eternal will!
> Thou gavest such nobility to man
> That He who made mankind did not disdain
> To make Himself a creature of his making.[46]

This prayer from Dante's *Divine Comedy* may serve us in these pages as our own. Cited by Jung in a section of his *Psychological Types* in which he discusses "The worship of woman and the worship of the soul," it can be read as well in terms of the sunken form of that worship that is its going under into psychology. *Hysteron proteron*: hysteria, too, is the Virgin Mother, daughter of its son, psychology.

"Generative chaos," which in all times and places appears as hysteria, challenges us to a higher kind of thinking. By this I mean a kind of thinking that can reflect each of the many theories that hysteria has inspired more deeply into itself while simultaneously comprehending them all at once. Freud, as we discussed at the outset of our venture, began in this direction, pushing off, first from the theory of inheritance, and then from the seduction theory. But no sooner had he deliteralized seduction and incest than he literalized them again with his theory of a positive Oedipus complex. With this move, psychology fell back behind even the level of reflection of the thirteenth century, which, as our prayer from *The Divine Comedy* shows, was already an age that could think dialectically by means of the incest motif.

But how is this higher kind of thinking to be achieved?

Earlier, in the introduction, we quoted a passage from the Renaissance scholar Edgar Wind. Wind, we may recall, makes the interesting point that "the exceptional cannot be understood by amplifying the commonplace . . ." for "both logically and causally . . . [it is] the exceptional . . . [that] . . . introduces the more comprehensive category."[47] Read in the light of this assertion we can say of hysteria that it is too exceptional, too fantastic, too "protean" and "more than" to be understood through reference to the commonplace. It cannot, that is to say, be reclaimed for psychoanalysis by means of mere clinical accounts as if it were just one more positively existing disease entity among all the others. On the contrary, as "the more comprehensive category," hysteria requires of psychology a more abstract kind of animus. But, alas, until psychology allows itself to pull out all the stops on its thinking, its failure to do so will continue to be acted out in our consulting rooms in the form of the conditions (hysteria reclaimed as merely one among them) that people have.

There are some indications that psychoanalytic thought is beginning to move in this direction. Juliet Mitchell, for instance, speaks in her book of hysteria being a universally present human potential, which appears, not only as a disease or illness, but in many other forms as well. Sighting at least a few segments of the

Midgard Serpent, she speaks of the political and cultural imperatives that hysteria, in the form of feminism, war trauma, and performance art, asserts. But then, reducing the Midgard Serpent to the cat, she lifts all this as if it could be accounted for by the regressive constellation of the Oedipus complex that sibling conflicts trigger.

It is painful to watch the Higgins in Mitchell fall back into the Mom-and-the-Kids vision of the psyche, which, in other respects, her reflections on hysteria move beyond. The same can be said for the Higgins in Bollas's *Hysteria*. For all that he has had to say about creativity and the work of the unconscious in other books, his bracketing of these insights from his analysis of hysteria is indicative of his unwillingness to give "that girl" that psychoanalysis has met in hysteria any credit. In contrast to Mitchell (who repeatedly refers to hysteria as a creative potential), Bollas is as dismissive of the generativity that hysteria would claim for itself as he is of the spirituality that the hysteric avows.

In support of my assertion here I offer a passage from Bollas's book in which he makes very much the same case we are making with regard to the psychology-generating role hysteria has played as inspiratrix of psychological reflection, but in a derisive, discrediting tone. Writing with reference to the "infatuation" with coining new psychiatric categories that was rife among psychoanalysts during the years following World War II, Bollas comments upon the proneness of hysterics to "always satisfy this desire, especially as it promised progeny out of the psychotic primal scene."

> Each analyst engaged in these new intercourses felt he or she was at a new frontier, espying a new psychic entity, ready for its writing and its naming. The fact that psychoanalysis in hospitals gradually expunged hysteria from its lists meant that it had to reappear in other forms.[48]

What Bollas here jaundicedly regards as mere mimetic identification on the part of hysterical patients with their analyst's desire for discovery and fame, I, with the anima concept in mind, regard more benignly as the opening of the clinical domain for psychological reflection. In taking this view, however, I do not wish to contest Bollas's observation that the expunging of hysteria from the diagnostic lists is what caused it to reappear as a plethora of lesser diagnostic terms. This, no doubt, is true. However (and this is a crucial point), *nothing is accomplished by simply bringing hysteria back in the positivistic sense it has already left beneath itself with its being expunged.*

To truly reclaim hysteria, we need a higher level of reflection. This level of reflection, were we to have it, would have to include hysteria's expungement – its negativization and multiplication – within the more comprehensive category that hysteria has shown itself to be. And have it we do! The anima concept, in its highest determination (not as the interior woman in us), is exemplary of the kind of reflection that psychology, through hysteria, shows itself to require.

Abrogating the complex

To be fair to Bollas, it must be said that there are a number of places in his writings where he makes what I, following Giegerich, have called the decisive, psychology-constituting move from positivity into reflection. Especially illustrative of this is a passage from his *The Mystery of Things*, published the year before *Hysteria* appeared. In this passage, Bollas dialectically turns against the positivistic, object-relations thinking in which he has been reared and upon which his mappings of various pathologies depends. "Object relations," he declares,

> is picture-book work, moving the story from one place to another, from the manifest content of the dream text to the manifest content of the analytical partnership. Freud's technique was more radical than this. By asking the patient to free associate he requested the breaking up of the object relational world and both patient and analyst felt the de-figuration of the dream text, broken up each time by the thoughts arising out of them. Left to itself, object relations theory will always return self to other through the here and now transference interpretation, enclosing the self in the cosy if solipsistic world of infant and mother; the Freudian action breaks this tie, sending the self into an uncertain and anxiously open-ended future.[49]

It is not just the neurotic patient who must destroy or abrogate, as Freud puts it, the Oedipus complex in the unconscious.[50] Psychoanalysis must do the same in the *form* of its thinking.[51] Taking an important step in this direction, Bollas icono-clastically contrasts the free association method, which is the basis of psycho-analysis proper, with the positivizing "picture book work" that object relations theory provides. The theoretical, or psychology-constituting, implication of his doing so, I believe, is most easily seen when it is compared with its correlative in the consulting room. Just as free association is said to facilitate cure by breaking up the pathological object relations that have foreclosed upon the patient's freedom, so the reconnection of psychoanalysis to its own inner infinity through a renewal of interest in free association and the work of the unconscious breaks up the rigid concepts that have accrued to psychoanalysis during the course of its history, freeing it to realize its theoretical trajectory in new formulations.

Physician heal (crack up, negate) thyself. This dictum applies not only to the physician as a person, but to the theories that the physician applies. The cosy solipsism of infant and mother, the anti-libidinal ego, the good and bad breasts, self, complex, and archetype even – these, and a whole host of other positivized concepts, must be dissolved, again and again, in the negativizing, mercurial bath of psychology's ongoing process. Or, to put this in terms closer to those Bollas himself uses, psychoanalysis, as analyst to itself, must repeatedly de-figure the theoretical dream-texts in which its thought is bound, returning these, via free association, to the genera-producing, idiom-disseminating work of the unconscious.[52]

Now, by "free association" and "the work of the unconscious" I do not in this context refer to a literal methodology (lying on the couch saying whatever comes to mind), a specific set of psychological mechanisms (displacement, condensation, symbolization, etc.), or a particular kind of unconscious content (introjects, interior objects, mental representations). To do so would be to inscribe both "free association" and "the work of the unconscious" back into the pages of the very picture book that has tended to divide psychoanalysis from its essence, as our quote from Bollas suggests. And yet it must also be recognized that this inscription has everywhere already taken place. Not only has the unconscious long been positivized in psychoanalysis; free association and the work of the unconscious have as well. Little wonder, then, that hysteria constellates again in our time. In one form or another, it is always the negative, or, better said, negativizing therapeutic reaction to the ruling dominant of external reflection.

Reflected into themselves (hysterically resisted), "free association" and "the work of the unconscious" are no longer merely what they positively, externally, or literally are – a technical method and a set of unconscious psychic processes. In addition to this, they are also all that they are not – imploded metaphors that designate, by virtue of their being imploded, the speculative nature of thought per se, "internal reflection" as such.

Sentences from Heidegger's "Letter on humanism" come helpfully to my mind in connection with this point. In a paragraph that begins with his stating that "thinking builds upon the house of Being, the house in which the jointure of Being fatefully enjoins the essence of man to dwell in the truth of Being," Heidegger continues a few lines later: "The talk about the house of Being is no transfer of the image 'house' to Being. But one day we will, by thinking the essence of Being in a way appropriate to its matter, more readily be able to think what 'house' and 'to dwell' are."[53] The same goes for "free association," "the work of the unconscious," "psychoanalysis," "talking cure," "hysteria," and every other term. One day we will, by thinking psychology's being-in-soul in the negativizing way appropriate to its matter, more readily be able to think what these are.

Divided from its essence by the positivization of its many terms and insights, psychoanalysis must do what it bids its patients do: submit to the fundamental rule, saying whatever comes to its mind, no matter how meaningless, embarrassing, or profound. And again, just as with its patients, it must listen with "evenly hovering attention" to everything it hears itself thinking. For only by this means can the pathological structure that psychoanalysis inevitably becomes by being positivized be broken up by the new thoughts arising out of it.

Bollas, despite his apparent focus on the consulting room, makes just this point in a passage in which he argues for the merit that the word "spirit" may have in psychoanalysis. After quoting a sentence from Heidegger – "the Unthought is the highest gift (*Geschenk*) that a thought can give" – which has come to him by way of Derrida, he writes as follows:

> In our place and in our time the word "spirit," perhaps unsaturated with meaning and yet evocative, may call forth associations, as did the word "id"

in the early half of the first century of psychoanalysis, as then did the word "ego" in the midcentury, and more recently as does the word "self." But our words often need displacing (as I may be doing with Winnicott's phrase "true self" by substituting "idiom" for it) because the overusage of a term, though transitionally essential to individual and collective efforts of objectifying the signified, eventually loses its meaningfulness through incantatory solicitation, devaluing any word's unthought potential.[54]

Bollas's proposal with regard to introducing the word "spirit" into psychoanalysis is very important. Its importance, however, is not limited to its merely being a freshly evocative word in a time when other terms have become shop-worn. More than this, the introduction of "spirit" as a term has a bearing upon the positivity–negativity issue we have been discussing. In marked contrast to the other terms that psychoanalysis uses, which are so easily positivized, "spirit," by definition, is *not* a positivity. On the contrary, in a very explicit way it is logically negative. And, thus, in using the term (and not just using it, but coming to it theoretically as Bollas does), psychoanalysis makes, or could be making, a decisive step in leaving empiricism and external reflection beneath itself.

What a contrast! What a shift! Reflected into itself, object relations sublates itself, giving way to talk of "subject relations" and "spirit."

In an essay dealing with the distinction between "mind" and "self," Bollas raises the question: "[b]ut how if at all do we distinguish between thoughts going into the thinking and the supposed object of thought, both of which it may be argued are mental and from the mind?"[55] In quoting this question our concern is not with the specifics of the answer Bollas provides. The distinction itself is what is important to us here. *"Thoughts going into the thinking"* as opposed to *"the supposed object of thought."* Or, said another way, the ongoingness of thought, its logical movement as internal reflection and negativity contrasted with thought in its positivity as this or that externally reflected idea, fact, or entity. How similar this opposition or contrast is to the psychology-constituting one through which we have been insighting psychoanalysis and analytical psychology in these pages!

In another passage, also from an essay included in *The Mystery of Things*, Bollas again discusses his proposal with respect to the introduction of the term "spirit."

[U]nder special circumstances the term "spirit" should be introduced into psychoanalysis, even though there would be many objections to a term laden with pre-psychoanalytic meanings. If, however, we understand spirit as the expressive movement of an individual's idiom through the course of his or her life, we may say that each of us is a spirit, and that we have spiritual effects upon others – who will indeed carry us as such within themselves, and we in turn will be inhabited by the spirits of others. Spirit is not the same as an internal representation although it does, I think, come very close to what we mean by an internal object: something deeper, more complex, beyond representation, yet there.[56]

Passing by Bollas's confining of the term "spirit" to the idiom of a person (a view which doubtless has much merit in the context of personal analysis), it is the move away from the materiality that the word "object" implies (even when we know we are speaking of internal objects) to the immaterial quality of the word "spirit" that is of interest to us here. Celebrating this movement in the language of our musical, we could say that the Higgins in Bollas would seem, in this passage, to have once again freed his Eliza-anima from the hysterical, (pre-)Oedipal solipsism of the object-relations picture-book work that would always, by conceiving of her as an infant, return her to mamma. Not easy, this, when the actual mother has long been put in the place of the Mother of God within the doctrines of psychoanalysis.

I say "seems to have freed" because in *Hysteria*, published only a year later, Bollas falls back behind this crucial insight. Not only is hysterical character described in the picture-book manner he had so recently decried, but the picture which he gives of it is then totalized. In contrast to the many other maladies of the soul that are broken up and ameliorated by the free association process, the hysteric's object relations are portrayed by Bollas as being so melded with his or her absence-erotizing utterances that the latter, for all their appearance of being spontaneously produced, merely reinforce the former. Far from breaking up the cosy solipsism of object-relations thinking, which would always return the infant to the mother in the here-and-now transference interpretation, free association, according to Bollas, is utterly sequestered there in the case of the hysteric.

How strange! The patient with whom Freud invented free association at the beginning of psychoanalysis is regarded by Bollas, a century later, to be almost totally resistant to what, in many other contexts, he regards as free association's inherently therapeutic effect. When writing about free association, Bollas (with our sympathy) characterizes object relations as a mere picture-book work by comparison. However, a year later when he is analyzing the structure of hysteria, the object-relations picture-book mode is empathically reaffirmed in precisely the terms in which he had previously decried it. Hysteria, in his view, is not only an all-out campaign to return to the solipsistic embrace of mamma-the-caregiver, its regressive power is such that it is able to suck the fundamental rule into the vortex of mamma and infant, as we discussed in detail above in our section dealing with baby-talk.

Possibly, what happened here is that Bollas, having cancelled out object relations as part of the movement deeper into internal reflection, felt, quite rightly, the need to rescue and retain it. This, however, he attempts to do positivistically by bringing back hysteria as a diagnostic entity and then, so to speak, throwing the picture book of object relations at it. This, I believe, is an unnecessary move. Object relations, with its keen sense of the fateful forces that disturb and ruin people's lives, does not need a class of ruined or disturbed people to bear witness to its merit as a theory. Were it to, it would be a part of the sickness of our times, and not a seeing-through of that sickness.

Looking carefully again at the passage from *The Mystery of Things* in which Bollas speaks of object relations as a picture-book work, we see, ironically enough, that vestiges of picture-book thinking are present in the very critique that he there levels against it. The problem is not with his reference to the solipsistic world of the infant and mother. This cosy view is what he is trying to push off from, to leave behind, or retain beneath the more comprehensive vision he is reaching toward. The problem, rather, is his reference to the "Freudian action breaking the tie." In referring to free association in this way, he locks it again into a familial, picture-book image – the paternal metaphor. Far from breaking up or abrogating the parental complexes through free association, he merely moves their Oedipal and pre-Oedipal story from one place to another such that the theoretical trajectory of free association, the spontaneous gesture of psychoanalysis itself, is foreclosed.

The same, of course, can be said for Juliet Mitchell's theory. Shifting the emphasis from parent–child relations to sibling relations does not really change the form of the thinking involved. Likewise, her characterization of the former kind of relationship as vertical and the latter as horizontal does little more than encapsulate these mighty vectors within the Oedipal horizons of personalistic psychology. Failing to genuinely revision itself through the negativization of its categories, psychoanalysis – both "Freudian" and "Jungian" – merely re-equips itself to say to another generation of patients, "Don't do what I do, just do what I say."

But cannot the same be said of Jung's characterization of psychology as being a translation of the archaic speech of myth into a modern mythologem? Is this not simply another example of "moving the story from one place to another;" Jungian psychology as a picture-book work where the picture book is a mythology text? Doubtless, in some quarters this is so. In the so-called "classical school" of Jungian analysis the archetypes are positivized, regarded as eternal verities. The "archetypal school," however, has pushed off from this position with its move away from the archetype as such, to the phenomenal or archetypal image. And then there is the work of Wolfgang Giegerich, which moves beyond imagination in its positivity to logical form, negativity, thought. His contribution, which we shall return to later, is a decisive breaking-free of analytical psychology from its own version of what Bollas rightly decries as "picture-book work."

Chapter 8

Voicing the Weather Oracle

It is not storms, not thunder and lightning, not rain and cloud that remain as images in the psyche, but the fantasies caused by the affects they arouse. . . . Man's curses against devastating thunderstorms, his terror of the unchained elements – these affects anthropomorphize the passion of nature, and the purely physical element becomes an angry god.[1]

C. G. Jung

He [the hysteric] can transmit his state of mind in adept ways, so much so that others of like temperament can identify with his plight. He could find himself in a community of kindred beings, all transmitting symptoms back and forth over their own psychic Internet.[2]

Christopher Bollas

Speaking out

In these pages we have provided a "supplement of reading" for many aspects of Bollas's theory of hysteria. That it has been possible to do so with such vigor, I believe, owes something to the fact that his account of the ways in which the hysteric resists analysis, even while seeming to take to it so well, is a very compelling one. To my mind, however, what is compelling about his account is not to be found in its literal meaning, but in the suspending or seeing through of this. Bollas's *Hysteria*, I submit, is not the clinical book it purports to be. Not at all an analysis of hysteria as a positively existing malady. On the contrary, if read from the more radical perspective that it carries within itself, it is a writerly *enactment* of the unthought known that psychoanalysis has itself become within the culture of the Western soul, a psychoanalysis (or nearly so) of analysis itself at its centenary.

Just as a poet or novelist explores themes of universal significance, indirectly, by examining the minute particulars of a specific time, place, and collection of characters, so Bollas's consulting-room account of hysterical character is transparent to the larger story of our time. The analytic couples discussed in his book, like any analytic couple, are a microcosm of the prevailing collective spirit. To listen in on their conversations is to listen to the discourse of society at large. This is so even with respect to the most personal of intimacies and private of meanings. For, as Lacan has argued, everything we say to one another or think to ourselves – both inside the consulting room and outside of it – is overdetermined by the tropological structures inherent in language itself.

Capturing the humbling implications of this insight in an arresting image, one analytic writer has described himself as "a ventriloquist's dummy of the culture" who is, at the same time, the author of sentences that no-one else has written.[3] This image is as apt a caricature of the analyst's and patient's work together as it is of that particular writer. Analytic couples are also ventriloquists' dummies through which the culture speaks. At the same time, however, they may also be the originators of new thoughts.

As constrained by the structure of language as the "talking cure" undoubtedly is, there is at the same time something uniquely generative about it. On occasions, at least, an analytic couple may reverse the direction of the ventriloquist act they are performing, throwing their voices beyond the sound-proofed walls of the consulting room into the world at large. Ironically, it is from therapy's most inarticulate moments that such potentially mutative and far-reaching articulations come. By silencing the newspeak of the culture speaking through them, resistances to the so-called "fundamental rule" may be the caesura through which the associative process is truly freed. To speak with one's own voice, one must first stop speaking with everyone else's.

In this connection I am put in mind of therapeutic impasses in which the existing repertoire of dynamic interpretations out of which the towering edifice of psychoanalysis has been built is no longer sufficient to think the anxieties, dreadful silences, and somatizations that a particular analytic couple are suffering. At such junctures, I believe, the "talking-cure" depends for its success upon the *parthenogenic* production of neologisms, new words, a whole New Testament even.

One such new word is the word "therapy" itself. An old word really, therapy (or *therapeutae* as it was once rendered) has been given a new and distinct meaning in the culture of our time. We are, as the phrase would have it, "a therapy culture." So much so, in fact, that it is not unusual to find a salesman who talks like Kohut or a hairdresser who sounds like Jung. Never mind that such men and women may never have darkened the door of a therapist's office themselves. Like the legendary hundredth monkey, they have picked up its patterns of thought and feeling, preternaturally, out of the air-waves or ether (and only later from the Oprah show). Freud, we may recall in this connection, was intrigued by the phenomenon of "thought-transference" and telepathy. And Bollas, similarly, begins *Hysteria* with the observation that "[the hysteric] can transmit his state of mind in adept ways, so much so that others of like temperament can identify with his plight. He could find himself [thereby] in a community of kindred beings, all transmitting symptoms back and forth over their own psychic Internet."[4] Jung, writing like the mystic he was derogatorily accused of being, speaks in more positive terms: "Neither propaganda nor exhibitionist confessions are needed. If the archetype, which is universal, i.e, identical with itself always and anywhere, is properly dealt with in one place only it is influenced as a whole, i.e. simultaneously and everywhere."[5]

Psychoanalysis, then, even when addressed to "the therapeutic community" as Bollas's *Hysteria* is, is not an exclusively clinical enterprise. It is not a sub-speciality within the Faculty of Medicine, like bone-setting or dentistry. On the contrary, along with Globalization, Down-sizing, and Money, it is the logical horizon, the truth of our age, the myth we are in, much as the religions were in earlier times. This is not to say that psychoanalysis is a religion. Like religion, however (whose sublated form it is), it has a totalizing character. This is so regardless of whether we consciously subscribe to it or not. In the same way that Christianity has inscribed its influence deeply into us during the past two thousand years, regardless of whether we identify ourselves as being believers or not, so too, after a century of psychoanalysis, everyone can be said to be "in" analysis.

Perhaps this is why our practices are down! The whole world is already inside that consulting room with no walls that Berggasse 19 and 1003 Seestrasse have become in our times. Who is there left to come in when there is no outside left to come in from?

Stormy weather

In its special end-of-the-century series, *Time Magazine*, with unerring judgement, placed Freud at the forefront of its list of the century's most influential scientists and thinkers.[6] Decades previously, Auden made a similar claim. In his famous elegy for Freud, he describes the great man as being "no more a person now but a whole climate of opinion\ under whom we conduct our different lives." Continuing the meteorological metaphor, the poet likens the originator of psychoanalysis to a "weather" which "quietly surrounds all our habits of growth and extends, till the tired in even the remotest miserable duchy have felt the change in their bones and are cheered . . . ."[7]

Auden's depiction of Freud's thought as a "climate of opinion" that surrounds our lives "like weather" brings us back to the assertion introduced in the previous section. There, it will be recalled, Bollas's *Hysteria* was declared to be a writerly enactment of the unthought known that psychoanalysis itself has become in our culture. Restating this declaration in terms of Auden's imagery, we could just as well describe the book as a writerly enactment of the "climate of opinion" that psychoanalysis has become in our life and times. Taking this analogy a step further, we could view hysterical patients, such as Susie, Heather, and Gerald, as passionate examples of the psychoanalytic weather that blows through our lives even as actual tropical storms and hurricanes are given names, such as Hannah, Alice, and Betty.

Psychologically speaking, climate and weather are suggestive of mood. We speak, for instance, of one person as having a "sunny" disposition and of another as being "stormy." A malcontented companion may be said to have "rained on our parade," while a lively visitor is celebrated as being "a breath of spring." Clearly, when it comes to the depiction of moods, meteorological, atmospheric, and climatic metaphors immediately suggest themselves.

Such associations, no doubt, owe something to the fact that our emotional state can be affected by actual climatic conditions. Gloomy weather can make us gloomy while bright days may lift our spirits. But there is also a weather that is generated from within ourselves. It is this inner, emotional weather that we especially have in mind when we speak of moods. Seasonal affective disorder notwithstanding, to understand this kind of weather we must resort to psychology.

In an earlier work, Bollas has written extensively about moods in relation to what he there calls "the psychoanalysis of the unthought known."[8] His view in a nutshell is that moods replicate the known, but as yet unthought, vicissitudes of the not-so-facilitating environments that stymied our development during our formative years. In the case of so-called "bad moods" this is obvious enough. The rough mental handling we give ourselves in the bad mood may be readily understood as being replicative of the inadequate care we received from our attachment figures during the tenure of our early dependency. It is more difficult, however, to see that our so-called "good moods" arise from the same background. The key to understanding here is the recognition that all moods are essentially "autistic structures."[9] We withdraw into moods even as the "weather" they generate surrounds us. While the "foul weather" of a bad mood is indicative of a self-state that recalls the forfeiture of one's spontaneous gesture in the face of an inhospitable familial environment, the "fair weather" of a good mood is indicative of a self-state in which the impulses, gestures, and desires that had been thwarted are prepossessingly withdrawn into as if into an imperious bubble of stubborn cheerfulness, insistent happiness, and the like. As Bollas, summing up his object-relational account of the psychology of mood, puts it:

> When a person goes "into" a mood, he becomes that child self who was refused expression in relation to his parents for one reason or another. Consequently, moods are often the existential registers of the moment of a breakdown between a child and his parents, and they partly indicate the parent's own developmental arrest, in that the parent was unable to deal appropriately with the child's particular maturational needs. What had been a self experience in the child, one that could have been integrated into the child's continuing self development, was rejected by the parents, who failed to perform adequately as ordinary "transformational objects", so that a self state was destined to be frozen by the child into what I have called a conservative object – subsequently represented only through moods.[10]

Can Bollas's analysis of mood be applied to the "climate of opinion" that Auden suggests psychoanalysis to be? If Freud's thought is "like weather," and weather a metaphor of mood, can the psychology of mood that Bollas has provided serve us in our attempt to think the unthought known that psychoanalysis has become for our culture?

These questions can also be asked in terms of hysteria. Is hysteria a mood disorder? Or, better said, could we learn something further about psychoanalysis by thinking about hysteria as if it were a mood? (Jung, we may recall in this connection, defined anima as "the *a priori* element in . . . moods, reactions, impulses, and whatever else is spontaneous in psychic life."[11]) In Jungian parlance, to be in a mood is to be identified with or "possessed" by the anima.

For the words "child" and "parent" in the passage from Bollas above let us substitute the words "psyche" and "psychoanalysis." Read in the light of these amendments, that complex of moods that Bollas subsequently attempted to assail with his year-2000 theory of hysteria is revealed to be the existential register, as it were, of a breakdown between the psyche and psychoanalysis.

But what is the cause of this breakdown? In Bollas's personalistic account (as we have just seen), moods are indicative of a breakdown between child and parent, a breakdown, moreover, for which the parents are largely to blame. Limited by an arrest in their own development, mother and father may be unable to meet the maturational needs of their child. When this is the case, those elements of the child's potential that have not been actualized through object-use live on into adulthood in frozen form as moods.

Rereading this explanation in the light of our substitution of terms, we are led to entertain the possibility that psychoanalysis, far from being the "transformational object" it aspires to be, may have become a "conservative object" due to a developmental arrest of its own. Constrained within the limiting horizon of an arrested analytic theory, the soul loses its meaning and withdraws into itself. The moods into which it withdraws, however, are also emitted by it. Released into the real, they envelop the world much as weather does. The economy, the stock-market, and institutional life generally become hysterical emotional systems. Answering this madness, the ancient notion of the *anima mundi* gains a new pertinence in our times.[12]

Of course, it is easier to see the speck of dust in one's brother's eye than the beam in one's own – hence the difficulty the various analytic schools have in appreciating each other's contributions. But this said, it seems to me, as an observer from the adjacent field of analytical psychology, that the developmental arrest afflicting psychoanalysis resides in its attitude toward the spirit. Unaware of the deficiency of its stance in this regard, psychoanalyis has tended to reject as pathology the very aspects of the collective unconscious that its patients have been called by their sufferings to integrate.

Bollas's *Hysteria* is a case in point. In its pages, as we have already discussed, the spirituality of the hysteric is taken to be nothing more than a pretty lie through which sexuality, reality, and the father are warded off. This despite the fact that the spirit has been an acknowledged dimension of human existence in every age and culture thus far. If spiritual investment is archetypal, the lack of it in psychoanalysis is more suspect than is the presence of it in the hysteric.

There are times in any thoroughgoing analysis in which the patient must be the therapist. Is this what hysteria is for psychoanalysis?

In a letter to the clergyman Pfister, Freud noted that "none of the pious ever discovered psychoanalysis," its discovery falling rather to him, "a completely godless Jew."[13] In a letter to Jung, Freud expresses a similar antipathy to things spiritual. Affecting a bemused tone, he disingenuously praises Jung for having "solved the riddle of all mysticism," signing himself, at the close of the letter, "your untransformed FREUD."[14] Heir to its founder's resistance to religion, psychoanalysis has been loath to consider the role of the spirit in the life of the psyche. When this arrest in its development is taken into account, however, the spirituality of the hysteric appears in a whole new light – not as a repression of sexuality, but as an expression of it that is compensatory to psychoanalytic atheism. Both sexual and spiritual at once, hysteria is the anima of psychoanalysis itself.

Suffering psyche

But what of our patients? Do they not come to us because they are ill? And hysteria – is it not the clinical problem that Bollas and others have once again claimed it to be? In these pages we have disputed the claim that hysteria is a particular kind of pathological structure that arises, trans-historically and trans-culturally, out of a particular set of aetiological causes. Hysteria, we have insisted, is not merely a psychological disorder that people have, something that can be explained personalistically in terms of the conflicts, traumas, and developmental arrests of childhood and family life. While we do, of necessity it seems, spend many hours in therapy working with our patients on matters of this kind (the personalistic mode being how psychology's absolute subjectivity, i.e., its lack of an Archimedian point of view, is currently compensated and positivized), hysteria is of a different order. It is as much collective as it is personal, as much of the group mind as it is of the individual mind. Or, to put this another way, hysteria (here used in a sense inclusive of the many diagnostic names by which the soul's maladies are known in our day) is the undifferentiated or sub-dialectical unity of personal and collective, individual and group, spirit and life, mind and earth.[15]

This idea – that psychical suffering at the individual level has an impersonal, transpersonal, or archetypal background – is a key idea in analytical psychology. In Jung's writings we find it stated and restated in various ways throughout his career. For instance, as early as 1914 he declared that there are not a few neurotics "who do not require any reminders of their social duties and obligations, but are born and destined rather to be bearers of new cultural ideals."[16] Some years later, Jung said much the same thing when he wrote that "neurosis is intimately bound up with the problem of our time and really represents an unsuccessful attempt on the part of the individual to solve a general problem in his own person."[17] And then there is this from his memoirs:

> A collective problem, if not recognized as such, always appears as a personal problem, and in individual cases may give the impression that something is out of order in the realm of the personal psyche. The personal sphere is indeed

disturbed, but such disturbances need not be primary; they may well be secondary, the consequence of an insupportable change in the social atmosphere. The cause of disturbance is, therefore, not to be sought in the personal surroundings, but rather in the collective situation. Psychotherapy has hitherto taken this matter far too little into account.[18]

The ubiquity of hysteria, its many guises in as many times and places, points not only to *its* ubiquity or universality as a diagnosis with such-and-such a cause, but to *universality* as such. Hysteria, in other words, is how the universals of the human situation reach us. Manifest in "our" lives as "our" symptoms, the fallen or, conversely, newly unfolding forms of culture are taken up into the *status* of subjectivity, the *status* of psychology, if only in the diminutive *form* of our personal concerns.

I say *status* of the subjective and *form* of the personal because, as Hillman has noted, it is precisely when we feel most intensely personal that we are in fact the least individual and the most collective. "This 'me,'" writes Hillman,

> even most deeply experienced as if from the ground of being, seemingly so unique, so truly my own, is utterly collective. For psyche is not mine, and the statements that express my deepest person, such as: "I love you," "I am afraid," "I promise," are collective universals whose value lies just in their impersonality, that they are said by everyone, everywhere. As collective-universals, these statements are archetypally personal, but not literally so.[19]

As the ancients knew (and Gaston Bachelard has reminded us with his notion of a "psychology of capital letters"[20]), Joy, Sorrow, Hope, Jealously, Fear, and the rest have a psychology of their own, quite apart from what the Polybus and Merope of our day – developmental psychology and Freudian positivism – have led us to regard as "our" psychology. And this is to list only emotional and affective states. In addition to these we may recall the figures which Hesiod identifies in his *Theogony*: Old Age, Envy, Doom, Strife, Destiny, Lamentation, Deceit, and Dreams.[21] In our contemporary world, hysteria finds still other epithets of itself: Globalization, Terrorism, Down-sizing, Profit-Maximization, Fundamentalism, Affirmative Action, Global Warming, Infotainment, Food Additives, Cyberspace, Money, and so on.

It is in terms of these affective constellations, existential typicalities, and titanic forces and concerns that our supplement of reading regards hysteria. If we are overly emotional in a seemingly shallow way, it is because the various epithets of hysteria in our day have a boundary-transgressing, inflationary effect upon the personal subject. If we are indifferent to the conversion symptoms that hystericize our bodies, it is because our bodies, far from being merely ours alone, are the incarnational register, as it were, for events pertaining to the body politic at large. The same can be said of hysteria's other famous traits. Its childlike innocence, usually taken literally as child*ish*ness, developmental arrest, and resistance to adulthood, may also be regarded as bodying forth what Jung has called "the child-hood aspect of the collective psyche,"[22] i.e, the newly-fledged symbolic value that is compensatory to or renewing of the spirit of the times. Likewise, the theatrical-ity so common in hysterical personalities. Usually seen on the model of the attention-seeking behaviour of an inadequately loved child (or in Bollas's view, as identificatory playing out of a parent's interior object world), this, too, may be viewed in archetypal perspective. For if the world's a stage, as Shakespeare said, we may find ourselves compelled to "act out" upon that stage roles that the powers and principalities that invisibly constitute our lives cathect us with. Suggestibility, it follows, is not only the false compliance of a false self, but the presence in the individual of psychology at the group level.

And what of love? The hysteric is said to have particular problems in this sphere. What has the coquettishness of hysteria to do with the collective soul?

In the "Suggestion and libido" section of his *Group Psychology and the Analysis of the Ego*, Freud states that "the 'Eros' of the philosopher Plato coincides exactly with the love-force, the libido of psychoanalysis."[23] But if this is so, is hysteria not just as exactly the Diotima, or anima-muse, that instructed Socrates that it is love that leads us to the archetypes or forms?

Within a few pages of making the above assertion about the libido of psycho-analysis and the Eros of Platonic philosophy, Freud writes that "there is no doubt that something exists in us which, when we become aware of signs of emotion in someone else, tends to make us fall into the same emotion."[24] This "something," which Freud also calls "suggestibility," is, in his view, "an irreducible, primitive phenomenon, a fundamental fact in the mental life of man."[25] Turning this around a bit, we could also say that suggestibility is the conduit of what is irreducible, primitive, fundamental – in a word, archetypal – about life and the psyche.

In analytical psychology the hysterically suggestible "something" through which we are each subject to the emotional concerns of the group is conceived of in terms of anima/animus theory. Classically defined, the anima and animus are mediating figures that both personify and projectively bring to bear the instinctual imperatives of the collective unconscious. The more unconscious we are of the suggestive power of these "mediating daimons" (as von Franz calls them[26]), the more collective or archetypally determined our relationship will be to the issues at hand. Obedient to the imperatives of the collective psyche, as these are manifest personally and interpersonally in our lives and relationships, we more or less live out the life of Everyman or Everywoman. When, however, the anima and animus are made conscious, when, that is to say, the transpersonal libido that animates our lives is related to in its otherness as other, a process of differentiation which Jung called individuation begins. No longer identified with the emotions and images reaching us from the collective, we find, rather, that by sustaining a lover's quarrel with them we can bring ourselves and them to unique, even culturally renewing, realization. This may happen in an entirely inward, or rather, introverted manner, as for instance when we explore a feeling or mood by making it the basis of a painting or poem. Hillman has written, in this connection, of a soul-sophisticating development of anima (symptoms, moods, fantasies) into psyche (reflection, imagination, and the culture of psychological mindedness).[27] Just as validly, the process of differentiating our own unique response to the collective emotions we have fallen into – the soul-sophisticating development of anima into psyche – may occur interpersonally through passionate debate with others in the *polis* of everyday life. If man is a political animal, as Aristotle observed, it is largely because he has an emotionally labile, hysterically suggestible soul.

In an earlier chapter we discussed Bollas's account of the hysterical couple on a date. The scenario as he described it was one in which "the hysterical lovers-to-be . . . meet up for a film, stumble into rationalized need to visit one lover's flat, make tea in the kitchen, bump into one another like two internal objects cut loose, giddy with the oddity of their release into the real . . . giggle a lot, and then talk and talk and talk."[28] But what, we may now ask, is it that these lovers-to-be are talking about? Down-Sizing, Terrorism, and the other sections of the Midgard Serpent we listed above?

Perhaps our hysterical inability to make it together sexually – just like that – is like Thor's failure to lift the cat off the floor – a sign of our being in touch with the archetypal level of existence. Likewise, the "blind-fucking" that Bollas says can also overtake us in our hysterical couplings may be regarded as an epiphany of the titanic divinities by which we are transcended in our day. Sex, after all, is not child's play. It is symbolic. Not because of the internal objects that we release so giddily into the real in our childish ambivalence about facing reality, but because of the powers and principalities of the real itself, which bear down upon it with that impossible weight that might yet be its sublation into love. Platonic love, it follows, is not the opposite of carnality and sex. Rather, it is the unity of both, inasmuch as it retains physical sexuality within or beneath itself as a sublated moment within its more comprehensive vision.

In a paper titled, "The indivisiblity of the personal and collective unconscious," Mary Williams writes that "nothing in the personal unconscious needs to be repressed unless the ego feels threatened by its archetypal power."[29] Further to this statement, we could say that *the repressed unconscious of personalistic psychology is, at the same time as it is that, a receptive unconscious with respect to an archetypal or transpersonal psyche.* This is especially the case when a civilization's culture becomes unstable through either decline or rapid growth. When the archetypes – those compelling forces of life's immensity – are insufficiently mediated on the cultural level, they become, in something of the manner of the persecutory anxieties of Klein's paranoid-schizoid position, the compelling forces in our lives as individuals, forcing us to behave or be the presence of what is not otherwise represented. Just as children impoverished of maternal care tend to become for themselves the missing breast (Jung has spoken of fatherless children "nominating a part of their body for a father"[30]), so the individual at every stage of life becomes the stand-in, however haplessly, for whatever he or she, with reference to an inborn sense of wholeness, senses to be missing in the collective sphere.

Our argument here is reminiscent of the adage which declares absence to be the most compelling form of presence. The presence referred to here, of course, is psychic presence, presence in the positivity-negating sense of image, reflection, or thought. Further to this we may say that the shadowy intercourse of the afore-mentioned absent parents is especially fertile psychologically. But what does this look like?

In his essay, "Hysterical phantasies and their relationship to bisexuality," Freud declares that "an hysterical symptom is the expression of both a masculine and a feminine unconscious sexual phantasy."[31] That this is so is never more true than when Zeus and Hera, Yahweh and Israel, Christ and his Church have come un-coupled. For it is precisely the demise of these symbols which has given rise to that new form of cultural-coitus unique to our time, the transference neurosis of psychoanalysis. Distributed interpersonally between the analyst and analysand in the transference, the masculine and feminine sexual fantasies which are the sunken form of the culture which preceded them come together anew in the psychology-generating intercourse of the talking-cure. That this process, true to its characteri-zation as "a most dangerous method,"[32] occasionally lapses back atavistically into the ethics-violating positivity of actual intercourse may have less to do with succumbing to the incestuous urges and traumatic repetitions of childhood than with the failure of psychotherapy to recognize the dynamics of the collective unconscious, writ small in the anima and animus, which it is cathected with. Infantile sexuality notwithstanding, we cannot, in our theory, have an infantile attitude toward sexuality, but must also understand, with Jung, "its spiritual aspect and numinous meaning."[33]

Echoing the statements we quoted from Jung above about neurosis being an attempt on the part of the individual to solve a collective problem in his or her own person, Jung speaks in yet another place of "the recrudescence of individual symbol-formation" that follows the decline of Christian symbolism.[34] The distinguished French Jungian Elie Humbert makes a similar point:

> If the collective has nothing to offer, it is up to each of us to try and understand what it is we need in order to be able to live. Thus, the analysis undertaken in the spirit of this process becomes an adventure in the recognition of . . . [interior, religious] space and in allowing it to develop freely; an adventure also in feeling, accepting, and coming to terms with the symbols that will, of their own accord, arise.[35]

Heraclitus, philosophizing in the late sixth century BC, said, "Even sleepers are workers and collaborators in what goes on in the universe."[36] To this statement we may add that it takes an immense amount of dreaming on the individual level to conceive a collectively significant dream. For not every dreamer is sufficiently conscious of his cultural abandonment to create very much beyond himself in his oneiric productions. Mostly, it is really only a question of one's own personal myth, if that. Indeed, as Jung observed, many still live the whole of their lives in past centuries and know nothing of the loneliness of a truly contemporary existence.

But to return to Heraclitus's point, in light of the views of Jung we quoted above, there are not a few neurotics who are destined, if only through work upon what is repressed in them, to be the bearers of new cultural ideals.

The obvious analogy to the problematic we are discussing is the child who must be the caretaker of a dysfunctional parent. Mimetic to such a child, the individual may become the hystericized container, as it were, of the culture, which no longer supports or contains him or her – *a situation that has led in our day to a virtual epidemic of iatrogenically produced false memories of being inadequately parented by one's personal parents.* Though we may, of course, have been inadequately and even abusively parented, and though this may well need to be explored in psychotherapy, *psychology* must push off from this preoccupation, even as Freud pushed off from the seduction theory, if it is truly to come of age. Bent though we may be by the burden of what the culture no longer carries, we are not, on this account, abused children. On the contrary, we are adults, or elders even, *of psychology.* As such, we may no longer ask what our country, profession, religion, parents, ideals, or culture can do for us, but what we can do for these.

An adage adapted from Freud states that we act out what we do not remember. This holds true as well for what our culture would seem to have forgotten. When the symbolic forms that had previously expressed the fullness of our human lives and the vicissitudes of our collective situation fade, the individual may be called to the front, sometimes at an unfortunately young age, to serve in their stead. Related to this, romantic love – larger than life in even the most ordinary of times – may become still more so as we projectively seek in a lover's face a semblance of what is missing in the culture. If Nancy's face, no less than Helen's, can launch a thousand ships, it is because "the collective unconscious *as a whole* presents itself to a man in feminine form . . ." and "to a woman . . . in masculine form."[37]

In a formulation that strongly resembles this one from Jung concerning the anima and animus, Freud writes of our tendency to fall in love via the projection of the ego-ideal:

> The sexual ideal may enter into an interesting auxiliary relation to the ego-ideal. Where the narcissistic gratification encounters actual hindrances, the sexual ideal may be used as a substitutive gratification. In such a case a person loves (in conformity with the narcissistic type of object-choice) someone whom he once was and no longer is, or else someone who possesses excellences which he never had at all. . . .[38]

In another place Freud writes of "sexual overvaluation," accounting for this in terms of the setting up of the love-object in the place of the ego-ideal.[39] Bearing this in mind as we read down the page from which we have just quoted, we can see still more clearly how Freud's formulation of the relations between the sexual ideal and the ego-ideal parallels Jung's concerning the transpersonal significance of the anima/animus and our own concerning hysteria.[40]

> The ego-ideal is of great importance for the understanding of group-psychology. Besides its individual side, this ideal has a social side; it is also the common ideal of a family, a class, or nation.[41]

Freud here is to our Jungian point: it is not just that the hindrances to "our" narcissism lead us to seek a love-object on the model of "our" ego-ideal; the personal sense of hindrance may also be located at the cultural level as a collective sense that something is missing there. For if the ego-ideal has, in addition to its individual side, a social side, which is also the common ideal of a family, a class, or a nation, then collective factors such as these may be expected to have a great importance for the understanding of love relationships. Our love relationships, that is to say, are not motivated only by personal transferences. Archetypal transferences – the common ideals of family, class, and nation – may also figure in them. Just as in a movie an actor such as Jeremy Irons may personify Britain, and his oriental mistress, Hong Kong, so also may we, in our lives and loves, personify impersonal factors.[42]

"Girls do it with guys who avoid the draft." As this slogan from the era of the Vietnam War suggests, it is not only pheromones and hormones, object relations, and physical build that figure in mate selection. Just as invisibly, the great themes of life, the fashions of political correctness, and sex-sells advertising play a part as well. Recognizing this, contemporary evolutionary theory has had to revision its understanding of natural selection, at least insofar as humans are concerned, in light of the consideration that culture – and hence the human psyche – is itself one of the environmental conditions under which selection takes place.[43]

Analytical psychology approaches psychical suffering on the individual level by linking it back to the archetypal. In doing so it assumes, as Hillman has put it,

> that the relationships in our contemporary humanistic culture are not humanly underdeveloped as much as overloaded with archetypal demands. What people expect of mothers and fathers, teachers and friends and lovers is far beyond the ability of personal human beings; people ask that archetypal qualities be present in each other which in other cultures are present only in Gods and Goddesses.[44]

At the same time, analytical psychology recognizes the role that the individual, called to adulthood and citizenship by symptoms and erotic entanglements, plays in the culture at large. Summarizing this point of view, so central to the ethos of analytical psychology's classical tradition, Neumann writes:

> To the extent that he does live in reality the whole range of his particular life, the individual is . . . an alchemical retort, in which the elements present in the collective are melted down and refashioned to form a new synthesis, which is then offered to the collective. But the predigestion of evil [let "evil" here refer to the titanic forces mentioned above – GM] which he carries out as part of the

process of assimilating his shadow makes him, at the same time, an agent for the immunisation of the collective. An individual's shadow is invariably bound up with the collective shadow of his group, and as he digests his own evil, a fragment of the collective evil is invariably co-digested at the same time.[45]

Oedipus at Delphi

In making the case that he did for the universality of the Oedipus complex Freud essentially created what we, following Jung, have been calling personalistic psychology. Personalistic psychology is a conception of psychology that is limited to our positivity as persons who have developed out of a particular set of empirically given human circumstances. The archetypal reach of personalistic psychology is thus limited to the universality of the family set-up, the tensions and conflicts occasioned by mother, father, and siblings, and the stages of psychosexual development – in short, by all that Freud had in mind when he declared that "the profound and universal validity of the old legends is explicable only by an equally universal validity of the . . . hypothesis regarding the psychology of children."[46]

Oedipus, however (and this is the rub as the archetypalist sees it), was not a *person* in the personalistic sense of today's psychology. Nor was he "psychological man" in the diminutive sense in which we now, in the wake of Freud, consider ourselves to be so. In the ancient world, "psyche" was a wider notion than "man." As such, it was not *in* Oedipus in the way we now, under the banner of his name, assume that it is *in* us. It was not, that is to say, limited by or to his empirical personality in the way we now limit it to ours. On the contrary, what was psychological about Oedipus was that in addition to his being this or that particular person (if such he was), he was also *"Person"* in the metaphysical, universal, or capitalized sense of the notion.

Analytical psychology holds the same to be true of us as well. Besides being the particular selves that we empirically are we are also living instances of what may variously be called Self, Anthropos, or Universal Person. In our times, however, the crucial-that-it-be-kept difference that the dialectical unity of the empirical and the metaphysical embraces, far from being retained under sublation within our vision of ourselves, seems utterly to have collapsed. Like the anti-heroic protagonist of Kafka's novella *The Metamorphosis*, who awakens to discover that he has been transfigured into a loathsome dung-beetle, we suffer the greater spirit that we also are in the form of symptoms, the negativity of what Giegerich has called "the soul's logical life" positivizing itself as thorns in our flesh.

Discussing precisely this state of affairs with reference to the faith-neurosis of his Protestant minister father, Jung characterizes his father as having "regarded his suffering as a personal affliction for which you might ask a doctor's advice; he did not see it as the suffering of the Christian in general."[47] In an extended commentary on Jung's account of this, Giegerich draws out its wider implications for psychotherapeutic practice:

[O]ne does precisely *not* do justice to the patient if one considers *him*, i.e., the patient in his positivity, to be the true patient of therapy. Who [then] is the true patient? It is the *prima materia*, it is the God or Gods, "the suffering of the Christian *anthropos* at large," the "truth" of the age, the logic of our mode of being-in-the-world, *as* they play through the life of the singular patient in the consulting room as well as through our real social life in the world.[48]

This vision, which Jung's "higher psychotherapy"[49] has in common with the ancient world in general and with Greek tragedy in particular, has been largely forgotten in our time. Restaging itself in our day, the tragedy of Oedipus resides in his having become *our* repressed, *our* complex – a Blanche duBois or Willie Loman. But the symptoms that are the remainders of this reduction remember otherwise. They remember shaping influences in addition to and beyond that lesser tragedy (terrible as this may have been) of our childhood in family with parents. Reflecting this "beyond" in its theory, analytical psychology conceives of the complexes as aggregates of personally acquired contents which have been drawn together by an archetype. Just as iron filings distributed around a magnet conform to the magnet's magnetic field, so the events that constitute our lived, experienced lives are apperceptively shaped by supra-personal, trans-subjective archetypes into the patterned happenings and thematized experiences that reflectively give to life its inner problematic and imperative of meaning.

Neumann has written in this connection of "secondary personalization." This "principle . . . holds that there is a persistent tendency in man to take primary and transpersonal contents as secondary and personal, and to reduce them to personal factors" via cycles of projection and introjection.[50] The idea here is that we experience life in terms of archetypal expectations, which are grounded in the psyche's archaic structure. Putting this another way, Neumann states that "the kind of experience we shall have is prescribed by the archetypes, but what we experience is always individual."[51] This is so even with respect to our parents in earliest childhood. The complex source of later transferences (as Freud so usefully described them to be), our parents are themselves the recipients of primordial projections, inasmuch as they are invested, from day one, with the "trailing clouds" of what we (following Jung) have called the archetypal transference.

Just as Oedipus had, in addition to the Polybus and Merope he grew up with as his parents, an even more royal set of parents, Laius and Jocasta, so, too, do we have both a personal and an archetypal set of parents. The fateful consequence of this positivity-negating double lineage is that each of us is doomed to live out the universality of the age-old patterns through the singularity of our individual lives.[52] At its highest determination, the interiorizing, family-negating tragedy of incest is figurative of the individuation process itself.[53] Like Oedipus, we all commit Self-generating acts of patricide and incest throughout our lives as life channels what may variously be called Great Mother, collective unconscious, Jocasta, on the one hand, and Great Father, symbolic order, or Laius, on the other, through our uniqueness or inner infinity. At best this process results in fresh, transvaluative realizations of the age-old patterns to which we are heir, a forging, as it were, in the smithy of our symptoms, what Joyce has called "the uncreated conscience of [our] race."[54] At worst there is merely repetition, without individuating acts of repentance, of what D. H. Lawrence has referred to as the "mistake which mankind at large has chosen to sanctify."[55]

Hillman, drawing upon the heuristically rich metaphor of polytheism as a way of thinking about the ego-transcending and, hence, God-like universality that reaches us through our symptoms and pathologies, makes a point similar to Neumann's. "[A]rchetypal psychology," he writes,

> can put its idea of psychopathology into a series of nutshells, one inside the other: within the affliction is a complex, within the complex an archetype, which in turn refers to a God. Afflictions point to Gods; Gods reach us through afflictions. . . . Our pathologizing is their work, a divine process working in the human soul. By reverting the pathology to the God, we recognize the divinity of pathology and give the God his due . . .[56]

Living in polytheistic Greece (himself, even, a part of its pantheon with his apotheosis at Colonus), Oedipus moved within a psychic field that was richly imagined by his culture. At the centre of this psychic field or mythological landscape was the oracle at Delphi with its famous injunction: "Know thyself." It was through consulting this oracle that Oedipus was led to discover the nature of the crimes he had committed.

Puzzling over the oracle's cryptic message with the help of questions posed to him by the prophet Teiresias, Oedipus enacts a dialectical process of self-discovery. Commenting on Sophocles' dramatization of this process, Freud likened it to the dialectic of the talking cure of psychoanalysis in modern times.[57]

But what of the mythological landscape and the oracle at its centre? How do these figure in analysis?

In making the comparison he does between Oedipus's enlightenment and the analytic process Freud lost sight of these transpersonal expressions of the psyche even as Bollas left the Magi from the East and the Star of Bethlehem out of the account when comparing the family of the hysteric to the Holy Family. Where originally, in the Delphi of the ancients, the injunction – "Man, know thyself" – conveyed the meaning "know you are a man and not a god,"[58] later, at Berggasse 19 in Vienna, the reference to divinity was dropped altogether. Humans would know themselves by themselves, or rather, through a human interlocutor, the analyst. And they would do so with reference to their childhood as its relationships were projected in the transference. That the relations of an earlier man or woman in us to the Gods might also serve as the basis of the transference was simply ruled out as illusion, if it was thought about at all. And so it was that psychology became the interpretative re-enactment of personalistically conceived familial incest, which it mostly is today.

In Zurich things went rather differently. In developing his own form of analysis, Jung was more faithful to the original intent of the oracle's adage. Jungian analysis, as our quotes from Neumann and Hillman above attest, is an analysis *with* Gods. At the heart of its practice is a version of the age-old "know thyself," which is based upon the recognition, cultivation, and revering of a distinction between I and not-I, ego and archetype, human and divine. Because consciousness, as Jung put it, "can only exist through continual recognition of the unconscious,"[59] the analytic effort is to differentiate an awareness of the archetypal configurations that are enacting themselves through our fantasies, thoughts, and behaviour. If symptoms thwart and inhibit, it is obviously not *our* will that is being done. But if not ours, then whose? This question – so basic to Jungian practice – is continuous with the oracular tradition of discriminating spirits and naming the Gods. What is the myth I am in? How do those involuntary productions of the night, our dreams, portray what is going on? What do the Gods in the symptoms want?

A patient in my practice dreamt about an accountant calculating sums. Like the ruminating Oedipus coming to recognize that he himself is the killer of Laius and the son-lover of Jocasta, my patient interprets the dream-figure as a personification of a subjective propensity in himself: "It is my obsessiveness," he says, "my compulsiveness." "But are those really yours?" I ask in reply. "Accountants are in the world. They have accrediting bodies, professional societies. The accounting mentality is universal, something any one of us may be recruited by."

Another patient, who hated himself on account of his extreme shyness, dreamt of a beautiful oriental woman in a kimono. Her hands were clasped, her gaze averted, her head bowed. The idea presented by the image seemed to be one of modesty. Mediating the compensatory potential of the collective unconscious through a geographic or trans-cultural metaphor, this anima figure brought the possibility of taking a different attitude toward his plight. For, what he, as a North American, experienced as a social liability and railed against angrily, was shown to have a deeper value inasmuch as it could be likened to a beautiful oriental virtue. While it did not cure him of his inhibitions, the dream brought meaning and allowed him to adopt a more respectful and caring attitude toward himself for a time.

These examples of what the Jungian question looks like in practice are also illustrative – if only faintly – of the diagnostic utterances, oracular prognostications, and ritual proscriptions given by the oracle at Delphi to suppliants such as Oedipus. In the ancient world, when difficulties arose, a pilgrimage was made to Delphi to consult the oracle. Approaching the oracle, the suppliant would be directed to ask, "To which God or Hero should I sacrifice?" In this way, his or her plight was placed immediately in its universal context. By discovering which God had been neglected, the suppliant could set right the offense of such an omission. Or to put this in the contemporary terms of analytical psychology, when revalued from the perspective of what it has excluded from itself, the neurosis indicated by the suffering (generally defined by Jung as one-sidedness) could be cured.

In a passage in which he discusses our contemporary difficulty in understanding the Greek world view, Hillman writes that "while we begin always with an ego, the Greeks always began with the Gods."

A man or woman in Greek polytheistic psychology placed the personal in perspective through cult, initiation, and sacrifice, or through activities in the civic world, or through the catharsis of tragedy, or erotic mania and its discipline, or through overcoming the ignorance and opinion of the personal through reason and dialectic – but never, *never was human relationship an end in itself*. The closeness of persons with each other in the smallness of Greek life, and even the stress of love and friendship in Plato and Aristotle, is not for its own sake.[60]

Elaborating further on this point, Hillman continues:

In this perspective the human task was to draw the soul through recognition closer to the Gods, who are not human but to whose inhumanity the soul is inherently and priorly related. To neglect or forget these powers – to believe one's life was one's own, or that one's feelings were personal, or that personal relationships alone could provide community or substitute for relationships with Gods – meant loss of humanity. The human was unthinkable without its inhuman background. To be cut off from personified archetypal reality meant a soul cut off.[61]

These reflections bring us back to hysteria. At Delphi a certain class of specially selected women was enlisted to pronounce the oracle. On account of what we would now refer to as their emptiness, suggestibility, and dissociative conscious-ness, these women were regarded as being susceptible to revelatory ecstasies. Hysterics by another, more dignified name, it was these women, possessed by the Gods whose mouthpieces they thereby became, who oriented the individual in relation to the imperatives of life over which the Gods were imagined to preside.

Of course, we cannot know today whether the women who served at Delphi were regressively bent upon restoring their relationship to mamma-the-caregiver, as Bollas has claimed is the case in hysteria. Nor can we know if their permeable ego boundaries, emptiness, and regressive tendencies were hysterical symptoms resulting from catastrophic displacement by a sibling, as Juliet Mitchell has argued in her rival account. We can, however, turn to these early figures as the touchstone of an archetypal perspective. When we do this, we notice several things. First, their status was not that of immature children, but, rather, one of immense importance for society. Second, the mother they regressed to was not their personal mother, but *Ge*, the Earth Goddess – "mother" in a more mythologically religious or arche-typal sense. And third, their oracular link to this mother was not at the expense of a cutting off from the father in the manner that Bollas has described in his personalistic account of hysteria. For Apollo, according to the myths concerning Delphi, had long ago slain Python, the snake of matriarchy, and appropriated the oracle to himself.

Servants (*savants* even) of Pythian Apollo, the mediums of Delphi expressed the dialectical unity of the maternal and paternal orders. And this, I would suggest, was so regardless of whether any one of them, as individuals in the contemporary sense, had navigated the crossover from mother to father and resolved *their* Oedipus complex. For that transition had already happened logically, i.e., on the level of the Gods, within Greek culture and religion generally. Apollo, like the "seminal father" Bollas describes, who can save his children from becoming hysterics, had already sublated the Pythonic Mother, taking her up into himself. There was no need for the individual to do so.

But what of our patients, their symptoms, our theories? How may these be revisioned in terms of this background?

When the cultural vision of the powers and principalities of life has been reduced to the vicissitudes of the Oedipus complex (as psychoanalysis has done in our time), the enervations of the hystericized mind and body are explained as the result of the individuals in question having failed to resolve *their* Oedipus complex. The same enervations, however, permit of a very different understanding within a culture that has itself resolved that complex on the higher plane of its logic. Far from being of mere personal significance, they are readily understood as pointing beyond the individual upon whom they have inscribed themselves. Like the "psychic Internet" referred to by Bollas,[62] "our" symptoms are, thus, indicative of a nervous capacity to go "on-line," as it were, and to follow the links, and even be a link, in the transpersonal scheme of things. Listening to our patients, we may find ourselves wondering whether the mother and father being discussed are not the personal parents, but rather, transpersonal registers constituted of their logical negation. For, as a symbolic process, the individual, in addition to being some Little Hans of a "budding Oedipus," is also the triangulated child of a Greater Mother and Greater Father – the maternal imaginary and then some, the symbolic order and then some. Mimetic to Oedipus, each of us is doomed to meet ourselves coming back as we move between these two sets of parents. The incest and patricide committed in this archetypally conditioned, know-thyself process is, however, as excusable as Thor's failure to lift the cat off the floor, once we realize that what appeared to be only a cat, a parent, or an infantile need is actually the Midgard Serpent. And yet we are responsible at the same time, each of us being an instance of the "existing Concept" (Hegel).

With its notion of a collective unconscious, analytical psychology is reminiscent of the oracle at Delphi. Working within this tradition, the Jungian analyst Laurie Layton Schapira has explicitly linked the contemporary hysteric with the Pythia who served at the oracle at Delphi. In a book entitled, *The Cassandra Complex: Living with Disbelief*, Schapira works out what she calls "a modern perspective on hysteria" by turning to the old myths for inspiration. Among these, it is the story of Cassandra that she finds most exemplary. "Cassandra," she writes,

> was one of the daughters of Priam and Hecuba, the king and queen of Troy. One day while she was in the temple of Apollo, the god appeared and promised her the art of prophecy if she would lie with him. After accepting his gift Cassandra refused to fulfil her part of the bargain.

It is said that divine favors once bestowed cannot be revoked. So Apollo begged Cassandra to give him one kiss and, as she did so, he breathed (some say spat) into her mouth, thus insuring that no one would believe her prophecies.

From the beginning of the Trojan War, Cassandra foretold its gloomy end. But no one ever listened to her predictions. She pronounced that the Greeks were hiding in the wooden horse, but the Trojans would not heed her warnings. It was her fate to know what disasters were coming and be unable to avert them.[63]

This scene of botched or, rather, negated ravishment, so reminiscent for us of Bollas's account of the hysterical couple on a date, is a depiction of Cassandra's being called to her station as a prophetess of Apollo at Delphi. The motif of Apollo's breathing or spitting into Cassandra's mouth indicates her divination as bride of the god. As Schapira, drawing upon E. R. Dodds, explains, "in the process of divination, the Pythia was known to become *entheos, plena deo*: the god entered into her and used her vocal organs as if they were his own."[64]

In elaborating on her argument, Schapira develops the notion of mediality. Hysterics, she claims, have an intuitive capacity, which runs deeper than the extroverted feeling that Jung held to be their main mode of interacting with the world around them. As "medial women," they are "driven to express the shadow aspects of [their] culture. . . ."[65]

The notion of mediality and of medial woman, significantly enough, comes into analytical psychology by way of Jung's own Pythian mistress of some forty years, Toni Wolff. "The medial woman," writes Wolff in her essay, "Structural forms of the feminine psyche,"

> is immersed in the psychic atmosphere of her environment and the spirit of her period, but above all in the collective (impersonal) unconscious. The unconscious, once it is constellated and can become conscious, exerts an effect. The medial woman is overcome by this effect, she is absorbed and moulded by it and sometimes she represents it herself. She must for instance express or act what is "in the air," what the environment cannot or will not admit, but what is nevertheless a part of it. It is mostly the dark aspect of a situation or of a predominant idea, and she thus activates what is negative and dangerous. In this way she becomes the carrier of evil, but that she does, is nevertheless exclusively her personal problem. As the contents involved are unconscious, she lacks the necessary faculty of discrimination to perceive and the language to express them adequately. The overwhelming force of the collective unconscious sweeps through the ego of the medial woman and weakens it. . . .[66]

Wolff continues:

> By its nature the collective unconscious is not limited to the person concerned

– further reason why the medial woman identifies herself and others with archetypal contents. But to deal with the collective unconscious demands a solid ego consciousness and an adequate adaptation to reality. As a rule the medial woman disposes of neither and consequently she will create confusion in the same measure as she herself is confused. Conscious and unconscious, I and you, personal and impersonal psychic contents remain undifferentiated. ... As objective psychic contents in herself and in others are not understood, or are taken personally, she experiences a destiny not her own as though it were her own and loses herself in ideas which do not belong to her. Instead of being a mediatrix, she is only a means and becomes the first victim of her own nature.[67]

Reading Wolff's account of medial women we will be reminded, with Schapira, of hysteria on the one hand and Cassandra on the other. And further to this, we may be put in mind yet again of the interest that spiritualism and mediums commanded during the early years of the last century among even the most prominent psychologists of that time. However, while noting this interesting and suggestive history, we must also bear in mind, with Giegerich, the fallacy of regarding psychology as the study of people with such-and-such a psychology. Since the psychological move, as Giegerich has shown, is always against positivity and into reflection, we cannot rest satisfied with revaluing the hysteric as a personality, now with the traits of mediality figured into the mix. Our interest – consistent with the aim of releasing the notion of the soul from its attachment to the notion of a human being[68] – is, rather, in the absolute negativization of hysteria, and all its supposed features and traits, into itself as the theory, the thought, of psychology. It is the psyche itself, as the absolute negative interiorization of anything and everything that comes within its Pythian purview, that is Cassandra-like and medial. But until this is realized once again, in a manner appropriate to our times, and the contemporary equivalent of the Delphic oracle is built anew in our theory, we will have to turn for guidance to those Pythian anima-states through which the shadow Gods of our culture reach us – our fantasies and symptoms. As Hillman has put it,

My fantasies and symptoms put me in my place. No longer is it a matter of where they belong – to which God – but where I belong, at which altar I may leave myself, within which myth my suffering will turn into a devotion.[69]

Chapter 9

The Jungian Thing

If it were possible to personify the unconscious, we might think of it as a collective human being combining the characteristics of both sexes, transcending youth and age, birth and death, and, from having at its command a human experience of one or two million years, practically immortal. If such a being existed, it would be exalted above all temporal change; the present would mean neither more nor less to it than any year in the hundredth millennium before Christ; it would be a dreamer of age-old dreams and, owing to its limitless experience, an incomparable prognosticator. It would have lived countless times over again the life of the individual, the family, the tribe, and the nation, and it would possess a living sense of the rhythm of growth, flowering, and decay.[1]

C. G. Jung

[L]ife in the maternal order – from a Freudian point of view – must be infant and mother affecting each other as impressions. Insofar as the infant is concerned, the unconscious will in the first place be composed of thing presentations, the traces of the self's experience of the mother. Indeed, in many respects, the relation between thing presentations – which constitute the primary repressed unconscious – *is* the psychical system between infant and mother. Thus not only is the unconscious formed out of the impact of the mother as thing, but the system unconscious sustains this mother within us for the remainder of our life. To understand the peculiar affliction and talent of hysterics, we must appreciate that they seek to live within a thing-presentational order, which in many respects constitutes their effort to usurp the symbolic order (itself linked to the father) with the power of the primary repressed system of unconscious communication. Very often this passion is the trace of maternal erotism.[2]

Christopher Bollas

What is a thing presentation?

This question follows from our previous discussion of Oedipus and the oracle. Oracles, such as the one which Oedipus visited at Delphi, were based upon images. When the supplicant approached the oracle with a pressing need for orientation and truth, answers were given in the form of cryptic sayings concocted of loosely associated auditory, eidetic, and proprioceptive impressions. The presupposition at work in this process was that the images arising from what we would now call the medium's syntonic countertransference shared points of comparison among themselves that were indicative of the supplicant and his situation. The same may be said of many other traditions. *I Ching* hexagrams, Norse runes, Navaho sand paintings, astrology and the tarot: however questionable these practices may be in our day, all testify to the importance images have had in the divining of truth in past ages. Drawing upon the same source (though in a less literally mantic way), legend and fable, fairy tale and myth have long done so as well. Contemporizing this legacy, poems, right down to our own time, have conveyed what is known as poetic truth, as have the arts generally, through the aptness of their images. And this is to say nothing of cave paintings, contemporary cinema, and, spanning both of these, that interior cave and inner cinema, the dream. In a passage that can be read as a summing up of all these sources and traditions, the Jesus of the Nag Hammadi collection's, *Gospel of Thomas* declares,

> When you see your image, you are glad. But when you see your images which came into being before you, which neither die nor are made, how much will you then endure![3]

With their emphasis on dreams, fantasies, evenly hovering attentiveness, and vicarious introspection via empathy and the use of countertransference reactions, the depth psychologies have much in common with the traditions we have just mentioned. The status of the image, however, changed considerably when the skin of the Python which Apollo wore at Delphi came to be worn in Vienna by Freud. Indeed, in the terminology introduced by Freud, the images that animate the unconscious (manifesting themselves in dreams and other psychic expressions) came to be regarded as "thing-presentations."

As with the companion idea, namely, that a dream's images are merely a disguise beneath which the tenets of psychoanalysis are hidden, the imposition of this term has been most consequential for psychology. With Freud's notion of *nachträglichkeit* or "deferred action" in mind, we might even say "traumatic." Indeed, just as a recent event may call forth a much earlier one in such a way that its traumatic impact is fully experienced for the first time, so the privileging of a conceptual distinction with respect to images over the logical possibilities that the images themselves tautegorically present is evocative of such earlier events as Apollo's usurpation of the oracle at Delphi, Moses' tablet-smashing wrath at the spectacle of his people dancing around the Golden Calf, and the Reformation campaign that militant Protestant leaders such as Cromwell waged against what they regarded as the idolatrous images of Roman Catholicism.

This is not to say that Apollo should not have usurped the Mother-Goddess who preceded him at Delphi or that Moses should have been gentler with his lapsed followers. Nor is it to suggest that the Reformation was wrong or that the

Enlightenment should not have happened. Rather, it is to understand that the depth psychologies, heir as they undoubtedly are of these sublating actions of the spirit, are charged, at the same time, with the task of rescuing and retaining the imaginal mode within a more comprehensive view – if only to the end that the animus or critical mind may turn against this mode again as the dialectic continues on new levels.

"Death once dead, there's no more dying now," psychology in its negativity triumphantly declares. Just as Herod is a facet of the same truth that is portrayed in the figure of the Christ-child, so too may Apollo, Moses, Cromwell, and Freud be seen as dimensions of the very images they would seem to put asunder. Indeed, as Giegerich has stressed in his insider's critique of archetypal psychology, the movement within an image against itself is not a movement against the imaginal mode per se, but against the positivity of its pictorial form.[4]

Having noted the dialectical necessity of the spirit's killing action, we must hasten to add (with Hegel's *aufgehoben* in mind) that sometimes it takes a poem to give a "thing" its due. Just as the beautiful fiancée in Keats's *Lamia* is changed back into a shameful serpent by the killing stare of the bald-headed philosopher who is her bridegroom's mentor, so the soul's images, when regarded through the baleful eye of a positivized concept such as Freud's notion of "thing-presentations," fade into "the dull catalogue of common things."[5]

Exploring something of the same dialectical tension in a poem of his own, D. H. Lawrence tells the story of how he pitched a log at a snake one day because the voices of his "accursed human education" had said to him "he must be killed." Rescuing the snake (if only through regret about the meanness of his action), Lawrence reflects that he had "missed [his] chance with one of the lords of life" and now had "something to expiate; a pettiness."[6]

Briefly mentioned by Freud in *The Interpretation of Dreams*, the main discussion of thing-presentations occurs in his 1915 essay "The unconscious." Writing with reference to schizophrenia on the one hand, and to the confabulating work of the dream on the other, Freud suggested, sensibly enough in light of his clinical referents, that the "difference . . . between a conscious and an unconscious presentation" resides in the fact that "the conscious presentation comprises the presentation of the thing plus the presentation of the word belonging to it, while the unconscious presentation is the presentation of the thing alone." Elaborating further, Freud writes,

> The system Ucs contains the thing-cathexes of the objects, the first and true object-cathexes; the system Pcs originates in a hyper-cathexis of this concrete idea by a linking up of it with the verbal ideas of the words corresponding to it. It is such hyper-cathexes, we may suppose, that bring about the organization in the mind and make it possible for the primary process to be succeeded by the secondary process which dominates Pcs. Now . . . we are in a position to state precisely what it is that repression denies to the rejected idea in the transference neuroses – namely, translation of the idea into words which are

to remain attached to the object. The idea which is not put into words or the mental act which has not received hyper-cathexis then remains in the unconscious in a state of repression.[7]

Said more plainly and completely, the idea here is that while thing-presentations signify the instincts and their objects in a pre-linguistic or imagistic manner, it is the words which in their turn are linked to these that make control, mastery, mature expression, consciousness, and sublimation of these instinct-cathected and object-cathecting images possible. Freud's famous dictum, "where id was, there shall ego be"[8] could just as well read, "where things were, let words be," or again, "where images are, let concepts be."[9]

In his theory of hysteria, Bollas picks up on this thing-presentation/word-presentation distinction, bringing it into line with both developmental psychology and Lacan's lexicon of registers in such a way that the psychoanalytic transformation of the pythonic mantle of prophecy into a baby blanket could hardly be more complete. Thing-presentations, according to Bollas, arise out of "the world of maternal image-making" while word-presentations bespeak what is variously referred to in French psychoanalysis as the Name-of-the-Father, the paternal order, and the Symbolic.[10] What is controversial here, at least from a Jungian point of view, is not the association of images with the mother and words with the father – Jungians make the same symbolic distinctions. Rather, it is the reduction of the archetypal categories that these figures designate to the literal parents that many analytical psychologists would question. Though Bollas states in the early pages of his book that mother and father, as represented psychically, do not correspond in the sense of a naive realism to the actual parents,[11] when writing about word- and thing-presentations he falls back into this kind of ontogenetic reduction, carried away, it would seem (as is much of psychoanalysis) by the crucial importance that parents have in the lives of their children. The result of this is that the imaginal loses its archetypal primacy and is devalued in relation to word-presentations. Viewed through the lens of an object-relational model, images are regarded as being redolent of the infantile bond to mamma-the-caregiver, whose primary thing-ness was impressed upon the child's psyche prior to the rupture that sexuality, language, and the father bring. In keeping with this, words (except where they are being used, as in hysteria, "not for what they mean or convey, but for what [they] affect"[12]) are regarded as more mature expressions. From this it follows that the best that can be done with images in the consulting room is to crack them up with free-associations. By demanding words, as Freud did when he directed his patients to say whatever came to mind, analysts of this tradition, according to Bollas, cut the umbilical tie to the mother as thing (which is what images are in this conception) to the end that the subject may "matriculate in the paternal order."[13]

Bollas's views here are consistent with the distinction that contemporary psychoanalysis, caught in the fallacy of psychology as the study of people with such-and-such a psychology, has drawn between subjects who are said to be able to symbolize and those unable to do so, who are said to be pre-symbolic. Hysterics for both Bollas and Mitchell are people of the latter sort. Though they do, of course, "talk and talk and talk," their speech, insofar as it is hysterical, is not representational, but presentational.[14] Words are treated as things, not in the concrete manner of schizophrenics, but in the literal manner that is characteristic of young children.[15] Hysterical language, writes Mitchell, "*does* something, it does not stand in *for* something."[16] In hysterical usage, words are not harnessed to the yoke of meaning, they are "not . . . in a signifying chain, but . . . things reduplicated."[17] Unable to admit, let alone accept, loss (of mamma, in Bollas's view; of exclusivity and specialness in Mitchell's[18]), the hysteric regresses to the thing-presentational order, where his or her infantile wants may be relentlessly asserted through symptoms, seductions, theatrical bids for attention, and lies.[19] This is not to say that the speech of hysterics is devoid of images and metaphors. On the contrary, these may be present in abundance. However, due to the hysteric's inability to tolerate loss, and his or her "'I will *die* if I don't get what I want'"[20] stance, such figures are not symbolical in the strict psychoanalytic sense.[21] They are not, that is to say, serving as the re-presentations or re-memberings out of which the inner world is constituted, but as performative bids for gratification on a much more infantile level.

The amazing mirror-thing

Jungian thought, where it has not lost its theoretical nerve and simply capitulated to the more dominant discourse of the psychoanalytic mainstream, has an entirely different understanding of images and their symbolic status. Images, in the view of analytical psychology, bespeak the cosmic wonder that the psyche, as an inner dimension of reality comparable in its scope to the immensity to the outer world and the universe at large, may be reckoned to be. As such, they are derived (if that is the word), not from the sensuous relations between infant and mother (as Bollas has suggested in the quotation at the top of this chapter), but from that "amazing mirror-thing"[22] and "psychic reflection of the whole world,"[23] the Great Mother or collective unconscious. While one's actual mother (for weal or woe) certainly is "the first/Poetic spirit of our human life," as Wordsworth so aptly put it,[24] the Jungian thing reaches back behind her early handling of us to the star that guided the Magi from the East to Bethlehem, the eye that Odin placed in Mirmir's well, and the oracle at Delphi – to name but three cultural representations of this primordial source.

"Yes, just look at him. That is the man-eater!" Jung's mother declares in his fateful childhood dream of an enormous underground "thing," which Jung recognized, years later, to be a phallus, and a ritual one at that.[25] Less darkly (canonical symbols being still within his reach) Angelus Silesius concurs: "What good does Gabriel's 'Ave, Mary' do/Unless he give me that same greeting too?"[26] Wordsworth makes a similar point: "The props of my affections were removed, and yet the building stood, as if sustained by its own spirit!"[27] If it were not for the death of his mother in the tender years of his boyhood, Wordsworth, for all his literary genius, could not have written *The Prelude* in the Platonic spirit in which he did, nor could he have borne such unmediated witness to the force of the object-ive psyche through our lives. Virgin mother, daughter of thy son? Seer blest prophet of pygmy size? Awesome immensity of a phallic mother? On all three scores, indeed!

Numerous passages from Jung's writings come to mind as being especially illustrative of what we are here calling "the Jungian thing." All of these, even when their specific reference is to the unconscious, fantasy, or the archetypes, have to do with the representational, or better said, presentational power of images. For in Jung's view (as the archetypal school of analytical psychology in particular has stressed), "the psyche consists essentially of images."[28]

Our first quotation is from Jung's essay "Psychological aspects of the mother archetype." Drawing upon an adage of Goethe's, Jung speaks of our being "inside," not our own mother during gestation or the sphere of her care during childhood, but that greater mother, the psyche itself, which, through its myriad images and forms, is the prime conditioning factor of all perception and experi-ence.

> "All that is outside, also is inside," we could say with Goethe. But this "inside," which modern rationalism is so eager to derive from "outside," has an *a priori* structure of its own that antedates all conscious experience. It is quite impossible to conceive how "experience" in the widest sense, or, for that matter, anything psychic, could originate exclusively in the outside world. The psyche is part of the inmost mystery of life, and it has its own peculiar structure and form like every other organism. Whether this psychic structure and its elements, the archetypes, ever "originated" at all is a metaphysical question and therefore unanswerable. The structure is something given, the precondition that is found to be present in every case. And this is the *mother*, the matrix – the form into which all experience is poured.[29]

Another quote. In "The soul and death," an essay which treats of the symbolism that the psyche throws up in relation to death, Jung again refers to the psyche's ego-transcending immensity. "The nature of the psyche," he writes,

> reaches into obscurities far beyond the scope of our understanding. It contains as many riddles as the universe with its galactic systems, before whose majestic configurations only a mind lacking in imagination can fail to admit its own insufficiency. . . . If, therefore, from the needs of his own heart, or in accordance with the ancient lessons of human wisdom, or out of respect for the psychological fact that "telepathic" perceptions occur, anyone should draw the conclusion that the psyche, in its deepest reaches, participates in a form of existence beyond space and time, and thus partakes of what is inadequately and symbolically described as "eternity" – then critical reason could counter with no other argument than the "non liquet" of science.[30]

We are a far cry here from cracking up images. In contrast to the disseminative work of free association that Bollas, with reference to Freud and Derrida, considers to be the appropriate response to dreams and other psychic images, the attitude conveyed by Jung is one of awe for the way in which the psyche as a whole presents itself in every image. In Jung's view, a dream is not a disguise but a natural expression. It does not need to be deconstructed in accordance with some postmodern metaphysic of absence or have all that it condenses within itself exposed and laid bare. On the contrary, rightly regarded it is the dialectical expression and epiphanic presence of all that it additionally is not – a dove in the consulting room. Putting this another way, we could also say that the spontaneously constellated images, such as those of which our dreams are made, are the self-representation of what Jung, with reference to the unconscious, called the Unknown, in that moment of truth which is its immediate effect upon us.[31]

Railing against "the Freudian[]'psychoanalytical' method" which "dismisses the manifest dream-content as a mere 'facade,' on the ground that the psychopathology of hysteria leads one to suspect incompatible wishes as dream-motifs," Jung writes,

> The fact that the dream as well as consciousness rest on an instinctual foundation has nothing to do either with the meaning of the dream-figures or with that of the conscious contents, for the essential thing in both cases is *what the psyche has made of the instinctual impulse*. The remarkable thing about the Parthenon is not that it consists of stone and was built to gratify the ambitions of the Athenians, but that it is – the Parthenon.[32]

Again Jung draws our attention to the majestic immensity of the psyche. Each dream-figure or image, as the Upanishads put it in a phrase often quoted by Jung, is "smaller than small, greater than great."[33] Each, just by being so absolutely what it is (that it is at the same time all that it is not) is as remarkable as the Parthenon – or the underground phallus of Jung's childhood dream for that matter. Putting this another way, we can also say that every image is archetypal, not because archetypes can be demonstrated to exist (with their essence in negativity, archetypes are not entities in need of empirical validation), but because each one, being itself and no other, is raised to the power of the nth number by the infinity of images that it potentially could have been, and, hence, verily is.

In a passage from his 1914 correspondence with Dr Loÿ, "Some crucial points in psychoanalysis," Jung, speaking with reference to "the tendencies and determinants that produce culture in man with the same logic as in the bird they produce the artfully woven nest, and antlers in the stag," makes the important statement that "the psyche does not merely *react*, it gives its own specific answer to the influences at work upon it, and at least half the resulting formation is entirely due to the psyche and the determinants inherent within it."[34] Whatever else it is – a work of art, a Greek temple, an attitude, idea, life situation or transference, the psyche's "own specific answer" has the character of an image.

In this connection another quote comes to mind, this time from Jung's "Foreword to Suzuki's *Introduction to Zen Buddhism*." "The unconscious," Jung writes,

> is an irrepresentable totality of all subliminal psychic factors, a "total vision" *in potentia*. It constitutes the total disposition from which consciousness singles out tiny fragments from time to time.[35]

The tiny fragments that Jung refers to as being singled out from time to time are images. Like the Pythia of Apollo, these images, potentiated as they are by the imagination's "total vision," bespeak the archetype. As such, they are not yours or mine in an exclusively personal sense. While they do, to be sure, pay tribute to our finiteness by drawing the stuff of our day-to-day existence into imaginal form, they are also conditioned, not merely by the signifying chain of established meanings that governs the word as it is positivized in our language, but (in a manner that is often compensatory to that) by the infinite set that the imagination as archetype may be considered to be. As Jung puts this, "The archetype represents *psychic probability*, portraying ordinary instinctual events in the form of *types*."[36]

Two further quotes. The first is from "The structure of the psyche." Reasoning in terms of his concept of the collective unconscious, Jung writes:

> If this supra-individual psyche exists, everything that is translated into its picture-language would be depersonalized, and if this became conscious would appear to us *sub specie aeternitatis*. Not as my sorrow, but as the sorrow of the world; not a personal isolating pain, but a pain without bitterness that unites all humanity. The healing effect of this needs no proof.[37]

Related to this quotation is another from a seminar Jung gave on dream analysis:

> [T]he dream presents an impartial truth. It shows the situation which by law of nature *is*. It does not say you ought to do this or that, nor does it say what is good or bad. It simply shows the dreamer in a situation. Man *is* so underneath. This is the truth.[38]

Presentation and representation

The vision of the psyche we have attempted to convey, citing passages from Jung's writings, has as many implications as there are differences between the Jungian and Freudian psychoanalytic traditions. At this juncture we may briefly discuss two or three of these, leaving it to be understood that others will be taken up in subsequent sections.

The first has to do with the status of the image in psychoanalysis generally, and analytical psychology in particular. With its emphasis on images, analytical psychology could easily be misread as being hopelessly mired in what Bollas, drawing upon Lacanian psychoanalysis, calls the "maternal imaginary." In marked contrast to Lacan, author of the Name-of-the-Father concept and renowned sceptic of images, Jung referred to himself as "the age-old son of the mother"[39] and was equally well known for the value he placed upon images. This contrast, however, should not lead one to the conclusion that Jung would have disagreed with Lacan's adage that "the mirror would do well to reflect a little more before returning our image to us."[40] It was Jung, after all, who introduced the concept of the imago into psychoanalysis, and Jung who declared that "there are very few beings yet capable of making a difference between mental image and thing itself," decrying this state of affairs as a "primitivity [that] is poisoning our human world and is so dense a mist that very few people have discovered its existence yet."[41] It would also be incorrect to assume that Jung, for all the resistance he felt toward the father of the primal horde that he met in Freud, did not give place to the realm of the fathers in his theory. On the contrary, in Jung's thought the father-imago plays an essential role in the destiny of the individual as "the representative of the spirit whose function it is to oppose pure instinctuality."[42] But this said, we must again emphasize, as our quotations above have indicated, that the image, "hard as granite,"[43] is the rock upon which analytical psychology has built its house.

That the image can provide so firm a foundation stems from an epistemological consideration. As Jung frequently pointed out, psychology lacks an Archimedean perspective with respect to its subject matter. There is no way out of the images that psyche and psychology are alike in consisting of. We are always in an imagining, always shaped by a fantasy, always in the psyche. Insufficiently cognizant of the mediating, even constituting, role that images have, psychoanalysis has tended to regard them as secondary, distorted reflections of more substantial realities such as sexuality, the breast, object relations, body, the family, etc. Of course, these positive facts of life *are* reflected in the image in distorted form. There is no denying that. And through its recognition of this, psychology has brought psychological reflection to bear upon all these areas. But like the fugitive stag of alchemy, the psyche – that unity in negation of subjectivity and subjectivity's own Other – has vanished with every knowledge claim that would reduce it to something more literal. Recognizing this, analytical psychology begins the other way around, with the primacy of image.

In an especially lucid discussion of the issue that concerns us here, Kugler has made the important point that,

> the psychic imago as defined by Jung is not a copy or representation of some other more primary reality, but is the very source of our sense of psychic reality. Our *experience of reality* is located within the human condition as an essential function of psychic imaging.[44]

In support of this reading of analytical psychology's imago concept, Kugler quotes Jung: "The psyche creates reality every day. The only expression I can use for this activity is *fantasy* ... Fantasy, therefore, seems to me the clearest expression of the specific activity of the psyche. It is, pre-eminently . . . [a] creative activity."[45] Continuing his point, Kugler then states that from a Lacanian perspective, analytical psychology would appear to be "caught in the imaginary order, in a world of deceptive imagos." But this critique, he writes,

> only holds *if the imago is assumed to be essentially representational in nature*, i.e. it re-presents some more primary reality. For Jung, however, the inner *and* outer worlds of an individual come together in psychic images, giving the person a vital sense of the living connection to both worlds. "Fantasy it was and ever is which fashions the bridge between the irreconcilable claims of subject and object."[46] *The experience of reality is a product of the psyche's capacity to image.*[47]

Quoting a bit more from Kugler, we learn further that, "[t]he psychic imago in Jungian psychology performs a synthetic function, integrating both external sensory experience and internal psychic reactions."

> The significant point is that the imago is not simply a *reproduction* of the outer or inner world (i.e. a copy of an historical event, object relations, or of a drive), but rather, a psychic *production*. The realm of psychic imagos is referred to in Jungian psychology as the imaginal, while Lacan refers to this realm as the imaginary. *The important difference being that the imaginal is constituted by productive and reproductive imaging, while the imaginary is constituted by reproductive imaging.*[48]

Building upon Kugler's clarifying distinction with respect to productive and reproductive imaging, we may now draw out a second implication of Jung's imaginally based vision of the psyche. This has to do with Bollas's and Mitchell's division of "people's psychologies" into symbolic and pre-symbolic kinds. As we have already discussed, working within the confines of a personalistic psychology, both Bollas and Mitchell approach the phenomenology of the psyche in general, and that of hysteria in particular, from the vantage point that the psychodynamics of childhood and family life affords. The psyche for them, wonder that it is, even in their diminutive sense of it, is not the *cosmic* wonder it is for Jung and Jungians. It is not, that is to say, the presentation of a "total vision," an image of "the situation as it is," or a picturing of life "*sub specie aeternitatis.*" On the contrary, as a complex template of self and other representations concocted from the vicissitudes of each person's experience growing up, it offers little more than an idiosyncratic, transference-blinkered, child's-eye view. While lip-service may be paid to the uncanniness of the unconscious by many psychoanalytic authors, what appears to be omnipotent or omniscient about the psyche is rationalized away, for the most part, by a consulting-room mentality, as infantile illusion. Where analytical psychologists speak of the numinous, psychoanalysts speak of idealization. And where Jungians speak of the objective psyche, their Freudian and their post-

Freudian counterparts speak of paranoia, omnipotence fantasies, precocious self-sufficiency, and the use of one's own mind as an object. Unrecognized as such, the grandeur of the psyche is forced to appear as something people have and are in need of treatment for: grandiosity or madness. Similarly, the hysteric, for all his or her theatrical displays, picturesque speech, and spiritual aspiration, is said to be pre-symbolic.

Hysteria, however, looks very different when the child at its centre is regarded as a metaphor, or symbol even, for the age-old psychic factor that is born anew in every individual. In the quotation cited at the beginning of this chapter, Jung suggests that if the unconscious were personified, "we might think of it as a collective human being combining the characteristics of both sexes, transcending youth and age, birth and death, and, from having at its command a human experience of one or two million years, practically immortal." Continuing with this analogy, he suggests that it would "be a dreamer of age-old dreams and, owing to its limitless experience, an incomparable prognosticator." With this proposal in mind, we may ask ourselves if the immaturity and childishness of the hysteric is, at the same time as it is that, an image, or conduit even, through which what Jung variously calls the collective human being, universal person, two-million-year-old-man, anthropos and archetype presents its imperatives through our lives.

"Unless you are converted and become like children, you shall not enter the kingdom of heaven,"[49] said Jesus, the second Adam, as he invited his followers into the new dispensation which his coming had inaugurated. "Thy Babe, O Virgin, is an old man; he is the Ancient of Days and precedes all time," writes Ephraem Syrus in an old verse quoted by Jung in *Mysterium*.[50] Drawing upon images from the religious traditions that preceded it, analytical psychology has a very different view of what in psychoanalysis is known as "archaic infantile grandiosity."

Hosea and the prostitute

"Everything in the unconscious seeks outward manifestation, and the personality too desires to evolve out of its unconscious conditions and experience itself as a whole."[51] Adapting this sentence from Jung's memoirs to our present purposes, we could say that only its second part refers to the subject as a person, while the part about "everything in the unconscious seek[ing] outward manifestation" refers to the "collective human being" mentioned by Jung in the previous quotation.

Following from this, the question arises: when we are listening to hysterical demands or watching hysterical performances, what is it in the subject that wants its way so badly that it will stop at no ploy or contrivance to get it, the childish, pre-symbolical ego or the anthropos, transpersonal self, universal person?

It is noteworthy in this connection that behaviour similar to that which Bollas and Mitchell regard as being childishly pre-symbolic in the hysteric is discussed by Jung, in a seminar he gave on symbolism, as being a preferred mode of symbolic expression used by such stalwart figures as the Old Testament prophets during times when their people's falling away from God had to be dramatically portrayed. In a section of *The Visions Seminars* in which he elucidates the dream of a patient whose uncanonical use of Christian images suggested that a post-Christian process of individuation had been constellated, Jung writes as follows:

> When the man [in the dream] picks up the lame sheep, he is picking up something that is in correspondence with himself, which expresses himself in a way, because these figures in the archetypal pattern are acting symbolically, . . . exactly as the prophets in the Old Testament acted prophetically or symbolically. You find that those Old Testament prophets did the most astonishing things to catch the eye, so to speak, to express an idea symbolically. The worst case was the prophet Hosea who symbolically married a prostitute because the Lord ordered him to do so, expressing in that way that the people had prostituted themselves to the heathen – he showed the people what they were by marrying a prostitute by divine command. That is symbolical doing or acting, and in a dream of this order such actions or gestures are equally symbolical. When the dream figures take up those animals, it is as if they were speaking through their action, as if they would convey a certain idea, as if they said, for instance. "This I do to show you that one should feel compassion" – or something like that."[52]

"Astonishing things to catch the eye," "symbolical doing or acting," "speaking through . . . action," "this I do to show you": are these not the tell-tale signs of hysterical character? From a Jungian point of view, they are something more besides, even as hysteria is something more. Indeed, as the analogy that Jung makes to the Old Testament prophets suggests, these behaviours also indicate that the collective unconscious has been constellated and that the archetype is speaking – not the wants of the ego, yours or mine, but of the Ancient of Days who seeks fresh realization through our lives.

In *The Psychology of the Transference*, Jung refers to psychotherapy in general, and the psychology of the transference in particular, as a "sphere but lately visited by the numen, where the whole weight of mankind's problems have settled."[53] By this he means to suggest that in addition to being the arena in which personal transferences are resolved, the consulting room of analtyic therapy is also the *temenos* in which archetypal transferences are asserted as a result of the failure of such institutions as the Church, marriage, and the family to renew themselves in the light of the changing times. "Eternal truth," he writes in that same work,

> needs a human language that alters with the spirit of the times. The primordial images undergo ceaseless transformation and yet remain ever the same, but only in a new form can they be understood anew. . . . Where are the answers to the spiritual needs and troubles of a new epoch? And where the knowledge to deal with the psychological problems raised by the development of modern consciousness? [54]

Heirs to the declining religious and cultural institutions that preceded them (the aforementioned failure of the Church to renew itself), do the depth psychologies now find themselves performing acts in the consulting room that differ little from the behaviour of the Old Testament prophets when their people strayed from God? Is hysteria, that is to say, the prostitute which psychoanalysis has been commanded to marry so that its unfaithfulness to the soul can be dramatically portrayed? Is Jung, with his concept of the anima, a latter day Hosea?

Besides the primal father and his horde, the parents-in-coitus, the good-enough mother, the ventriloquist's dummy of the culture, and the polymorphously perverse child, Jung's reference to Hosea and the prostitute suggests another image of the psyche and of analysis, that of an old man and young girl. In *Memories, Dreams, Reflections*, Jung writes that in the "dream wanderings" of active imagination, such as those he himself engaged in during his famous period of "confrontation with the unconscious,"

> one frequently encounters an old man who is accompanied by a young girl, and examples of such couples are to be found in many mythic tales. Thus, according to Gnostic tradition, Simon Magus went about with a young girl whom he had picked up in a brothel. Her name was Helen, and she was regarded as the reincarnation of the Trojan Helen. Klingsor and Kundry, Lao-tzu and the dancing girl, likewise belong to this category.[55]

The figure of the old man mentioned by Jung (and known to him in his own dreams and fantasies as a character named Philemon) is a wisdom figure. We could even regard him as a personification of "eternal truth," or to express this in more theoretical terms, of the archetypal unconscious. The young girl corresponding to the wise old man is the anima (in Jung's fantasies, Salome). She is the personification of the life-giving, renewal-seeking, projection-making factor. As such, it is she who brings the psyche's archetypal background erotically into play, she who compels its timeless potentials to be lived, so that all we are heir to, from time immemorial, may be brought to fruition again. Taken together, the old man and young girl present the same idea that the term "archetypal libido" expresses in a more abstract, conceptual way.

The figures that belong to the phenomenology of this archetype are legion. We have already mentioned Eliza and the professor in an earlier section. The blind Oedipus on the arm of his daughter, Antigone, is another couple of especial importance, as are Mary and Joseph, and Jesus and Mary Magdalene (especially in the Gnostic tradition). And, then, in our own time, there is the psychoanalyst and the hysteric (to borrow from the title of an early article by Bollas[56]). Joseph Breuer and Anna O., Freud and Lou Salomé, Jung and Sabina Spielrein, Ferenczi and Gizella Pálos, Rank and Anaïs Nin: behind the all-too-human dramas of these couples (to say nothing of those we must sit in judgement over on ethics committees) the objective psyche, like some Old Testament prophet (or randy veil-rending new one), enacts its wants and needs through our lives in a powerful symbolism.

This is not to say that the rule of abstinence is to be dispensed with. By no means. The messianic libido of the anthropos does need to be optimally frustrated if it is to realize itself anew as that logically negative and, hence, love sublating form we call psychology. A more fitting model of this process than those based upon child-development, however, may be one drawn from the religious traditions to which psychology is heir: that of eschatological waiting.[57] While we work in the consulting room with this or that patient on this or that problem it is sobering to realize that although its advent has certainly begun, we still await the arrival of a true psychology.

Symbolic life

The expression, "symbolic life," comes from Jung. It derives from the title of a seminar that he gave to the Guild for Pastoral Psychology in London in 1939.[58] In the present context, it serves our efforts well to explicate more fully what we mean by "the Jungian thing." But here we must take care. To speak of the expression "symbolic life" as serving "our efforts" is already to be too personalistically reductive. For what is at stake with regard to the Jungian thing is not how we, as optimally frustrated, disillusioned egos, *represent* it psychologistically to ourselves (important as this may be in a certain respect), but, rather, how it *presents* itself in its living immediacy or symbolic life through anything at all.

This point – as subtle as it is important – trades upon Kugler's discussion of the imago in analytical psychology as well as certain observations that Mitchell has made with respect to hysteria. If we speak of psyche presenting itself, in contradistinction to the ego explicating *its* representations, it is to recognize with Kugler the *productive*, even creative, character of the Jungian thing. And tilting now at Mitchell's theory, if we here insist upon this distinction, it is because it seems apt to do so, given her claim about the trumped-up imperative that hysterics make of their wants.

Be it on the model of the overweening child or on that of the Ancient of Days, there is something about the psyche (and not just the psyche of the hysteric) that will not be denied. And psychology, too, will not be denied, except that everywhere it is denied through its refusal to be psychology, with the result that its patients are compelled to want in its stead.[59]

Like the infant hallucinating the breast, the child tantrumming at the candy counter, and the Ancient of Days outfitting itself in new forms, psychology's imperative is to generatively discover, and even itself be, truth. And it is in this spirit that we, speaking the language of equations and lists, which Mitchell regards as typically hysterical,[60] assert the Jungian thing *to be* the symbolic life. Cathected with truth-seeking libido, and giving its own specific answer to the influences at work upon it, the autonomous psyche, in concert with the world, creates reality from out of itself – symbolic life.

"Split a piece of wood, and I am there. Lift up a stone, and you will find me there," declares Jesus in the *Gospel of Thomas*.[61] Seeing its own Other – in a stone on the beach, a phrase from a book, the analyst, or some other person – the Jungian thing reverberates within us, "this is it!"

But if the Jungian thing is the symbolic life, what is a symbol? *Ignotum per ignotius* – it would be tempting to answer this question by listing a whole series of mysterious and affecting terms, such as psychic reality, life instinct, archetype, or libido. Or, better still, to simply say tree, rock, man, woman, bridge, flower, beer can, star, ad infinitum. In alchemy, the symbolical essence of the philosopher's stone was conveyed by the fact that it is known by a thousand names.[62] Our touch-stone for this discussion, however, is psychoanalysis. We are attempting to look at the Jungian thing in relation to the very different status that mainstream psycho-analysis assigns to the image. Our approach, therefore, must vary accordingly.

We have already noted in passing the views of Bollas and Mitchell relating to this question. Influenced by Lacan, both of these writers regard the symbol in the light of his concept of the symbolic order. The symbolic order, for Lacan, consists of the vast chain of interconnected signifiers of which our common speech and language is composed as well as of the laws and institutions of society at large. Conceptually speaking, it is the realm of the father, the paternal order. Bollas, as we have seen, speaks of the hysterical patient as needing to matriculate from the thing-presentational order of maternal image-making into the paternal order of the word. In his view, cure depends upon this transition from thing to word, maternal to paternal, imaginary to symbolic. For her part, Juliet Mitchell, restricting the notion of the symbolic to the representational order of language, regards the hysteric as using words, which would otherwise be symbolical just by virtue of their being words, in affecting, presentational, non-symbolic ways. Cure of the hysteric, in her view, is a function of passing through an analytically facilitated death experience, which initiates the subject into loss, thereby changing the valance of language usage from presentation to representation.[63]

Doubtless, there is much of merit in these views. Bollas and Mitchell describe familiar developments in the sphere of the personality and its disorders. Loss, defeat, and death – all that psychoanalysis places under the rubric of castration – change the way language is used, even as language, according to French psycho-analysis, is itself something of a castrating father inasmuch as it brings about loss, defeat, and death by coming between us and the maternal immediacy of life. The necessity, even rightness, of passing through this linguistically conceived castra-tion ("softened . . . down into circumcision," as Freud said[64]) is confirmed by the sense of *gravitas* it yields. The "Songs of experience" are more weighty than the almost pre-linguistic "Songs of innocence" we sang in our lamb-white days. With the leaving behind of immediate gratification, people do enter the semiotic world of adult meanings, responsibilities, and institutions. Drawing upon the prior work of Lacan, Bollas and Mitchell give an account of this transition and of its failure to occur.

The problem with this approach, however (in terms of the perspective we are developing), is the positivization of language, the positivization of the word. Though language, to be sure, has its essence in negativity, its words become fixed, so much so, in fact, that deconstruction has arisen, where this has been recognized, as a means of restoring or maintaining their logically negative character. The language of psychoanalysis is a case in point. With its strong, referential roots in biology and family (body parts and developmental phases), "psychoanalese" is particularly prone to be being positivized, as the frequent use of rote interpretations attests. Recognizing this, Lacan, wielding Saussure's signifier/signified distinction as if it were the primal father's cleaver, brought that distinction down upon the talking cure by boldly asserting that the unconscious is structured like a language. However – and here is the problem – the language, which the unconscious is said to be structured like, is itself structured like a family. The shadow of those old objects still falls upon the representations that the ego makes to itself. Positivity holds fast to the negation that would sunder it. And thought itself – that essence of psychology proper – is locked in an "ontologized text" of familial metaphors, the Lacanian trinity of imaginary, symbolic, and real being but a variant of the Oedipal triangle.

When Freud, like some Old Testament prophet, proclaimed the universality of the Oedipus complex, the *logic* constituting our reality became familial, family a religion in an increasingly secular way, the analyst a priest. Free association, contrary to the promise of its name, became an Oedipal soliloquy. For no matter what was said, analytic listening, falling far short of the ideal of evenly hovering attention, returned it to the transferences of the family constellation.

Celebrating free association, at the centenary of the psychoanalytic movement, Bollas, as we have seen, continues to speak of it in familial terms, even while decrying object relations theory as a picture-book work. The ebb and flow of free association – now condensing into images, now cracking up and disseminating itself via words – is conceived by him as being a dynamic interaction of maternal and paternal registers. He uses the same language when he is discussing the psyche itself. Holding to the view that "the mother and the father are always the foremost psychic structures to any self," Bollas draws upon primal-scene imagery to account for psychic life in general.[65] "In the inner world," he writes in *Hysteria* (with reference not only to the hysteric but to everyone),

> the internal mother and the internal father have essential intercourse every day. Indeed, so too in Freud's theory itself, as thing presentations can only become available to consciousness by attaching themselves to words, so the inner mother world and the inner father world constantly link and create third objects that shall be born of this coupling."[66]

It is interesting to place this analytically conceived "holy family" alongside Bollas's disrespectful use of the Christian symbol. Unable to sublate itself, unable, that is to say, to move beyond the positivity of its primary objects, psychoanalysis resorts to destroying the mighty images of the religion that preceded it, envious of these for having already long ago made the movement against positivity into reflection which psychology and psychoanalysis have yet to make within themselves with respect to the times in which we live at present.

"If, as it is, I cannot soften heaven, I will at least move hell," declares Freud, quoting Virgil at the dawn of psychoanalysis.[67] "He who denies the great must blame the petty," writes Jung, opposing this attitude, which he took to be the basis of a vast interpretative attempt "to put an end . . . to the larger aspect of the psychic phenomenon."[68]

In connection with these references some related thoughts of Julia Kristeva's come to mind. In her essay "Credo in unum Denum," the distinguished French psychoanalyst treats the Holy Trinity as if it were consubstantial with the Lacanian trinity of imaginary, symbolic, and real, on the one hand, and the Freudian Oedipal triad on the other. Referring specifically to the "Symbol of the apostles," a credo of dogmatic formulations concerning the triune God and the Virgin Mary, she writes that, "to the analyst . . . the representations on which the Credo is based are fantasies which reveal fundamental desires or traumas but not dogmas." Continuing with this line of thought, heedless of the work Jung has done on the psychological value of dogma, she states further that "analysis subjects these fantasies to X-ray examination. It begins by individualizing: What about your father? Was he 'almighty' or not? What kind of son were you? What about your desire for virginity or resurrection?"[69]

Adapting Lucifer's anguished cry in *Paradise Lost* to that of the freely associating analysand in psychoanalysis, we here could say on the latter's behalf, "Which ever way I fly is Oedipus, myself am Oedipus." Kleinian and Lacanian amendments to analytic theory do nothing to change this situation. Indeed, far from releasing the soul from its Freudian fate, the addition of the prefix "pre" to the word Oedipal, or the abrupt ending of sessions after five minutes in "The-Name-of-the-Father," merely instills that fate more deeply. Mom's house or dad's, inner parents or outer, psychology is still locked in the family metaphor, each new thing that is learned about family life and child development – from the trauma that sexuality inflicts upon all children to the sadness of the child just prior to language acquisition – becoming a place where psyche is misconceived as an attribute of individuals by a psychology fallen into the trap of seeing itself as a subdivision of socio-anthropology.[70]

But there is another tradition, in which a freer conception of free association arose. Geographically headquartered in Zurich, even as psychoanalysis was headquartered in Vienna, artists of the Dada movement, writers such as the Irish expatriot James Joyce, and the former President of the International Psychoanalytic Association, Jung, sought the inspiration of an unconscious very differently conceived. In radical contrast to the bleak, Oedipally foreclosed views of Freud, the Dada movement emphasized the unconscious as creative source, Joyce the Finnegan-awakening, new-anthropos-constituting "stream of consciousness," and Jung the actively imagined, archetype-renewing, individuation process. Common to all of these was the sense that art, image, the unconscious, thought, consciousness, fantasy, and words have a creative significance of cosmic proportions. Jung, in particular, emphasized this, speaking of the psyche as "the world's pivot"[71] and of reflecting consciousness as being tantamount to a "second cosmogony."[72]

"I know that without me/God can no moment live;/Were I to die, then he/No longer could survive."[73] The song of experience that is the correlate of Angelus Silesius's child-like verse about God being as dependent upon him as he is upon God is not Freud's myth of Oedipal urges and crimes in the family, but Jung's myth of the role of the human creature in rendering creation conscious of itself. In Jung's view, the human psyche, with its imaginative and reflective capacities, "is set up in accordance with the structure of the universe" such that "what happens in the macrocosm likewise happens in the infinitesimal and most subjective reaches of the psyche," that is, in the very ways we apperceive the world.[74] "Liberat[ing] itself from the concretism of the object," the imagination again and again "attempts to sketch the image of the invisible as something behind the phenomenon."[75] In this way, creation continues negatively, so to speak, on the plane of the mind, passing through a series of changes in the way it is logically constituted, experienced, and lived.

Returning to our question – What is symbol? – we may now quote a definitional statement from Jung's writings that is so admirably unencumbered by assumptions that it can hardly be improved upon. "A symbol," he writes, "always presupposes that the chosen expression is the best possible description or formulation of a relatively unknown fact, which is none the less known to exist or is postulated as existing."[76] The value of this definition lies in the justice it does to the unconscious. If the unconscious really is unconscious, which is to say, unknown, what else could a symbol be but "the best possible expression for a complex fact not yet clearly apprehended by consciousness."[77]

Anticipating the present discussion, in which we are attempting to differentiate the symbol in the sense of analytical psychology from the language-based notion of the symbolic order, Jung adds in connection with the above statements that "the concept of a *symbol* should . . . be strictly distinguished from that of a *sign*. Symbolic and *semiotic* meanings are entirely different things."[78] This point is most important. Viewed from the perspective of the Jungian critique that follows from it, Freudian psychoanalysis, being mainly semiotic, is as pre-symbolic as are the patients it has characterized as being unable to symbolize. Or, said another way, being contained within the Oedipal confines of its positivized view of the unconscious, the Freudian symbols (as they are sometimes called) are not symbols at all but signs. Making this point to a correspondent, Jung writes,

> The irrational factors that manifest themselves indirectly as "incest complexes" and "infantile fantasies," etc. are susceptible of a quite different interpretation. They are psychic forces which other ages and other cultures have viewed in a different light. To experience this other side one should have the courage, for once, not to rationalize the statements of the unconscious but to take them seriously.[79]

The difference Jung points out between symbols and signs is like the difference between the terms potency and castration as these are used in common parlance. The symbol, or Jungian thing, is immensely potent. It is not, as were the sons of the primal father whom Freud discusses in *Totem and Taboo*, subject to castration. Nor is it heir, in the manner of the semiotic, to the textuality of the social contract that the brothers in the horde substituted for the father they had dispatched. Though it can, to be sure, be expressed through the symbolic order of language, law, and social institutions, it cannot, like the brotherly order of circumcised signs that make up the signifying chain, be reduced to these without remainder. On the contrary, should any of these cease to be symbolic, by becoming too familiar and known, the Jungian thing may constellate in a compensatory manner. With the force of a neglected deity, it may, under such conditions, assert a new image, one with the power to utterly change the way in which reality is constituted.

But whether compensatorily constellated or not, the main thing about a symbol is the link it makes to the unconscious as the source of life. In contrast to what is rightly said of signs – that they are severed, both from the concepts they signify and the objects to which they seem to refer – the symbol, as the "best possible description or formulation," presents the unknown in a manner that coheres and unites. It is by linking back to the "all-uniting depths"[80] that underpin our conscious lives that the symbol creates anew the links between the dissociated elements of our lives. In the wasteland heaped with broken images which Eliot regarded modernity to have become, creation begins again in what Yeats has called, "the foul rag-and-bone shop of the heart."[81]

Writing with reference to the unconscious symbolic background which potentiates life, Jung states that "compared to it even the external world is secondary, for what does the world matter if the endogenous impulse to grasp it and manipulate it is missing?"[82] Here again, this idea of grasping. The symbolic life, or Jungian thing, like the aforementioned nursing baby, tantrumming child, and Ancient of Days, is an "endogenous impulse" to grasp hold of life and to make use of the world's bounty, a generative will to find sustenance and truth. And, of course, the same can be said with reference to that mediatrix of the unknown, the anima or "unknown woman," whom medicine and psychiatry have presumptuously claimed to know by another name, hysteria.

Jung continues. With reference to what we are variously calling the Jungian thing, symbolic life, endogenous impulse, anima, infant, hysteria and Ancient of Days (tree, stone, beer can, star) let us hear him out to the end. "In the long run," he writes, immediately following from where we left off quoting him above,

> no conscious will can ever replace the life instinct. This instinct comes to us from within, as a compulsion or will or command, and if – as has more or less been done from time immemorial – we give it the name of a personal daimon we are at least aptly expressing the psychological situation. And if, by

employing the concept of the archetype, we attempt to define a little more closely the point at which the daimon grips us, we have not abolished anything, only approached closer to the source of life.[83]

Chapter 10

The Advent of the Notion

Just as the Creator is whole, so His creature, His son, ought to be whole. Nothing can take away from the concept of divine wholeness. But unbeknownst to all, a splitting of that wholeness ensued; there emerged a realm of light and a realm of darkness. This outcome, even before Christ appeared, was clearly prefigured, as we may observe *inter alia* in the experience of Job, or in the widely disseminated Book of Enoch, which belongs to immediate pre-Christian times. In Christianity, too, this metaphysical split was plainly perpetuated: Satan, who in the Old Testament still belonged to the intimate entourage of Yahweh, now formed the diametrical and eternal opposite of the divine world.[1]

C. G. Jung

Although the mother creates an illusion of unity with her infant, this illusion recedes during the late Oedipal period, when the child discovers that the complexity of his internal world and the shifting matrix of group life dissolve the simpler – and simplifying – psychic structures such as those built around the mother–infant relationship or the Oedipal triangle. Neither an affiliation with the matriarchal order nor identification with the patriarchal order will resolve this Oedipal recognition, when the child finds that his mind generates a complex world that defies cohering fables. Then latency inaugurates a lifelong creative retreat from this recognition: the child who realizes that mental life and group processes are too complex to be adequately thought has learned something, though he will also insist on his ignorance. As each person develops there is always this split between the wise self and the fooled self, the shrewd and the innocent.[2]

Christopher Bollas

Sublating the covenant

A Leonard Cohen song, "Anthem," declares that "there is a crack, a crack, in everything. . . ."[3] Wolfgang Giegerich agrees: "A psychology that does not know about the rupture in the soul, that is not responsive to it in the very constitution of the categories of its thinking and thereby does not allow the brokenness to find adequate expression in it, is a psychology which cannot do justice to the soul's wound."[4]

The issue that Giegerich here challenges psychology to attend to is history. Time passes. Nothing is immune to it. Not that universal truth and eternal form that Freud declared the Oedipus complex to be. Nor even the "ageless and ever-present"[5] archetypes that Jung conceived the psyche to be structured by.

Mythology understood this. And religion, too. Indeed, as Giegerich points out, the immortal gods that were spoken of, propitiated, and worshipped in these traditions were all subject to time, coming into being and passing away when their time had come.[6] The contradiction here, if there is any, is a dialectical one. Just as Christ would not be what as Christ he was, had he not exposed himself to the winds of history and died on the cross of time, so the soul, as the sublated form of all that history has negated, arises from the sundering blow that time metes out.

In reminding us of the rupture in the soul, which it is psychology's task to know about and constitute itself in terms of, Giegerich, fittingly enough, provides a post-Jungian update of Jung's often-repeated statement about eternal truths requiring new forms that are in keeping with the spirit of the times. Acknowledging this himself, Giegerich quotes a sentence from Jung's 1935 Tavistock Lectures: "My problem is to wrestle with the big monster of the historical past, the great snake of the centuries, the burden of the human mind, the problem of Christianity."[7] "Time," Giegerich concurs, "is what determines whether an archetypal image has the status of psychological reality."[8] Though we may with some justification speak of archetypal potentials as being "eternal," it is only in time that these potentials become real.

It was ever thus. In his book *Primitive Mythology*, Joseph Campbell, like Freud before him, indulges in a "phylogenetic fantasy" that is most suggestive in the present context. Directing his visionary eye into the deepest reaches of human pre-history, the great mythologist wonders what became of humankind's instinctive responses to life when the environmental triggers that released those responses receded from view as conquest over nature was gradually won. Thinking of this in terms of the ethologist Tinbergen's notions of "sign stimuli" and "innate releasing mechanisms,"[9] Campbell writes:

> Who will claim to know what sign stimuli smote our releasing mechanisms when our names were not Homo sapiens but Pithecanthropus and Plesianthropus, or perhaps even – millenniums earlier – Dryopithecus? And who that has knowledge of the numerous vestigial structures of our anatomy, surviving from the days when we were beasts (for example, the muscles of the caudal vertebrae that once wagged our tail) would doubt that in the central nervous system comparable vestiges must remain: images sleeping, whose releasers no longer appear in nature – but might occur in art?[10]

What a remarkable suggestion! As our primordial forebears evolved, certain action-potentials or "innate releasing mechanisms" fell into a dormant state. No longer exposed to the kinds of situation that triggered a particular instinctual response, no longer, that is to say, incited to action by the sign stimuli that wild nature had provided, humans became more and more divided from the fullness of their evolutionary make-up. In this way, a gap or cleavage opened up between what their archaic heritage potentiated them to be and what, in fact, they actually were. But as Freud would say, our species is unable to abandon a satisfaction it has once enjoyed. Out of the dialectical tension occasioned by this angst-filled rupture, art emerged – art, culture, and religion too. Needing to express their pent-up poten-tial ("the endogenous impulse to grasp," which we have already heard about from Jung), humans created for themselves – on the walls of their caves, in their rituals and dances, and in their relationships with one another – a semblance of the numinous sign stimuli that had formerly released their various instincts. In this way, the connection that had been broken between the organic and the inorganic, humanity and nature, mind and earth was renewed and renewed again on other levels.

Many associations spring to mind that enrich this idea. We may think of Jung's many references to the Anthropos and to the perennial challenge of its renewal; of our First Parents in the Garden of Eden (especially in those accounts where they are depicted as having tails); and of their fall from that oneness with nature that was at the same time their oneness with God.

The covenant theme, as this figures in the Bible, also comes to mind. In the Jewish and Christian traditions, the story we are telling of the broken and yet soul-constituting connection between the world of the instincts within us and the external world without is told as the story of the making, breaking, and making again of agreements with a God who visited tribulations upon his people in the form of earthquake, whirlwind, flood, and war. This making of covenants began with Abraham. In my mind's eye, I see the old patriarch looking much like his forefathers "Pithecanthropus and Plesianthropus, or perhaps even – millenniums earlier – Dryopithecus." I see him dreaming that dream that served as the basis for the ceremony of the covenant, the one in which the spirit of God, in the form of a smoking fire pot and flaming torch, moved between the sections of a slaughtered beast.[11] And this, in turn, brings Giegerich's work on ancient ritual slaughtering as primordial soul-making to mind.

In Giegerich's view, the move against positivity into negation, which consti-tutes psychology, began in the dim reaches of human prehistory with sacrificial slaughter. "Killing," he writes, with reference to both hunting and the bloody sacrifice of animal and human victims,

> was . . . the main act in which the first negation of the animals' *environment*, and *ipso facto* the primordial opening of what we call the *world* of man, takes place. It is the pivot between the immediate, natural life of the living creature and the cultural existence of man which is posited, mediated from the outset. With the early hunter's terrific killing thrust of the spear, with the sacrificer's shocking blow of the axe, man did not merely hit, as did the beast of prey, some indifferent Other and thus something of no further concern beyond its food value. He also hit and killed his own Other, and thus himself. In this he

did not literally destroy himself as a living creature, he only killed himself logically as the *merely-biological* creature. The one who died as merely-biological being had simultaneously risen as mental, conscious human, and thus made his first entrance into the state of being as *soul*.[12]

Explaining further how the soul constituted itself by killing, Giegerich continues a paragraph later:

> It was the soul itself that with the shock of the killing blow shocked itself out of the darkness of merely-biological existence. In this darkness it violently opened up for itself for the first time soul-space as a small island. Within vegetative and animal life's impenetrable, pasty substantiality the mercilessly descending blow tore open a certain free space, and the blood gushing forth from the open wound ignited a light.[13]

The crack in everything, the rupture and wound in the soul, is mirrored or reflected into itself in the killing blow of the ancient sacrificer. The blood that gushes forth is the igniting of a light – the same light, we may surmise, that moved as a smoking fire pot and flaming torch between the halves of the sectioned animal in the dream in which the ceremony of the covenant was revealed to Abraham. And from Abraham we can leap past his son Isaac to Christ, who, as "the Lamb that was slain from the foundation of the world,"[14] was, at the same time, the light of the world through his bloody death on the Cross.

Taking different forms at different times, the heart of Christ burns forever, unconsumed. In the line following his reference to there being "a crack in everything," Leonard Cohen adds that "that's how the light gets in."[15]

But what have these reflections to do with psychoanalysis and hysteria? From a history-of-psychology perspective, plenty. In 1983, a previously unknown essay of Freud's was discovered. Titled "Overview of the transference neuroses," this essay set out to reconstruct, if only in the form of a "scientific myth," a phylogenetic account of the various kinds of contemporary neurosis. In Freud's view, the rupture in the soul (which we, following Campbell, have imaged as a disjunctive gap between innate releasing mechanisms and their associated sign stimuli) is the result of a severe curtailing or "anticathexis" of libido, which was brought about by the dramatically altered living conditions that were associated with the "exigencies of the Ice Age."[16] "[T]he temptation is very great," writes Freud,

> to recognize in the three dispositions to anxiety hysteria, conversion hysteria, and obsessional neurosis regressions to phases that the whole human race had to go through at some time from the beginning to the end of the Ice Age, so that at that time all human beings were the way only some of them are today, by virtue of their hereditary tendency and by means of new acquisition.[17]

We will not review here Freud's bleak picture of our forebears living out the Ice Age in caves. It is basically the same picture he presented in *Totem and Taboo*, but with the addition that reproduction came to cross purposes with survival owing to limitations with regard to food and shelter, giving rise to the perversions. Of more interest in the present context is his contention that the dissociations of the hysterical and obsessional patients of our own day are heir to or redolent of the primordial split that the Ice Age brought about in the lives of our ancient forebears.

> [M]ankind, under the influence of the privations that the encroaching Ice Age imposed upon it, has become generally *anxious*. The hitherto predominantly friendly outside world, which bestowed every satisfaction, transformed itself into a mass of threatening perils. There had been good reason for realistic anxiety about everything new. The sexual libido, to be sure, did not at first lose its objects, which are certainly human; but it is conceivable that the ego, whose existence was threatened, to some extent abandoned the object-cathexis, retained the libido in the ego, and thus transformed into realistic anxiety what had previously been object-libido.[18]

Here, in the partial abandonment of object-cathexis (the disconnect between the innate releasing mechanisms and the objects that are their releasers) is the beginning of that "amazing mirror thing," the imaginal psyche. The libido, which has been diverted from its natural goal and anxiously retained in the ego, obtains, through this frustrating process of anti-cathexis, the form of an image. Or, said another way, as the shadows of our forebears' lost libidinal objects fell upon their egos, they were taken up into their egos in the form of images. Redolent of the instincts, this hypercathected imagery even now exerts a compelling force, prompting us to act out what we no longer remember (or even personally experienced) in such a way that we return, at new levels, to some semblance of the primordial situations out of which we once evolved.

This, of course, is a Jungian reading of the passage we have quoted from Freud. To be more accurate in our presentation of the Jungian position, we must add that the anti-cathected libido which has been transformed into imagery is not to be thought of as being inside an ego. Rather, since it is archetypal and, thus, greater than the ego, it is more apt to say that the ego is inside it. Filling our subjective experience with images and dreams and our lives with fantasies and projections, the imaginal psyche takes us "back to the future," as it were, as it transferentially searches for new editions of its primordially lost objects. This is not to say that the psyche's images are direct copies of what once was. On the contrary, as Jung often reminded his readers, in the process we are describing it is not a case of specific images being inherited – as the defiantly Lamarckian Freud maintained – but of an inherited or constitutional predisposition to create images of certain types.

Freud's account of the soul-constituting dynamic we have just described is a decidedly pessimistic one. Like the father of the horde, the collective unconscious, in Freud's conception of it, is more a tyrannizing superego constituted of fixed images than a life-giving id, though id it is as well. Discussing the fate of the libido in the aftermath of object-loss, Freud states in *The Ego and the Id* that "the character of the ego is a precipitate of abandoned object-cathexes and . . . contains the history of those object-choices."[19] Later in the same work he gives this observation a phylogenetic twist: "in the id, which is capable of being inherited, are harboured residues of the existences of countless egos; and, when the ego forms its superego out of the id, it may perhaps only be reviving shapes of former egos and be bringing them to resurrection."[20] Again, it is important to notice that in Freud's account of the collective mind, it is superego that is being formed. What Freud imagines being resurrected are archaic vestiges of the horrible deeds that the Primal Father wrought in prehistoric times.[21] Little wonder, then, that he came to such dour conclusions in *Civilization and its Discontents*.

It is interesting, however, especially in light of Campbell's idea that humankind provided itself with new sign stimuli in the form of artistic creations, that Freud introduces a measure of hope into what would otherwise be a completely bleak picture by granting to the artist and to artistic creation a degree of negentropic freedom and form-creating power. In a letter to Ferenczi (the actual originator of the Ice Age hypothesis), Freud wrote, "Don't we now know two conditions for artistic endowment? First, the wealth of phylogenetically transferred material, as with the neurotic; second, a good remnant of the old technique of modifying oneself instead of the outside world (see Lamarck, etc.)."[22]

Addressing this theme more fully in the postscript of *Group Psychology and the Analysis of the Ego*, Freud again speaks of the artist – the epic poet to be more precise – imagining how this figure emerged out of the early human situation that had arisen in the wake of the horde. Against the backdrop of all that we have had to say about the rupture in the soul and about the imperative to create, via the archetypal transference – what we have variously referred to as new sign stimuli, new forms, and new expressions of eternal truth – let us briefly examine Freud's account of the origins of the artist/poet.

Cognizant of the changes that take place in the spirit of the times, Freud imagines a period some generations after the slaying of the primal father;

> It was then, perhaps, that some individual, in the exigency of his longing, may have been moved to free himself from the group and take over the father's part. He who did this was the first epic poet; and the advance was achieved in his imagination. This poet disguised the truth with lies in accordance with his longing. He invented the heroic myth. The hero was a man who by himself [or so he gained prestige by claiming] had slain the father – the father who still appeared in myth as a totemic monster. Just as the father had been the boy's first ideal, so in the hero who aspires to the father's place the poet now created the first ego-ideal. The transition to the hero was probably afforded by the youngest son, the mother's favourite, whom she had protected from paternal jealousy, and who, in the era of the primal horde, had been the father's successor. In the lying poetic fancies of prehistoric times the woman, who had been the prize of battle and the temptation to murder, was probably turned into the active seducer and instigator to the crime.[23]

Reading this passage today, it is hard not to hear in it a reference to Jung. Jung, after all, in the early years of the psychoanalytic movement was regarded by Freud as a favourite son and future heir. Enthusiastically promoting Jung to this end, Freud had wanted to make him President for Life of the International Psycho-analytic Association. However, coinciding with the ideas he was developing with respect to the primal father's murder, Freud's doubts about this took the form of fainting spells in Jung's presence, which he explained in accordance with his belief that Jung harboured a death-wish toward him. But, beyond these well-known connections, Jung's likeness to the epic poet of Freud's speculative vision is most evident in the fact that he, too, at least in Freud's estimation, had "disguised the truth with lies in accordance with his longing," writing a book on the myth of the hero, in which he suggested that incest with the unconscious as mother leads to rebirth and renewal. And this is to say nothing of the woman who "had been the prize of battle and the temptation to murder." In connection with this "active seducer and instigator of the crime," we may think of the many hysterical patients in dialogue with whom psychoanalysis was invented. More particularly, we may think of Jung's early patient and "test case,"[24] Sabina Spielrein. Complaining to Freud about Jung's treatment of her, Spielrein gave a rather unvarnished glimpse of the exigency of Jung's longing.

Tracing analytical psychology's concept of the anima back to what Jung, writing to Spielrein, called "[t]he love of S. for J. [that] made the latter aware of something he had only previously suspected,"[25] it is possible to see the human spirit renewing itself in terms of new sign stimuli arising out of the psychoanalytic situation in the form of the love fantasies of the transference.[26] For it was the "art" and "poetry" that Jung (in Spielrein's words[27]) made with his patient that brought Jung to the awareness of what he called, in the same letter to Spielrein, "a power in the unconscious that shapes one's destiny, a power which later led him to things of greatest importance,"[28] i.e., to the theories of analytical psychology.

Imagining herself to be carrying a child named Siegfried, who was both a son she had conceived with Jung and Jung himself, Spielrein gave birth to this child, in the period after her cure, in the form of a medical diploma dissertation entitled, "Destruction as the cause of coming into being."[29] In the pages of this treatise, she advanced the thesis that sexuality poses a threat, not to the relations with mamma-the-caregiver, as Bollas now contends, but to the individual's personal identity as an ego. As Kerr, succinctly summing up the essence of Spielrein's theory, explains:

> If one grants that sexuality is always concerned with racial or species-wide aims (procreation), then it follows that sexuality will, in cases where there is a divergence, seek to override the ego's unique prerogatives. Sexuality "wants" (by teleological metaphor) children, and is ready to dissolve the ego in the act of sexual fusion to get them. Similarly, when one shifts to the hypothetical terrain of "sublimation," sexuality "wants" new artistic creations which the race can share. Sexuality does not care what this new creation "costs" the indi-

vidual. . . . Thus, from the standpoint of the ego, sexuality contains an implicit threat of dissolution. As the species-wide aims of sexuality make themselves felt, they come into conflict with the purely personal motives of the individual "I." Accordingly, and this is the main point, *against sexuality the ego always responds with an attitude of resistance.*[30]

We should not be surprised that a hysterical patient with such powerful insight into the rupture in the soul should have served as the sign stimulus that activated the archetypal libido latent in Jung's unconscious. Nor should we be surprised that Jung had an equally releasing effect upon Spielrein's energies. Still less should we judge this Ur-couple by the bloodless standards of contemporary ethics tribunals. For whether they ever had intercourse or not, the love that they learned to logically negate has kindled through their sacrifice of it a light of insight from which generations of analysts and analysands have since drawn.

Writing to Freud a short time after his relations with Spielrein had come, almost scandalously, to a head, Jung had the following to say about sexuality, religion, and psychoanalysis, the three themes that had been so intensely constellated between him and Spielrein in her treatment:

The ethical problem of sexual freedom really is enormous and worth the sweat of all noble souls. But 2000 years of Christianity can only be replaced by something equivalent. An ethical fraternity, with its mythical Nothing, not infused by any archaic–infantile driving force, is a pure vacuum and can never evoke in man the slightest trace of that age-old animal power which drives the migrating bird across the sea and without which no irresistible mass movement can come into being. I imagine a far finer and more comprehensive task for psychoanalysis than alliance with an ethical fraternity. I think we must give it time to infiltrate into people from many centres, to revivify among intellectuals a feeling for symbol and myth, ever so gently to transform Christ back into the soothsaying god of the vine, which he was, and in this way absorb those ecstatic instinctual forces of Christianity for the *one* purpose of making the cult and the sacred myth what they once were – a drunken feast of joy where man regained the ethos and holiness of an animal. That was the beauty and purpose of classical religion, which from God knows what temporary biological needs has turned into a Misery Institute. Yet what infinite rapture and wantonness lie dormant in our religion, waiting to be led back to their true destination! A genuine and proper ethical development cannot abandon Christianity but must grow up within it, must bring to fruition its hymn of love, the agony and ecstasy over the dying and resurgent god, the mystic power of the wine, the awesome anthropophagy of the Last Supper – only *this* ethical development can serve the vital forces of religion.[31]

Though Jung, when shown this letter some fifty years later, was reminded by it of the long period of time he spent in his younger days in "cloud-cuckoo-land" and of his equally long descent "by a thousand ladders" to what he called "the little clod of earth that I am,"[32] quoting it here may serve to heighten our awareness of the rift in the soul that psychoanalysis and analytical psychology unwittingly act out in our time through having forgotten their larger aspect.

The advent of the notion

The crack in everything is not merely a dissociative split in ourselves as persons. On the contrary, as Leonard Cohen unequivocally declares, it truly is in every-thing. That this is so is taugetorically confirmed by the other images in his song. Explicitly referring to the "holy dove," even as we have referred to the dove in the consulting room, the poet sings of its being "caught again," "bought and sold/and bought again," and of its being "never free." In other verses the same truth is presented in other ways: "We asked for signs/the signs were sent; the birth betrayed/the marriage spent/the widowhood/of every government/signs for all to see." And then, letting his voice deepen to become the "thundercloud" of which he simultaneously sings, he expresses the soul's outrage that "killers in high places say their prayers out loud." Finally, bidding us in a chorus to "ring the bells that still can ring," he strikes a chord of sombre affirmation. "Every heart/every heart to love will come/but like a refugee."[33]

Writing to Spielrein a little more than a decade after her analysis with him had ended, Jung said much the same thing to her. The letters to which I refer are those Jung wrote in response to a number of long, psychologically astute letters he received from Spielrein between 1917 and 1919.[34] In these, his former hysteria patient, now a psychoanalyst and analytic theoretician in her own right, presented something of her own theory of symbol formation, queried Jung regarding his views on this issue, and attempted to gain further insight into the "youthful Siegfried symbol" which had figured so centrally in her analysis.[35]

In Jung's letters, not surprisingly, Freud and his brand of psychoanalysis are represented in terms more or less equivalent to the image in our Cohen song of the "killers in high places [who] say their prayers out loud." Siegfried, on the other hand, the transferential love-child and solar-hero about whom Spielrein continues to be puzzled, is valued by Jung in much the same way that the light which gets in through the crack in everything is valued by Cohen. Far from being what Bollas has referred to as a fixated "'child within' who castrates the self's achievements in the real by periodic uprisings that shed the self of the accoutrements of accomplishment,"[36] this figure, according to Jung, is an irreducible symbol with a prospective tendency, that, if related to correctly, would contribute to Spielrein's self-realization.

"You are always trying to drag the Siegfried symbol back into reality," Jung cautions in one letter,

> whereas in fact it is the bridge to your individual development. Human beings do not stand in one world only but between two worlds and must distinguish

themselves from their functions in both worlds. That is individuation. You are rejecting dreams and seeking action. Then the dreams come and thwart your actions. The dreams are a world, and the real is a world. You have to stand between them and regulate the traffic in both worlds, just as Siegfried stands between the gods and men.[37]

Clearly, as the idea here of there being two worlds indicates, Jung was familiar with what Giegerich has more recently called the rupture in the soul, and had even conceived his theory in terms of it. When his *Collected Works* are consulted, we see that this is a theme to which he returned repeatedly throughout his career.[38] The example of this that is nearest in time to the exchange of letters with Spielrein from which we are quoting is his 1916 paper, "The transcendent function."[39] In this paper (which lay unpublished for some 42 years), Jung gives an account of his departure from Freud's method of free association in favour of what has come to be known in Jungian parlance as the dialectical approach to the unconscious. By actively engaging the counter-position of the unconscious at both personal and collective levels (rather than running away from these as analytic interpretation has been doing ever since Breuer took flight from the hysterically pregnant Anna O.), Jung found that it was possible to constitute a dialectical tension that produces symbols, ideas, and attitudes of a more embracing and far-reaching quality.

In psychotherapy, of course, this process is distributed interpersonally between the analyst and analysand, each mediating the counter-position in the unconscious for the other. The resultant symbol, if one comes at all, is thus a co-creation of the two partners (as Spielrein had insisted with reference to herself and Jung in relation to Siegfried[40]). But hard on the heels of this recognition comes a disturbing question: How is a "transference neurosis" that has been so prospective and soul-constituting to be resolved? Or, to ask the same question in terms of the lyrics of our Cohen song, how is the refugee heart that has come to love by way of analysis to be resettled apart from analysis? In his letters to Spielrein, as in his earlier paper on the transcendent function, Jung addresses this question, giving advice about how the dialectical relationship with the unconscious may be sustained on an independent basis by the patient after treatment has ended.

The counsel Jung gives to Spielrein in his responses to her might also be read in the light of the idea that what has been born of a wild analysis can live on (if, in fact, it can live on) only as a capacity for wild self-analysis.[41] In a letter written some sixteen months after the one from which we have just quoted, Jung gives further guidance to Spielrein concerning how she should relate herself to the figure of Siegfried. Here, as before, Jung's tone leaves us with the impression that his former patient continues, to some extent at least, to have the constellating power of an anima in his lingering countertransference.

How you must accept Siegfried I cannot tell you. That is a secret. Your dream can help. Dreams are compensatory to the conscious attitude. Reality and the unconscious are primary. They are two forces that work simultaneously but are different. The hero unites them in a symbolic figure. He is the centre and the resolution. The dream contributes to life, as does reality. The human being stands between two worlds. Freud's view is a sinful violation of the sacred. It spreads darkness, not light; that has to happen, for only out of the deepest night will the new light be born. One of its sparks is Siegfried. This spark can and will never be extinguished. If you betray this, then you are cursed. What has [the dream-figure] Liebknecht to do with you? Like Freud and Lenin, he disseminates rationalistic darkness which will yet extinguish the little lamps of understanding. I kindled a new light in you which you must protect for the time of darkness. That must not be betrayed externally and for the sake of external arguments. Surround this inner light with devotion, then it will never turn into danger for your little daughter.[42] But whoever betrays this light for the sake of power or in order to be clever will be a figure of shame and will have a bad influence.[43]

Heard in Midgard, Jung's advice to Spielrein is entirely bizarre. If all that is at stake is Spielrein's resolving her personal neurosis, why speak in such bombastic, inflationary terms of new light being born out of the deepest night and of the danger of being cursed if this is betrayed? In Midgard, after all, symptoms, like cats, are just what they seem to be – a nuisance (however agonizing) and nothing more. If your analyst can't lift the one or cure the other, well maybe EMDR or Prozac can.

Jung, however, is not speaking from Midgard. Nor is Spielrein (advocate though she often is for Freud's theories in her letters). Their conversation, rather, is taking place in Utgard. That Spielrein is still, even after all the intervening years, struggling to understand her Siegfried fantasy, suggests that she is in touch, by means of it, with the great Serpent that encircles the earth. Or, to say the same thing in other terms, that she cannot understand her fantasy suggests that it is the best possible expression of the unknown in the immediacy of its psychic impact upon her – a symbol in Jung's sense of the term.

In the letters, it should be noted, there are virtually no references to splits in Spielrein, though doubtless, like all of us, she had them. When Spielrein mentions her vocational conflicts with respect to being a musician, a doctor, or a wife and mother,[44] Jung merely states that in order to be real in this world certain exclusionary commitments must be made, but that "You have not thereby become yourself."[45] To become yourself, something else is needed than the resolution of personal conflicts and the bridging of one's personal dissociations (as important as such resolutions and bridgings may be). This something is the relationship to the infinite, the relationship to the symbols that spring, not from the gap between what we take to be our conflicts, but from the crack that is in everything, the rupture in the soul, i.e, the two worlds that we, as humans, stand between. It is only when we realize that the splits within us and between us are at the same time in the world that the true light comes in.

Jung's counsel to Spielrein, especially the part of it in which he warns her to protect the figure of Siegfried from Freudian interpretations (such as those he had once tried out on her himself), has much in common with certain divergent views which Kohut introduced into psychoanalysis several decades later.[46] Freud, it will be recalled, believed that all children are subject to a nightmarish encounter with instinctual conflicts – infantile sexuality, the incest taboo, and the triangular family set-up being what they are. Placing a seal upon this, his notion of the Oedipus complex, Freud even went so far as to declare acceptance of it to be "the shibboleth that distinguishes the adherents of psychoanalysis from its opponents."[47] These words, which Freud added to the 1920 edition of his *Three Essays on the Theory of Sexuality*, were, of course, a very pointed allusion to Jung, who was being drummed out of the tribe by Freud's utterance of them.

Writing in the late 1970s and early 1980s, Kohut had less to fear with regard to his tenure as a psychoanalyst. Revisioning the Freudian account of the Oedipus complex in the light of the self psychological concepts he had formulated in the course of his study of narcissism, Kohut quietly advanced the unorthodox view that the Oedipus *complex* was not an inevitable experience of childhood instinctual conflict and anxiety, which "every new arrival on this planet is faced with the task of mastering,"[48] but a secondary corruption or derailment in the lives of some children of an Oedipal *phase* of development that is under optimal conditions entirely benign.

In Kohut's view the difference between a line of development that passes heartily through the Oedipal phase and one that becomes sequestered in the conflicts associated with the Oedipus complex is based upon differences in the quality of the child's selfobject milieu. In the best case scenario, the parents, in their crucial role of esteem-supporting selfobjects, are able to empathize with the affectionate feelings and assertive strivings that their child feels toward them, assisting thereby in the child's healthy integration of these potentials into his or her self-structure. If, however, the parent of the opposite sex responds too seductively or the same-sexed parent in too envious or competitive a manner, the child will have to mobilize defenses against the lustful longings and hostile wishes that his or her potential for love and self-assertion become under such conditions.

As commonsensical as Kohut's revisioning of the Oedipus complex in the light of his notion of an Oedipal phase constituted of adequate selfobject responsiveness now seems, it is important to recognize that it is a radical departure from the traditional account. Contrary to Freudian theory, guilt about patricidal and incestuous wishes, terrifying dreams and fantasies redolent of the brutal acts that were committed during the period of the primal horde, and castration anxiety are not, for Kohut, the primary motors of conflict that motivate development during the fateful Oedipal period. On the contrary, raw, drive-determined expressions of sexuality and aggression such as these, as well as the super-ego that Freud envisioned as sternly opposing them, are secondary formations, or as Kohut also calls them, "disintegration products." It is when self-esteem fails, or was never properly achieved, owing to inadequacies in selfobject responsiveness, that the child or self-disordered adult is likely to come unravelled into sex, aggression, anxiety, guilt, and the lurid despair of the so-called narcissistic behaviour disorders.

These reflections bring us back to Jung and Spielrein. In the course of his analysis of Spielrein, Jung made much the same shift away from interpretations based on the Oedipus complex as Kohut did many years later. Influenced by the writings of Flournoy on teleological mechanisms,[49] he was quick to credit the figure of Siegfried with creative meaning in terms of Spielrein's future development. He had earlier come to the conclusion that his medium cousin Frl. S.W.'s sub-personality "Ivenes" was an anticipation of her more mature future personality,[50] and he regarded Siegfried in the same way. Though these are, admittedly, very different ideas from those Kohut developed, they equipped Jung, for all his countertransferential acting-out, to be a better selfobject for his patient than he would have been if he had continued to view her and her images through the pathologizing lens of Freud's notion of the Oedipus complex. Siegfried, in Jung's view, was a figure of light and wonder, a figure compensatory to the darkness of the times. In esteeming this figure as it appeared in Spielrein's fantasies, Jung was in effect conveying to Spielrein that the "great relationship"[51] (if we may here use an expression from Jung's later writings) was not her relationship to him but rather her relationship to what he (again in his later work) called "the transpersonal control-point,"[52] or self.

Toward the end of his life, Jung reiterated this point – so key to his theory – in his memoirs:

> The clash, which is at first of a purely personal nature, is soon followed by the insight that the subjective conflict is only a single instance of the universal conflict of opposites. Our psyche is set up in accord with the structure of the universe, and what happens in the macrocosm likewise happens in the infinitesimal and most subjective reaches of the psyche. For that reason the God image is always the projection of the inner experience of a powerful vis-à-vis.[53]

Releasing psychology

Nietzsche declared that one must have chaos in oneself to give birth to a dancing star.[54] Revising this statement in the light of the ideas we have been discussing in this chapter, the following formulation suggests itself: *the crack in everything, the rupture in the soul, is the dialectical abyss, or rent veil even, from which that new art form, sign stimulus, symbol, selfobject, and transferential love-child – psychology – has hysterically emerged.*

This chaotic formulation (if not yet to say star) may here remind us of another. At the beginning of our enquiry (with Anna O., and now Sabina Spielrein, in mind) we boldly declared hysteria to be "the anima, or Madonna even, of the therapeutic psychology that came to prominence during the last century of the Christian aeon." In this way we pushed off at the outset from the empirical conception of psychology as the study of something or other which it is supposed to be about, and followed, as in a "wandering womb" of internal reflection, the aforementioned movement against positivity into reflection through which psychology (in the sense of its highest determination as logical, i.e., notional life) constitutes itself. Reflected in the mirror that we established in this way (true psychology always beginning as the sublation of immediate psychology[55]), hysteria appeared to us, not as the analyst-destroying siren envisioned by Bollas, nor as the Mad Men and Medusas of Juliet Mitchell, but in the varied guises of Shahrazad, Eliza Doolittle, and most surprisingly of all, the Holy Mother – as, say, Leonardo da Vinci painted her during a period of our history in which Christianity still served as an adequate sign stimulus, selfobject, and symbol of the soul.

To be sure, there is no going back to Christianity, or to any other religion for that matter. For these, even while continuing to exist, are now subsumed under psychology. That this is so is particularly evident when we consider how Christianity is preached and practised as the star under which it began now sets at the end of its aeon. Today, in the twilight-glow of that star's setting, it is not even necessary to darken the door of a church, let alone to read the Bible. A brief perusal of a self-help book or an hour or two of the Oprah show is all that is required to know Christ as he is spoken of from the pulpit of what has become the Place of Bingo on the corner. The Bible, meanwhile, has become a psychology text. While Christianity seeks to stay current by incorporating pop psychology and New Age glitter, the higher psychotherapy furrows its brows over this old book as part of its attempt to come to terms with the religious libido to which it is heir. "We must read the Bible or we shall not understand psychology," states Jung in *The Visions Seminars*. "Our psychology, our whole lives, our language and imagery are built upon the Bible."[56]

Other end-times ironies appear in the sphere of worship, prayer, and ritual: none of these are any longer what they were in the past – the human half of that *symbol-on* or broken token which connected our forebears to the truth that was the essence of their times. On the contrary, on the model of God becoming man, we humans have become increasingly identical with ourselves as persons, ego personalities – the epistemological criticism that psychological consciousness has brought to the religion that preceded it having largely miscarried into humanism and its attendant ill, the modern "identity crisis."

Jogging through the Wasteland, we feel hounded by a sense of not being ourselves. In weekend retreats, still fleeing from the meaninglessness by which we are pursued, we seek truth in the form of more intense experiences, closer intimacy, stronger orgasms, goddess worship. Unable to bear the jagged edge of the broken token that we are, we try to become complete in ourselves – if only by toning up our muscles at the gym. Meanwhile, that Willie Loman of an old Adam in us, looking like Kevin Spacey in *American Beauty*, has a panic attack, overwhelmed by his longing for . . . he knows not what. And always those irksome lyrics, intoning themselves over and over again in the head: "I'd like to buy the world a Coke and keep it company." Jesus! If it could only be that easy.

The gyre widens. Christmas comes round again, barely able to keep within its orbit. But, here again, the kids in the chancel playing "Jingle Bells" on their guitars are no help – even though they are our kids and we got the whole thing on video. Their twanging notes simply cannot trigger our releasing mechanisms as choir and organ once did. But no matter, come Monday we can see the minister for an hour of counselling or take that seminar on how to be a better mom or dad.

Does this mean that the Holy Family and the Holy Trinity are an Oedipus complex after all? With Kohut's ideas in mind we arrive at a very different conclusion: the Oedipus complex, for all its ubiquity, is a disintegration product of the religious phase that preceded what Heidegger, with reference to Rilke, so aptly called our "destitute times." And the same can be said of the psychoanalysis that has arisen alongside this disintegration as the form of its sunken meaning. Its knowledge, *as necessary as it is each day in our practices*, is fallen knowledge, infernal knowledge. As Freud himself noted, it is a learning from pathology, about pathology. In the same way that ethologists must now make it their business to know all about what caribou do when a ruptured oil pipeline tears their world in twain, so psychoanalysis must know about how humans behave in the absence of the symbolism that had until very recently supported and sustained them.

"We are actually living in the time of the splitting of the world and the invalida- tion of Christ,"[57] wrote Jung in a letter to Fr Victor White some forty-three years after he had written to Freud expressing his hope that through its "feeling for symbol and myth" psychoanalysis could revitalize Christianity with "that age-old animal power which drives the migrating bird across the sea."[58]

But if symbolless modernity and deconstructed postmodernity are the pipeline that has divided the psyche into that dualism of id and superego between which the ego sits, as upon a "seat of anxiety"[59] (as Freud put it), what were things like before such divisions arose? The following passage from Jung's essay "On the nature of the psyche" sheds light on this question:

> Instinct and the archaic mode meet in the biological conception of the "pattern of behaviour." There are, in fact, no amorphous instincts, as every instinct bears in itself the pattern of its situation. Always it fulfils an image, and the image has fixed qualities. The instinct of the leaf-cutting ant fulfils the image of ant, tree, leaf, cutting, transport, and the little ant-garden of fungi. If any one of these conditions is lacking, the instinct does not function, because it cannot exist without its total pattern, without its image. Such an image is an *a priori* type. It is inborn in the ant prior to any activity, for there can be no activity at all unless an instinct of corresponding pattern initiates and makes it possible. This schema holds true of all instincts and is found in identical form in all individuals of the same species. The same is true also of man: he has in him these *a priori* instinct-types which provide the occasion and the pattern for his activities, in so far as he functions instinctively.[60]

Compared to this paradisaical (but in no way fantastical) vision of humankind's instinctual adaptedness to its earthly environment, Freud's metapsychology division of the psyche into id, ego, and superego is an east-of-Eden vision of disintegration. Though conceived by Freud and Jung in the polarizing spirit of the rivalry between them, these visions complement each other, even as the life in the Garden is followed by the Fall. Revising Jung's statement in a manner more inclusive of Freud's concepts, we could say that there is no id of amorphous instincts and no prohibitory "ideologies of the superego"[61] *unless or until* one of the conditions necessary to the pattern of behaviour is lacking. Putting it this way acknowledges that there are indeed amorphous instincts, or, as we might also call them (with our previous discussion of Kohut in mind), disintegrated instincts. For what Jung calls the necessary conditions within which a pattern of behaviour operates often *is* lacking, as, again, we noted earlier in our discussion of the remaindering of the innate releasing mechanism that occurs as a result of the loss of habitat and the sign stimuli which had previously shone forth from within it. And to the extent that these are lost, Freud is quite right in showing us the Leviathan and Behemoth at the bottom of that abyss that he calls castration and death instinct – the id and the superego. The value of Bollas's and Mitchell's theories of hysteria may be seen in terms of the dark light of this background as well.

But does this mean that we must live our lives in some sci-fi nightmare of sex, violence, and devastating unconscious guilt? Or can the jostling revenants of our sadism, psychopathy, narcissism, obsessionality, masochism, and schizoid aloofness be redeemed on the level of a new ideal, symbol, god-term, or image? Campbell, it will be recalled, spoke of the function of art, religion, and culture in general as one of providing a new sign stimulus. But the new sign stimuli that they have provided have become outdated. Something else is needed now. Something else and something more than just another provisional symbol or image.

We are coming round to asking our ultimate question. It is the question Spielrein addressed to Jung: who is Siegfried? As asked by us, however, this question has a different addressee. It is not Jung that we put it to but psychology. Addressing Jung in his negativity, *as* psychology, negativizes Spielrein and Siegfried as well. And as the positivity of these figures gives way to reflection, Spielrein's question finds its universal form: who or what has hysteria, as the *negative* Mary of our times, been carrying in the pregnant emptiness of her womb, beneath the void of an absent star?

But first let us take stock of where we are. Campbell's vision is largely of prehistoric happenings. The new sign stimuli that arose in the course of humankind's development in the logical form of art and religion have come and gone many times. Now, however, as we make the transition from a religious ontology into a psychological one, we witness another kind of tearing asunder and passing away. The art that once vitalized culture by releasing our pent up nature into itself is no longer able to do so. Religion, likewise, has become effete. Cut off from the numinosum, we experience nausea in its stead.

Speaking of the rituals of the Church in much the same way that he had written of the instinct of the cutting ant, Jung told the Guild for Pastoral Psychology:

Man expresses his most fundamental and most important psychological conditions in this ritual, this magic, or whatever you call it. And the ritual is the cult performance of these basic psychological facts. That explains why we should not change anything in a ritual. A ritual must be done according to tradition, and if you change one little point in it, you make a mistake. You must not allow your reason to play with it. For instance, take that most difficult dogma, the dogma of the Virgin Birth: it is absolutely wrong to rationalize it. If you leave it as it is, as it has been handed down, then it is true; but if you rationalize it, it is all wrong, because then you shift it over to the plane of our playful intellect, which does not understand the secret. It is the secret of virginity and the virginal conception . . . a most important psychological fact.[62]

Jung is not making a case here for a return to "that old-time religion" any more than I was in my critique of the contemporary Church service earlier in this section. While being respectful of those who can still find their way back to a traditional faith (Jung was speaking to the clergy in this talk), he knew that with the end of the aeon approaching a change was in the offing. His advice, if that is what it was, had thus already arrived too late. For everything that he cautioned against had already happened – perhaps not for those individuals whom the members of his audience would be ministering to – but, in a more general sense than that, for all. (Straddling the split in the world he would write to Fr White about some years later, Jung writes in the same letter that "Christ is still a valid symbol. Only God himself can 'invalidate' him through the Paraclete."[63])

For our purposes, the important thing in Jung's talk to the Pastoral Psychology Guild is the vision he provides of the dogmas and rituals of the Church as instincts. Like actual instincts, dogmas and rituals work by virtue of their total character. Everything must happen as it has always happened in order for the archetypal libido to invest the ceremony. As Jung says, to change even one little point is to make a mistake.

Whether it is by mistakes being made or simply by the force of history, the rituals and dogmas of the Church have become obsolete. As Jung put it, we have an intellect now that no longer understands them. They have become antiquated. The moment of their becoming so, however, is the beginning, the nativity even, of psychology.

In this connection (and bearing in mind our Jungian adaptation of Kohut's account of the Oedipus *phase* and its disintegration into an Oedipus *complex*), let us again recall Jung's statement about psychology's having arisen as the consequence of what he calls "an unparalleled impoverishment of symbolism":

Since the stars have fallen from heaven and our highest symbols have paled, a secret life holds sway in the unconscious. That is why we have a psychology today, and why we speak of the unconscious. All this would be quite superfluous in an age or culture that possessed symbols. Symbols are spirit from above, and under those conditions the spirit is above too. Therefore it would be a foolish and senseless undertaking for such people to wish to experience or investigate an unconscious that contains nothing but the silent, undisturbed sway of nature. Our unconscious, on the other hand, hides living water, spirit that has become nature, and that is why it is disturbed.[64]

The stars that Jung refers to are the archetypal images or sublated sign stimuli that triggered our releasing mechanisms during the long, religious phase of our Western history. Christ, of course, has been the principal symbolic form, the most important star, of the past two thousand years. Others mentioned in these pages are Mary, Joseph, and the dove. According to Jung, we speak of the unconscious today because of the demise of symbols such as these. It is their irrevocable fall that gives rise to psychology, even as it is through their fall that analysis could come upon the twentieth century like an annunciation.

In this connection, we may recall again Jones's grotesque account of Christian symbolism with a new appreciation. In his essays, "The Madonna's conception through the ear" and "A psycho-analytic study of the Holy Ghost concept," Jones portrays the Oedipus complex of amorphous instincts, or part-drives, that the Christian Anthropos unravels to become under the conditions brought about by the impoverishment or emptying out of the symbolic matrix in which the soul had previously found its dignity and metaphysical sanction. But is this truth? Is it really enough to just have knowledge of how humans behave when what Freud pejoratively called their illusions have been stripped away?

Our quote from Jung raises a different possibility. The stars that have fallen from the heavens have activated the waters below, i.e., the interior waters of the unconscious. A "recrudescence of individual symbol-formation" follows the decline of Christian symbolism, albeit in the form of symptoms.[65] At first this forming of new symbols bears, as does any transference, traces of the figures that preceded it. Dora, according to Freud, gazed at the Sistine Madonna in silent admiration. Jung, as the subject of an association experiment given to him by Ludwig Binswanger, gave away something of the complex underpinning his countertransference to Spielrein (who shows up as "Russia" in his responses) when he said "Star of Bethlehem" and then, debriefing this association, "Unto us a child is born."[66] In a complementary way, Spielrein, writing to Jung years later, explicitly identified the Siegfried figure of her dreams and fantasies with Christ – "Siegfried for me = Christ," she said, "and yet it is not exactly the same."[67] And this is to say nothing of Lacan, who was celebrated within his coterie as "the Hysteric," and whose teaching, it has been said, "reproduced the annunciation scene with Lacan playing all the parts. Sometimes he was the space that welcomes the word; sometimes, as Christ born of the Virgin, he transmitted it; sometimes, as man-God, he sowed it in others."[68] Such references indicative of the negativization of Christian ideas into psychology could be multiplied. The history of psycho-analysis is rife with them. Even today, Juliet Mitchell speaks of the hysteric's "parthenogenetic fantasies" and gives to a long section of one of her books the title, "The Holy Family and femininity."[69] And, of course, there is also Bollas's frequent use of religious metaphors in *Hysteria* as we have already seen.

So who is Siegfried? We will not quarrel with Spielrein's suggestion that Siegfried was a symbol for an integrated theory of psychology combining Freud's and Jung's views.[70] Nor will we contest Jung's interpretation of Siegfried as a bridge to Spielrein's future development, or take the time here to examine Jung's grappling with the whole problem of German nationalism as this showed up in his dreams as a blond youth to whom he gave the same name.[71] These, among other things, are what Siegfried was for Spielrein and Jung. For us, Siegfried is something else. Letting his specific image drop away (Spielrein's image of a child, Jung's of a blond youth), and forgetting his proper name as well, we may understand this figure in the light of all that has come after. Indeed, when interpreting the dreams of our analytic forebears, we need only look at the work that they subsequently produced. The interpretation of any dream of Jung's, or any countertransference he ever had to a patient for that matter, is analytical psychology, the discipline, the science, as he himself acknowledged in the aforementioned letter to Spielrein in which he speaks of what her love of him had taught him about the psyche.

Just as the philosopher's stone was known by a thousand names, so there are any number of alternative terms for the *negative* Siegfried: complex, archetype, self, sexuality, psychic energy, personal myth, anima/animus, collective unconscious, transference, transcendent function, synchronicity, psychic non-ego. For, whatever these terms literally refer to or mean in their positivity and in their difference one from another, they are, as Jung said of the symbol, the best approximation of the unknown in relation to which we are constituted as subjects. Said another way, all of these concepts, insofar as they are psychological (having their essence in negativity), are sublated symbols, modes of thinking. Compensatory to the amorphous instincts which have fallen out of the keep of the mighty images of religion (the id, ego, and superego of Freud), they are, as Campbell said of art, a new habitat of sublated sign stimuli and sublated instinct, but now beyond art: the soul as logical life or, more simply put, thought. Psychology, in its highest determination as logical negativity, is what now releases the *totus homo*, the New Anthropos (though this is everywhere brought down to the level of personal egos even as the Self in much of Jungian discourse seems mostly to mean *my* self). Vice versa, psychology is generated only as the action or contribution of the *totus homo*: your thinking and mine as universal, your thinking and mine lived in the spirit of Kant's categorical imperative, Nietzsche's *amor fati*, and the *Auseinandersetzung* of Jung.[72] As Jung expresses this (retaining the language of religion beneath the sublation of it, which psychology is): "Whoever knows God has an effect on him."[73]

Storks' nests, neologisms, *kenosis*, and negativity

Jean Laplanche, co-author of *The Language of Psychoanalysis* and a translator of Freud into French, justifies the occasional creation of neologisms on the part of the translator by drawing an analogy to an ethological story about storks' nests. When the French government consulted ethologists regarding how storks, which had long deserted France, might be brought back, they were advised to construct artificial nests for them. The theory was that the birds would be attracted to these nests and return, making a new adaption to the environment they had left. And this is exactly what happened. Storks were attracted to the artificial nests and populations of them were re-established. According to Laplanche, the successful neologism works in the same way in the making of translations, like those he made of Freud, from one language to another.[74] Pushing this analogy further, we could say that the word, or better yet, the notion "Psychology," is, in a more literal sense than Laplanche intends, a neologistic storks' nest, a new sign stimuli. "Transference," "libido," "repetition compulsion" – these psychoanalytic terms, as well as those we listed from Jung, and besides these the many other terms of other thinkers, are likewise neologistic lures and sublated sign stimuli, a whole new habitat even, of logical negativity extending inward in every direction toward an infinite, interiorized horizon.

In a turn on what Bollas said of the speech of the hysteric, we may say that in a sense these terms are also being used, not so much for what they mean or convey as for what they affect and release. Or, putting this another way, these terms retain the affect and demandingness of the hysteric, the affect and demandingness of the soul, within and beneath themselves as a part of their meaning. Though we take them literally and study them as such, looking to evolutionary genetics in an effort to prove the existence of archetypes, or to events in the consulting room to substantiate ideas such as projective identification and repetition compulsion, it is their negativity as variations of the logically negative notion "soul," or their having arisen as the result of the interiorization of phenomena from extra-psychological domains into themselves in terms of that notion, that I wish to stress here.

Jung can be read as making a very similar point to this himself when he speaks of the interchangeability of words such as "mana," "daimon," and "God" with their scientific synonym "the unconscious," or again when he speaks of psychology as a translation of the archaic speech of myth into our modern mythologem, science.[75] In keeping with his recognition that eternal truth needs new forms that change with the spirit of the times, Jung recognized that we cannot really go back to these antiquated terms, except as a *façon de parler*. On this point, however, he equivocated. It is precisely as a manner of speaking to or engaging with "the unconscious" that these terms retain a lasting value. "The great advantage of the concepts 'daimon' and 'God,'" he states in his memoirs,

> lies in making possible a much better objectification of the *vis-à-vis* [with the unconscious], namely a *personification* of it. Their emotional quality confers life and effectuality upon them. Hate and love, fear and reverence, enter the scene of the confrontation and raise it to a drama. What has merely been "displayed" becomes "acted." *The whole man is challenged and enters the fray with his total reality*. Only then can he become whole and only then can "God be born," that is, enter into human reality and associate with man in the form of "man." By this act of incarnation man – that is, his ego – is inwardly

replaced by "God," and God becomes outwardly man, in keeping with the saying of Jesus: "Who sees me, sees the Father."[76]

For Jung, the advantage of the terms "daimon" and "God" has to do with their objectified form and personified vividness, their emotional quality and effectiveness. These, he maintains, invigorate the *vis-à-vis* with what science too knowingly calls the unconscious such that "the whole man is challenged and enters the fray with his total reality." While we can agree with Jung about the importance of the whole man's entering the fray, the most recent thought in analytical psychology would critique his emphasis on objectification, personification, emotion, and vivid experiencing as a lapse into pre-psychological positivism. For psychology, it may now be argued (and here again we follow Giegerich), must push off from all such outside facts and external foundations (authenticating dreams, feelings, and experiences) if it is to speculatively plumb the abyss of its own inner infinity or logical life as thought.[77]

Late in his life, Jung came very close to recognizing that psychology must move beyond both scientific empiricism and the sensory-intuitional mode of myth and religion if it is to come home to itself more completely. In the paragraph in his memoirs immediately following the one we have just discussed, he dialectically turns against what he had said in praise of mythological terminology to consider its shortcomings. In this connection, significantly enough, he anticipates our present emphasis on negativity by making a passing reference to the theological notion of *kenosis*.

> The Christian's ordinary conception of God is of an omnipotent, omniscient, and all-merciful Father and Creator of the world. If this God wishes to become man, an incredible *kenosis* (emptying) is required of Him in order to reduce His totality to the infinitesimal human scale. Even then it is hard to see why the human frame is not shattered by the incarnation.[78]

Of course, the human frame is shattered, as we see each day in our practices, and in the church on the corner every Sunday. God's emptying himself has led to every imaginable ill. Our positivity as persons with this or that kind of psychology and this or that kind of body is at once both inflated and negated by the symptoms that the emptying out of the God-image gives rise to. Clinging to old identities and former worlds, we resist the negativizing revelation of the greater figure that we are within the new constitution of reality which consciousness has created. If, however, we recognize with Jung that the day of judgement for our littleness and the littleness of our psychology has dawned, we may also discover that we are capable of facing what has befallen us. Rising to the challenge as to an initiatory ordeal, we may find that we can accept the shards of our suffering, not as *our* neurosis only (the cat *we* cannot lift), but as *the* neurosis, the Midgard Serpent, the crisis of the times. Just as Jacob wrestled with the angel at the ford (and Jung and Spielrein with the figure of Siegfried), so we must wrestle with the mysterium of

God's absence just as we find it (or it finds us) at the abyss-edge of the world's split.

Responding in this way we are no longer only the children of our parents. Nor are we, on that model, any longer in the parent–child relation with God. For the all-encompassing psyche, which God has become in our time, "giv[ing] its own specific answer to the influences at work upon it,"[79] plays through our responses now, as if God in the form of his absence were releasing the thought of our hearts as surely as any previous sign stimulus had ever released any previous action in any earlier world. Or, revising this statement in light of the consideration that thought has a degree of freedom that the instinct it retains within and beneath itself never had, the sunken initiation that neurosis is in our times requires that we come forward to be this response. As St Paul declared to the Galatians, "I live, yet not I, but Christ liveth in me."[80] It is in this way (i.e., through our being at one and the same time the concrete individual what we are and exponents of that spirit through which God has emptied himself into us in our times) that psychology pushes off from the religious prefiguration of itself to become, or rather comprehend itself as, the utterly new and radically interiorized habitat that it is.

But what, then, of our problems? Existing as the persons that we are in the particular bodies that we have, our problems continue; there is no end to that. Comfort comes, however, as Christ said the Paraclete would, when these are understood dialectically in terms of the initiation we have just described and when psychology, pushing off from these as its focus, reaches out to the highest to become, in itself and for itself, the new constitution of reality.

A page further on in his memoirs from the passage in which he speaks of *kenosis*, Jung examines this incarnational emptying of the Godhead from the point of view of creaturely man. It will be recalled that for Jung the outpouring of the Holy Spirit upon the apostles at Pentecost meant that they, *and everyone after them*, "received the *filatio* – sonship of God. . . ."[81] The result of this, he explains, is that the opposition – God and man – gave way such that humans were invested with the (newly effective, i.e., existentially constellated) opposites within the God-image. With this development, the human process (except where it has disintegrated to become an Oedipus complex) becomes, in Jung's view, the vehicle of God's continuing incarnation; individuation, as the synthesis of the divine antinomies in creaturely man, the human challenge. We could also say that with this development, God (i.e., the whole mythological mode of being-in-the-world) sublated himself to become the *form* of human consciousness.

> [T]he necessary incarnation of God – the essence of the Christian message – can then be understood as man's creative confrontation with the opposites and their synthesis in the self, the wholeness of [man's] personality. The unavoidable internal contradictions in the image of a Creator-god can be reconciled in the unity and wholeness of the self as the *coniunctio oppositorum* of the alchemists or as a *unio mystica*. . . . That is the meaning of divine service, of the service which man can render to God, that light may emerge from the

darkness, that the Creator may become conscious of His creation, and man conscious of himself.[82]

Negativizing phylogenesis in the vessel of hysteria

God's emptying himself of his divinity to become man is a difficult idea. Jung, as we have just seen, connected this up with the human individuation process. Perhaps, however, it would be better to say that the notion of God's emptying himself to become man is Christianity's way of depicting the negativizing movement from positivity into reflection which we, following Giegerich, have claimed to be generative of psychology. But let us be clear: the term psychology, as we use it in these pages, does not refer to a particular kind of psychology. It is not something positive – a practice that one can be trained in or some kind of method. Still less is its form that of some woodsy New Age church of self-worship in which the word "sacred" is bandied about – heir though psychology is of the religion that preceded it. Rather, in its highest, or (putting this less grandly) its proper sense, psychology is consciousness – not in the personalistic sense of a particular state in someone's mind, but as the logical status in which the whole of reality is now constituted.

There was a time when consciousness existed only as the faintest glimmer of awareness. It was transcended on all sides by matter as by the severest of gods. Everything was created in the image and the likeness of everything else in a seething turmoil. It was an immense step in the history of consciousness for these obdurate conditions to be mythologically reflected. And then it took a series of other momentous steps – each one a step against the outwardness or positivity of what had been before – to culminate in the situation we are in today in which what had once been but a faint glimmer has increased to the point where it completely permeates the world and even throws its beacon light into remote reaches of the universe. This being our situation now, we can no longer claim to be transcended by powers acting upon us from without in the way we could before such a turning-of-the-tables upon creation occurred. The world is in the status of psychology now, more so even than Jung realized when he looked out over the immense herds of zebra, gazelle, gnu, antelope, and warthog while travelling in Africa and felt within himself, as he later put it: "Man, I, in an invisible act of creation put the stamp of perfection on the world by giving it objective existence."[83]

By definition, God is not an existing entity in the sense that people, cars, and buildings are. His existence, if we may use that word, is logically negative – in our times absolutely so. But this was not always the case. From ancient times right up to the dawn of Christianity the gods actually were manifest in things; they did exist in positive form, or rather, in the first negation of this, as the frost-demons and boulder-giants which animate the whole of creation in the mythological mode of being-in-the-world.

In the Garden of Eden, Adam and Eve could hide from God, or at least they tried to. God for them was a sensual reality that they could invoke and try to propitiate.

It is even recorded that their illustrious descendant Moses saw God from behind! With the birth and death of Christ, however, the Light of the World (as Christ came to be known) was negativized into us. And since this change in the world's metaphysical status has occurred we can no longer say, "I don't know," when asked about the fruit we have taken from the Tree of Knowledge and of the whereabouts of Eve. How can we when, through our having eaten that fruit and digested it at the Last Supper, we have been equipped to say with Paul that it is no longer merely we who speak (out of *our* faint glimmer), but the great universal light that has been achieved through the long period of earthly phylogenesis that speaks through us at the same time? There is no place to hide under the conditions of such an all-permeating and all-comprehending consciousness; no hiding place except, of course, the one we make for ourselves through neurosis.

This reference to neurosis, following as it does upon our discussion of God's emptying himself to become a man, brings us back to hysteria as the Mary of psychoanalysis. If the *kenosis* or emptying of God is Christianity's way of depicting the negativizing movement from positivity into reflection, all the more so is the story of the Virgin Birth as this was told at the beginning of the Christian aeon and, again now, in analysts' consulting rooms at that aeon's end.

In an earlier section we have already made the link between the Virgin Mary and hysteria, showing this fantasy to be at work in the theory and practice of both psychoanalysis and analytical psychology. We have named names (Anna O., Dora, Sabina Spielrein) and quoted authorities (Bollas, Jung, Kristeva, Lacan). We have followed Jung's account of falling stars and the recrudescence of individual symbol formation in the forming of the psychology of the unconscious. It remains to follow this movement, which is at once Mary's womb and the wandering womb of hysteria, logically, from the positivity of inorganic matter to (the darkness of this made visible) psychology.

We said that it was a momentous journey from matter in its "lifeless" state as matter (if matter ever was "lifeless") to the emergence of organisms and, beyond that, to the first glimmer of consciousness. In *Beyond the Pleasure Principle* Freud speculated about that development, that movement. Beginning with lifeless, inorganic matter, he imagined a tension building up and quickly cancelling itself out – or, to insert our word here – negating itself. But the crack in everything was even then in everything. The cancelling, negating, and falling back movement became divided against itself. Interferences imposed themselves. Resistances queered the pitch. The road to inertia – what Freud called the death-drive – became more and more circuitous; and in this way life dialectically constituted itself in what Freud describes as a moment of which we can form no impression, but which we might think of as like the moment (more easily represented) in which consciousness first emerged from the unconscious.[84]

It was then a tremendous step, an infinity of steps even, from the emergence of life to the dawning of consciousness as we know it now. In Freud's account, a simple vesicle at some point emerged, which became conscious by acquiring a surface boundary. As this vesicle's outer surfaces were perturbed by the energies of the surrounding universe (even as were Odin's as he hung on the windy tree, and Christ's as he hung on the Cross), their death saved the interior layers from a similar fate. The dead surface, thenceforth, worked as a protective shield and threshold of perception, filtering out some stimuli while letting minute intensities of other stimuli pass through.[85] In this way, life became sentient. What Freud would later call "evenly hovering attention" had made its first appearance in the scheme of things.

Turning, now this way, now that, the simple vesicle developed very specific tropisms; and by virtue of these it was able to worship the sun as well as other things such as moisture, wind, and night. Religion had made its first appearance. At this point in the process (which could only be measured in geological time) the simple vesicle, a more complex organism by now, began to display more diverse instincts and to respond to various sign stimuli. And as these were lost and replaced again and again, the world reflected itself in many gods. This certainly was an important milestone. With the appearance of the gods – even angry, persecutory ones – the world became a friendlier place. Swaddled in what Freud called "its protective shield against stimuli,"[86] the living being perceived the world outside and beyond itself as a containing mother. Moving into crevices and caves it found another mother on the level of a new sign stimulus. And with the passing of the millennia, caves become catacombs, churches, families, universities, and analytic offices. At the same time, developing skin, hide, shell, kaftan, toga and designer fashions, it became sexual, a sign stimulus for its mates. Brightening its hues ostentatiously, even hysterically, beyond those made available to it by nature – through the use of nose-rings, scarification, jewellery, and other aphrodisiac adornments – it even became what is called in ethology a "super-normal sign stimulus" for itself and its sexual objects.[87] With this development, the inwardness of being became a source of sur-natural selection, or spiritual election, operating alongside the naturally selective effect of the outwardness of things. The archetypal transference and the anima–animus syzygy had made their first, appreciable appearance.

The reference to the mother archetype we have just made does not occur in Freud. It is our addition (as are the references to Odin, Christ, evenly hovering attention, sign stimuli, and the syzygy). We add it in order to locate the womb of Mary within the larger framework of what Freud called the phylogenetic fantasy. In squaring Mary with the phylogenetic fantasy and evolutionary theory in this way, we make no claim against the immaculateness of her conception, but merely show to what extent she ever and always was the daughter of her son.

Most personalistic psychologies, of course, start with the mother and with the "facilitating environment" that she and the family, as "social uterus," provide for that highly complex vesicle suspended in their midst, the human infant. We, too, go back to the mother, not the personal mother who was the source of our lives, but to the mother-image as the precursive form of (psycho)logical life.

Logically speaking, the mother idea is that of nourishing containment. Leaving the important phenomenon of nourishment to one side, we will concern ourselves here with the second aspect of this idea, the notion of containment. The mother is all that carries and bears; she is a container, a cave, a vessel, a womb. Her symbols are legion: Mother Earth, the goddesses of antiquity, the Gnostic *krater* (mixing bowl), the alchemical *vas*, and the *temenos* of the analytic consulting room. The important thing in all this for our discussion, and the point of our phylogenetic fantasy, is that the essence of the containing mother vessel is its emptiness or negativity. The emptying of God, the advent of consciousness or psychology, began already long ago in the refuges and hideaways, grottoes, holes and sheltering caves that were reflected mythically as the mother goddess.

Linking these thoughts up with analytical psychology's distinction between the mother and the anima, we can say that the difference between them is the same as that between sign stimuli and super-normal stimuli. Though both partake of the "emptiness" that Jung called "the great feminine secret,"[88] the mother is a more concretely positive presentation of emptiness or negativity. The anima, by contrast – now attracting interest, now fading away like a mirage – is a more reflected, super-normal or aesthetic image of negativity, a lure, in the last analysis, for the animus of thought. At the empty tomb of Christ (a tomb that we regard as being already present from the foundations of the world) the mother and anima are represented by Mary, the mother of Jesus, and Mary Magdalene respectively.

Negativizing the vessel

In an essay on the feminine principle in which he reflects critically upon some of Jung's late ideas concerning the Virgin Mary, Giegerich gives the following psychological account of two important forms in the history of the soul: the Gnostic *krater* (mixing bowl) and the alchemical vessel or *vas*. "Their essence," writes Giegerich,

> is in the nothingness that they enclose, and the surrounding substantiality or materiality is, so to speak, no more than a necessary evil whose sole function it is to give that nothingness a determinate presence. *Krater* and *vas* are not supposed to be a "something" in their own right, but mere receptacles *for* things or substances. Thus they are images for *(logical) negativity* (even if still natural, concretistic images of such negativity).[89]

Continuing his argument, Giegerich reflects specifically upon the alchemical vessel. "[T]he alchemical vessel," he writes

> was supposed to be made out of glass, transparent. This transparent nature of the containing *vas* can be interpreted as an attempted negation of the opaqueness and impenetrable substantiality of its material nature and, by extension, of matter as such. What is actually intended (although of course not fully realized in practical reality) by the transparency and hollowness of the vessel is the negation altogether of the material reality of the vessel. Ideally the vessel

is supposed to be immaterial, absolutely inconspicuous, totally disappearing from our vision as a thing in its own right, in order to give exclusively room for, and allow one's attention to go all the more to, the substantial contents it may contain. Ultimately, it is in itself the image *of* absence or a self-sublating, self-negating image, a non-image. This negativity does not mean that the vessel should not *exist* as a container. It only means that it should not do its containing *in a material, natural way*. While the Gnostic *krater* as a kind of baptismal vessel was merely *filled* with spirit, the alchemical vessel, at least in the last analysis, is supposed to be, in itself a *spiritual* container, a *vas* that, *contra naturam*, contains in a nonphysical, nonliteral, that is, in a "spiritual" way.[90]

We can transpose Giegerich's logical analysis of the alchemical vessel backwards in time to the aforementioned caves and grottos of the primeval landscape and forwards in time to the womb of Mary and the negative symptoms of hysteria. For the *tertium comparationis* of all these vessel-like forms is their cavernous non-materiality and containing emptiness. Or, turning this around (even as Freud's anamnesis of hysteria found it already present in the caves of the Ice Age), we can follow the wandering womb of hysteria through a series of successive negations through time from the planet's primordial beginnings to the present day, in which consciousness itself exists as the unseen spiritual container of the whole world. Just as Christ was "slain from the foundations of the world," so too, within the inner reaches of matter itself, have Mary and hysteria been present all along as the empty womb-like tomb from which Christ and psychology, in the feeblest anticipation of their later forms, even then resurrected themselves, first in the form of the *lumen natura* or light of nature, and then, pushing off from nature, as reflectedness *per se*, logical life.

There is more that is helpful to us from Giegerich's article. In another passage he describes the sublation of the alchemical vessel as this occurred in the constitution of the mind during the alchemical stage of its soul-making:

> For many centuries the psyche of Western man, through the eyes of all the individual alchemists, stared at the alchemical vessel and what it contained. What happens when you stare long enough and soulfully at an object before your eyes? You become assimilated to it in your consciousness. To put the same thing another way, the object is (as we are wont to say in psychology) "integrated" into consciousness. Consciousness itself is, as it were, "infected" by its own content: what as long as you look at the thing in front of you exists as a *content of*, or *image in*, consciousness slowly turns into your attitude, your mindset, into the very *form* or logical constitution of consciousness itself. The object comes home to you, comes home to the subject. It loses the form of object and takes the form of the subjective style of thinking and experiencing, and thus the form *of form*. The original "object" of conscious-ness is dematerialized, spiritualized – sublated. This alchemical process of

distillatio, sublimatio, evaporatio is what in the history of the Western soul happened with the alchemical vessel itself. The alchemical vessel slowly ceased to be an object or content of consciousness and a literal instrument for its operations in the laboratory and was "interiorized" so as to become the logical form of consciousness. This transition has . . . two distinct aspects. First, it is the transition from "out there" (*in* reality, *in* nature) or "in front of consciousness" to "in here", "in ourselves" as subjectivity in the sense of "inherent in the *structure* of human consciousness itself"; secondly, it is ipso facto the transformation from "substance" or "content" to "form", from imaginal shape to attitude, category, perspective, spirit, or thought (in the sense of the act of thinking, comprehending).[91]

Again, we can read what Giegerich has to say back into the earliest phases of our phylogenetic fantasy. In such a reading, the alchemical laboratory appears in its most rudimentary or elemental form as the seething turmoil of phylogenesis itself. The observing alchemist gazing at the vessel (interiorizing it, thereby, into the form of his consciousness) corresponds, likewise, to the sentient vesicle looking out from the protective shield. And what of the alchemical vessel? This would be "the without of things," to use Teilhard de Chardin's expression,[92] the without within which the immanence of consciousness, even back at the beginning of time and within the merest of chemical processes, had already appeared.

Moving forward, as world-cleaving history commands, we find as well that we can say of Christianity and of contemporary science all that Giegerich has said of the alchemical vessel and its negation and interiorization into the form of contemporary consciousness. Centuries of meditation upon Christian symbolism have led in a similar way to the sublation of the container these once provided. Indeed, the Enlightenment mode of consciousness and the sciences associated with it can be seen as the interiorized form of religious objects, which were the content of much previous theological reflection. Meditating upon such things as gods and angels in the period prior to the Enlightenment (when such beings could still be experienced epiphanically), consciousness eventually became "infected" by these contents, even as it had been, long before this, when it reflected its first religious objects – the elemental forces beyond its protective shield – into itself as mythological figures. Taking its theophanic and symbolic objects into itself, consciousness ceased to observe them any longer "out there." As Giegerich argues with respect to the alchemists gazing soulfully at the *vas*, the content observed gave rise to a new form of consciousness. No longer was awareness focused upon gods and angels and points of doctrine concerning these, for it had itself become, in the manner of, say, an Aristotle, a Plato, or a Bertrand Russell, angelic and divine.

Giegerich's account of the alchemists staring at their alchemical retorts holds true for psychoanalysis and hysteria as well. Inserting these terms into his text in place of his references to the alchemist and alchemical vessel, we arrive at the following statement:

For more than a century now the psyche of Western man, through the hearts and minds of individual psychoanalysts, has focused its attention upon its version of the alchemical vessel, the hysterical patient. And what happens when you direct your clinical attention long enough and soulfully enough at the patient before you? You become assimilated to him or her in your consciousness. To put the same thing another way, the patient or hysterical syndrome (as we say in psychology) becomes "integrated" into consciousness.

With this Giegerichian analysis of hysteria analytical psychology's first alchemist concurs. As we discussed in an earlier section, having interiorized the hysteria and the other conditions he observed "out there" in his patients into himself as the "inner woman" and into his psychology in the form of the anima concept, Jung told the audience of his 1925 seminar about how, earlier in his career, "I could only admit the fact [of an autonomous fantasy life] in myself through the process of projecting my material into Miss Miller's. Or, to put it even more strongly, passive thinking seemed to me such a weak and perverted thing that I could only handle it through a diseased woman."[93]

Jung was not alone in making the kind of projection he describes himself as having made with respect to Miss Miller. Regarding themselves as scientists, all analysts during that period studied psychic phenomena as positive facts "out there" in front of them. They did not yet have the critical means to comprehend that psychology was being born in the rude stable of hysteria (i.e., as a condition that patients have) because it could not yet provide room for itself in the inn of its own self-comprehension. Little wonder, then, that psychology's first patients suffered the symptoms they did. Psychology was itself a wandering womb after the fashion of its two mothers, Mary and hysteria.

Even today, psychology exists in hysterical form, seeking to mirror its unapprehended inner infinity outwardly in its patients, as if their problems were the limit or horizon of the soul. Existing everywhere in this disintegrated state, psychology, even in its Jungian school, has lost or repressed the awareness of itself it attained through Jung. It has quite forgotten (if it ever knew) what it is about, or rather, that it is not *about* anything. Unstable in its identity, it is riven by numerous dissociations. These, more and more, it acts out by masquerading as another kind of science with a more "solid" foundation. Or, turning promiscuous, it shamelessly consorts with other disciplines. Unable to comprehend its own negativity, it continues to project this into patients, once again in the name of hysteria, such that they, by virtue of their symptoms, become the positive bearers of its own logical negativity.

But like cures like. Reflecting upon what it finds of itself in its patients, psychology begins to learn again now, at the beginning of a new millennium, what it is to be truly psychological. It learns again, if it ever learned before, of the *un*-ness of consciousness, which is to say, of the negativity that consciousness within itself is founded upon. Losing its senses, even as the hysterical patients with whom psychoanalysis began had lost theirs to the sensory amnesias from which they suffered, it develops a sublated form of perception – putting the lie to the adage that there is "nothing in the mind except by way of the senses."

Sight gives way to insight, hearing to comprehending, smell to intuition, taste to aesthetic discernment, and touch to sensitivity in the subtle sphere of mental life. And with this development the body (as Freud might have put it)[94] ceases to be a messenger that can deliver its message only through being shot. For having been transfigured by the psychology which its negation has ennobled and crowned, it returns to its senses, relieved of the burden of having to perceive what cannot be perceived by its sense organs, but only known, i.e., imagined and thought by the mind.

The lessons of hysteria continue. Suspecting physical causes (such as the family psychodynamic issues discussed by Bollas and Mitchell), psychology gradually learns to leave these beneath itself (not untreated, but unhallowed). With something of the *belle indifférence* it first glimpsed in its patients, it turns away from matter and the body, medicine and the natural sciences. Freed from these empirical touchstones, it learns to think on its own authority – fantastically, speculatively, psychologically – out of the depths of its own notion. Seduced into reductive theories by the allure of its patient, it learns again the age-old lesson that must be learned at every level of creation: to reject the seduction theory, in whatever form it presents itself; to push off from all materiality and positivity, negating these into consciousness and reflection. Or, gathering all of these statements into one simple expression, we can say that from hysteria psychology now learns again, at the dawn of a new aeon (and in a more subtle way than ever before) to concern itself with the annunciatory musings of its own virginal conception.

Christopher and Christ, the soul's child and the dove

In the previous few sections we have reflected motifs and images from Christianity, alchemy, psychoanalysis, and the phylogenetic fantasy into themselves and into each other in a very concentrated manner. The effect of this exercise was that the positivity of each area of interest negated the positivity of the others, such that the Mercurius imprisoned within them all could be freed as thought. It should also be noted, however, that each of the areas of interest that we played off against the others in this way is deeply rooted in psychoanalysis. Our references to phylogeny, for instance, connect up with *Beyond the Pleasure Principle*, *Totem and Taboo*, and "Overview of the transference neuroses," – three seminal works of Freud's that were written in terms of what he called the "phylogenetic fantasy," that is, in the "scientific myth" genre. Also traditional to psychoanalysis is thinking in terms of religious figures. Jung's works are very strongly informed by this approach. Among Freud's works, the obvious references are to his writings on Moses and on Leonardo da Vinci. More to our present point, however, is a passage from *Group Psychology and the Analysis of the Ego*, in which Freud employs a religious riddle to express his dissatisfaction with suggestion as a viable explanation or theory:

"Christopher bore Christ; Christ bore the whole world; say, where did Christopher then put his foot."[95] Freud attempts no answer to this "old conundrum," as he calls it. He takes it for granted that the problem is insoluble. But the answer is plain. Christopher's foot, while being *literally* planted in the stream across which he carried Christ was *logically* planted in Christ, i.e., in the world as it had been logically constituted within Christian consciousness.

As we said above, what was once a faint glimmer of light in the darkness of matter at the dawn of time, has become in the meantime (and in no small measure due to the development of the spirit within Christianity) an all-pervading consciousness in which all our lives are contained. Just as Christopher bore Christ, the bearer of the whole world, so we have a consciousness that is not only in us, but all around us now, in an all-comprehending way.

What a different turn psychoanalysis would have taken had it accepted the challenge presented to it in the form of the riddle Freud mentions, the challenge to think dialectically. Had it done so, I dare say, the form of its thinking would have provided the Joseph and Mary of our times – psychology and hysteria – with the Ave Maria that they so desperately need. But Freud set up his psychology rationalistically, in terms of a dichotomy or split. On the one side of this divide, he placed reason, the reality principle, and the secondary process; on the other side he placed the pleasure principle, the primary process, and the various modes of the dreamwork. With this move Freud dished the whole problem of the rupture in the soul, reducing it, with his characteristic pessimism, to the divisions within people. Castrated in this way, his psychology could never be the answer to the rupture in the soul, i.e., it could never be the new, sublated sign stimulus that our times require. And as Giegerich has shown, though Jung was as aware as Freud was of civilization's discomfiting "split in the world" as he called it, he, too, foreclosed the possibility of fully responding to it in his psychology by his positivistic insistence upon empiricism.[96]

It is all very well to distinguish on empirical grounds between "two principles in mental functioning" (Freud) or between "two kinds of thinking" (Jung),[97] so long as psychology takes this division into itself theoretically as its own, not in the this-then-that mode of Bollas's cycles of condensation and dissemination, but as that one kind of thinking that is the union of these opposites, dialectical thought.

But pushing off from these traditions at the outset of a new century, in which psychology will no longer be a function of people's narcissism, *we* can hear the self-negating, self-sublating, *totus homo*-releasing Ave Maria that psychology utters for our times with a clarity with which our analytic forebears could not. And hearing this, we can also know (as did Joseph and Mary at the beginning of the aeon that has just ended) the spiritual legitimacy of that pregnancy, seemingly so false and hysterical, which psychology is.

But once again, the question raises itself: who is the child that psychology is both pregnant with and born from? The answer, which is as near to us as thought itself, has been the open secret of this book: psychology itself. Like the vessels and wombs – Marian, alchemical, hysterical – from which it has emerged, psychology is logical negativity, logical movement, logical life. Indeed, as Giegerich (the Gabriel, Magi, and Herod of its negativizing nativity) has stated, in words that leave the religious imagery of this book behind as yet another seductive positivity to be rejected,

> the soul of a theory is the Notion or Concept whose unfolding the theory is. Psychological theory is a singular case. Psychology is the only discipline in which the life-giving *soul* of the theory happens to be the Notion *of soul* and where what it is the notion *of* is itself nothing other than *Notion*. For Soul is Notion. It is not the notion of an empirical "factor" or "fact" called "soul." The soul does not exist (out there in "reality"), it is not an entity, nothing ontological. It is (only?) *logical*, "just" a Notion, a thought, a word (but word not merely as *flatus vocis*). The word soul is not a significant having a signified. It refers to nothing outside of itself, only to the notion or thought that it means *within* itself or posits in and through itself.[98]

The "soul's child" is the notion of soul itself – self-reflection, self-relation, i.e., the logical life of the pregnant thought that it is. As such, it is not (merely) a notion in someone's head or a feeling in someone's heart; rather, it is the all-encompassing, all-encircling neotic inwardness of whatever real situation we are in. Psychology, that is to say, is apocalyptically or logically the truth of whatever we grapple with if we grapple with it thinkingly, as the unity of individual and universal, on the one hand, and of rupture and order (at the same time) on the other. As Jung (speaking as a psychologist) said, the *vis-à-vis* with God has been emptied into humankind. Ultimately, our situation, at least since the temple veil was rent from top to bottom by the death of Christ, is that we find ourselves between the effective opposites of a split world. For even the cross was emptied into us. Psychology, under these conditions, is the negative, interiorization of this split (which it would be neurotic to deny in favor of the quick fixes of sham meanings and fantasied visions of unity) into itself as the logical form of dialectical thought.[99]

So what about the image that has provided the title for this book? Leonard Cohen, we will recall, spoke of the "holy dove" and of its plight of being "never free." The poet is right. The dove is never free, for while it is a symbol of the spirit, it has the determinate form of a bird. And this is why, as we indicated in the introduction, it too must be negated, sublated. Its image-form, though rarer to be sure than the object relationships, drives, and clinical facts that psychoanalysis has founded itself upon, is still too determinately positive and external to truly present the absolute (i.e., embracing) inwardness of the soul, which now, as the logical constitution or home of reality, has taken all externality into itself. As Giegerich has expressed this to me in a personal letter,

> "The dove" as image or metaphor is self-contradictory. It unwittingly undoes itself that which it wants to suggest. The image of the dove holds the mind

back and down in the mode of thinking in terms of objects, things, while aiming for the spirit, the spirit that does not even blow like a wind (which is still too sensible), but is completely not-sensible, unimaginable, because it is sheer spiritual (logical) movement. The dove cannot fly! This is the contradiction. It is too fat, too heavy. Even if it literally flies, it stays a flying *object* in material reality, that as imagined object is, at each moment in time, motionless in one spot, as Zenon of Elea has shown. That is not real flying. What real flying is is *suggested* (no more) in a (German) poem that I lack the skill to adequately translate. It goes somehow like this: on its gay songs (i.e., using its own gay songs as if they were a ladder), the lark blissfully ascends into air. – The lark thus loses its material heaviness and begins to go under into its own songs. This is real flying. The flying movement is no longer a movement of a flying object, and no longer movement in space, but in spirit, and into spirit, the breakthrough from spatial imagining into thought, into bliss, into colourfulness ("gay songs": lit. colorful songs). . . .

Final Thoughts

The status of hysteria in the vision of psychology

Freud regarded psychoanalysis as toiling in the wake of the intuitions of the poets. The truth of this assertion is nowhere more evident than in the analysis of hysteria. Poetically conceived, hysteria corresponds to the figure of the inspiratrix, the figure of muse. What Beatrice was to Dante, Laura to Petrarch, and Fanny Brawne to Keats, Anna O., Dora, and Sabina Spielrein were to Breuer, Freud and Jung. The prose of these early analysts, however, often obscured this affinity. Coming from the fields of medicine and science, they developed a rather loveless language for the love with which they worked – words such as object-cathexis, transference neurosis, psychic energy, and projection. And yet, had Freud and Jung not been the wonderful stylists that they were, it is doubtful that psychoanalysis would have ever amounted to very much. Physicians though they were, they were in another sense poets.

Touching upon this issue himself in the "Prefatory remarks" to his paper on Dora, Freud writes reprovingly of the "many physicians who (revolting though it may seem) choose to read a case history of this kind not as a contribution to the psychopathology of neuroses, but as a *roman à clef* designed for their private delectation."[1] With this remark, Freud adroitly skirts the issue of his having been inspired to write his case histories in such a way that they could be read as novels. Surely, however, he is too defensive on this point. Just as an analysis can suffer from too little eros flowing between the partners (and not only from its sexualized excess, as is so widely feared), so analytic writing can suffer from a lack of liberal flourish, imaginative execution, and narrative richness. Indeed, when reading such stark and anonymous reports one is left to wonder if the dove (avatar of the love goddesses of Greece and Syria long before it became the emblem of the Holy Ghost) ever penetrated the consulting rooms of these authors. In the absence of this spirit, it is difficult to know how to credit what is being communicated. As much as one seems to learn on the technical side, one senses at the same time that the heart of the matter has not been touched. And on the heels of these reflections follows another: is the "borderline" patient, so ubiquitous in the literature today, an artifact of the analysts' own dull prose – a jilted form of hysteria, a disintegrated form of the muse?

In his essay "Psychology and literature" (originally published as "Psychology and poetry"), Jung gives an account of the psychology of the artist and of artistic creativity that is highly pertinent to the themes that have concerned us in these pages. Leaving clinical categories behind (as was his tendency in the clinical situation as well), Jung discusses the inspiration of the poet, taking care as he does so not to reduce the poet psychologistically to the man. As might have been expected, his own anima-inspired theory of the collective unconscious is key to his approach. Just as the unconscious has a personal dimension, it has, also, a collective one, the collective unconscious. In Jung's view, it is through access to material from this source that poets and artists are inspired to create symbolical works that are replenishing of, or compensatory to, not merely their spirit in a personal sense, but the spirit of their age.

But how is material from this source brought to light? And what has this to do with hysteria and psychoanalysis? The answers we have given to these questions in the preceding chapters are succinctly summarized in Jung's text.

Writing with reference to the *Shepherd of Hermas*, the *Divine Comedy*, and *Faust*, Jung points out that in each of these works (which together span almost the whole of the Christian aeon) "a preliminary love-episode . . . culminates in a visionary experience." Further to this, Jung states that the "undisguised personal love-episode" is

> not only connected with the weightier visionary experience but actually sub-ordinated to it. This testimony is significant, for it shows that in the work of art (irrespective of the personal psychology of the poet) the vision represents a deeper and more impressive experience than human passion. In works of art of this nature – and we must never confuse them with the artist as a person – it cannot be doubted that the vision is a genuine primordial experience, no matter what the rationalists may say. It is not something derived or secondary, it is not symptomatic of something else, it is a true symbol – that is, an expression for something real but unknown.[2]

Reading this passage, we may be reminded of the adage that states that we fall in love when we need to learn something.[3] This wise saying is, of course, a contemporary version of a wisdom tradition that goes back to Socrates. According to Plato, Socrates had been taught by his muse, Diotima, that love was one of the ways that led to knowledge of the archetypes, knowledge of the forms. In Platonic tradition, the other ways to this highest form of knowledge include dialectical reason, ritual (i.e., initiation into the mysteries), and divine madness. In psychoanalysis, significantly enough, all these ways to knowing come together. Love corresponds to the transference, dialectic to the talking cure, ritual to the structure of the sessions, and madness – well, that speaks for itself. Psychoanalysis was invented as a treatment for neurotic madness in general and hysterical neuroses in particular. As for the idea that madness could have a divine aspect, it can reasonably be said that it was over this issue above all others that Freudian and Jungian psychoanalysis took leave of one another.

But let us return to our passage from Jung, picking up from where we left off above. "The love-episode," he writes,

> is a real experience really suffered, and so is the vision. It is not for us to say whether its content is of a physical, psychic, or metaphysical nature. In itself it had psychic reality, and this is no less real than physical reality. Human passion falls within the sphere of conscious experience, while the object of the vision lies beyond it. Through our senses we experience the known, but our intuitions point to things that are unknown and hidden, that by their very nature are secret.[4]

The vision-inspiring love-episode to which Jung refers has many other names within the psychoanalytic tradition. We may immediately think of the names by which the heroes and heroines of the great case histories are known. For each of these patients, at least in their negativity, was the Diotima/Xanthippe in relation to whom a particular analyst was led to knowledge, even as each analyst fulfilled this very role for his or her patient.[5] But this is just the half of it. Heir to the Ave Maria which the Angel Gabriel recited to Mary, psychology constituted itself as the sublated form of these experiences. Seeing its own Other in these cases, even as Helen, according to Goethe, may be seen in every woman, it entered two more names into its list of vision-inspiring, or better, notion-releasing loves: "hysteria" and "anima." Above all others, these are the names for that love-episode that psychoanalysis would subordinate beneath itself as beneath a weightier vision.

But what more can be said of the vision that hysteria, Spielrein, anima/animus, Anna O., Dora, Frank Miller, and so on have afforded? At this point, we can be no more specific than we have already been with respect to these questions. Nor need we be. For these names, appearing now in their negativity within the annals of psychoanalysis, are but as many question marks tacked onto the end of that most fundamental question of all psychological and psychotherapeutic work: what is psychology, what is soul?[6]

On the small scale of people's lives, one answer to this never-finally-answerable question is a new life-picture born from the achievement of a more comprehensive and comprehending attitude. Contained within the greater vision that psychology itself is when regarded from the standpoint of its being a symbolic form (in Cassirer's sense), analysts and their patients daily work through disorders, resolve complexes, and forge new attitudes.

Often this work goes very quietly. As the beneficiaries of the wild analysis through which the pioneering analysts and patients of the past created analysis, our own practices seem comparatively tame. Living off the visions inspired by the love-episodes of our forebears (or as this is more often expressed, having learned from their mistakes), it seems that we can get away with practising analysis as a merely clinical enterprise – like medicine or dentistry. But this is only how things look from the standpoint of external reflection. Viewed from within, every analysis, even the quietest, is a wild analysis or, at the very least, potentially that.

For as patients and analysts we are not only who we literally are in our positivity. Psychologically conceived, we are also all that we additionally are not – instances of the universal person, Christophers, even, of a consciousness that is greater than our own.

It is difficult for us to realize that we are not merely what we take ourselves to be. The psyche, and the unconscious too, have been literalized in our conception of them. In an unpsychological way, we have come to view them as something we have, something that is in us as an attribute of ourselves as persons – the untoward effect of some seductive cause or, equally suspect, our personal/archetypal journey to wholeness and self. But the psyche of psychology, the notion of soul, is not any of these things – not any *thing* at all. Rather, it is a whole new mode of being-in-the-world and a whole new sense of our responsibility as agents in the world.

In this connection more can be said. To draw upon an analogy to the justice system and the law courts, our daily work in neurosis (if we may call it that) can be conceived to have, in addition to its small-scale significance, a more-than-personal importance, analytic cases no less than legal ones setting precedents and amending statutes in the soul-at-large. Of course, on the surface it may not look like this. Even in a court of law, the participants in a legal action may be quite unaware of the importance of their case. Callow and self-interested, they may want nothing more than personal justice, which is to say, to have the case settled in their favour. But there is no such thing as "personal justice." Every trial reflects the human situation at issue in the notional mirror of the law. And the outcome of this impacts everyone to a greater or lesser extent, even as it generatively contributes to the notion of the law itself. It is the same with analysis. A patient may simply want to get well, which is reasonable enough. But in this aim, truth must, at the same time, be served, the level of the universal faced. For, indeed, before the bar of psychology's notion of itself, and in the all-pervading light of that truth-comprehending, truth-generating consciousness and conscience that Freud misnamed unconscious guilt, there is no cure without it. Forgetting this, ironically enough, analyst and analysand must sometimes confront their statute-changing, precedent-setting importance by holding their sessions before a magistrate in an actual court of law. But here we must note that their failure of each other may be less theirs than psychology's. For more deeply comprehended (the shadow of the analyst notwithstanding), they may have merely acted out on the level of actual behaviour a dimension of the notion, a dimension of the soul, that psychology has not yet brought home to itself.

In *The Question of Lay Analysis*, a work written as part of an unsuccessful effort to defend his fellow-analyst Theodor Reik from a legal suit that had been brought against him, Freud comments on the tendency of psychoanalysis to "[transform] every neurosis, whatever its content, into a condition of pathological love. . . ."[7] Freud's characterization of transference love as pathological brings us back to Jung's discussion of the vision-inspiring love-episode and to the connection we have drawn between this and hysteria. Though psychoanalysis itself, as we have pointed out, owes its existence to a whole series of just such love-episodes and is itself such a vision, its tendency has been to reductively recast all subsequent episodes and all further visions into its own interpretative terms. But love is unanalyzable except as the vision it would ever newly bring. Recognizing this, psychology must release itself from its horde mentality. It must let go of the facts, images, and ideas that are its wives and daughters; free the intuitions that are its sons. For only by pushing off from the positivity of all these former loves and conquests, even as the negativizing anima of hysteria seductively calls and fades, can it truly be psychology at all.

We said above that consciousness is all-pervading, and that as a result of this the world is in the status of psychology now. In a passing remark, we linked this up to the need for truth and suggested that this need is the real background to what Freud called unconscious guilt. Further to this, we may now add that unconscious guilt is what consciousness disintegrates into when psychology conceives of itself as anything less than or other than the logical form of truth itself.[8]

This insight is most important for psychotherapeutic work. Indeed, it throws much light upon the hysterical transferences that we must deal with in our practices. Under the conditions prevailing in our world today, people feel as guilty as Mary would have felt had she thought of herself as an unwed mother. But like a necessary angel, analysis comes upon us as an annunciation to remind us of our spiritual charter. It teaches us, that is to say, that we have to assume responsibility for the change that consciousness has brought to our metaphysical status, if only by making us face the many lesser truths that we hide from in neurosis.

A passage from *The Psychology of the Transference* comes to mind in connection with these final thoughts. In it Jung speaks of the connection between the psychotherapeutic enterprise and psychology itself, in the highest sense of their meaning. Amended slightly in our own minds as we read it (such that what Jung says about the psychotherapist is said also of the patient), it strikes just the right chord to bring these reflections to their end.

> [T]he bond established by the transference – however hard to bear and however incomprehensible it may seem – is vitally important not only for the individual but also for society, and indeed for the moral and spiritual progress of mankind. So, when the psychotherapist has to struggle with difficult transference problems, he can at least take comfort in these reflections. He is not just working for this particular patient, who may be quite insignificant, but for himself as well and his own soul, and in so doing he is perhaps laying an infinitesimal grain in the scales of humanity's soul. Small and invisible as this contribution may be, it is yet an *opus magnum*, for it is accomplished in a sphere but lately visited by the numen, where the whole weight of mankind's problems has settled. The ultimate questions of psychotherapy are not a private matter – they represent a supreme responsibility.[9]

Notes

Introduction: Hysteron proteron

1 C. G. Jung, *Memories, Dreams, Reflections*, New York: Random House, 1963, p. 333.
2 C. Bollas, *Hysteria*, London: Routledge, 2000, p. 179.
3 Cited in F. McLynn, *Carl Gustav Jung: A Biography*, New York: St Martin's Press, 1996, p. 326.
4 S. Freud and O. Pfister, *Psychoanalysis and Faith: The Letters of Sigmund Freud and Oskar Pfister*, London: Hogarth Press and the Institute of Psycho-Analysis, 1963, pp. 86–7.
5 As Freud wrote to Pfister, "A squeamish concern that no harm must be done to the higher things in man is unworthy of an analyst." Freud and Pfister, *Psychoanalysis and Faith*, p. 87.
6 I allude here to the phrase of Gregory of Nazianzus, who spoke of the effort to integrate the pagan world into Christianity as "tak[ing] prisoner every thought for Christ." Cited in D. Miller, *The New Polytheism: The Rebirth of the Gods and Goddesses*, Dallas: Spring Publications, 1981, p. 74.
7 E. Jones, "The Madonna's conception through the ear: a contribution to the relation between aesthetics and religion," in E. Jones, *Psycho-Myth, Psycho-History*, vol. ii, New York: Stonehill, 1974, pp. 266–357.
8 E. Jones, "A psycho-analytic study of the Holy Ghost concept," in E. Jones, *Psycho-Myth, Psycho-History*, vol. ii, pp. 358–373.
9 Jones, "A psycho-analytic study of the Holy Ghost concept," p. 363.
10 Jones, "The Madonna's conception through the ear," pp. 353, 355.
11 S. Freud, "Analysis terminable and interminable," in *Collected Papers*, vol. v, ed. J. Strachey, London: Hogarth Press and the Institute of Psycho-Analysis, p. 326.
12 C. G. Jung, "The state of psychotherapy today," *CW* 10: 367.
13 N. Coltart, *How to Survive as a Psychotherapist*, New Jersey: Jason Aronson, 1993, p. 15.
14 S. Freud, *Civilization and its Discontents*, in *Civilization, Society and Religion*, trans. J. Strachey, Pelican Freud Libarary 12, Harmondsworth: Penguin Books, 1985, p. 305.
15 C. G. Jung, *C.G. Jung Speaking: Interviews and Encounters*, ed. W. McGuire and R. F. C. Hull, Princeton, NJ: Princeton University Press, 1977, p. 294.
16 Cited by Bollas, *Hysteria*, p. 28.
17 E. Wind, *Pagan Mysteries in the Renaissance*, New York: W. W. Norton, 1968, p. 238.
18 C. G. Jung, "The spirit Mercurius," *CW* 13: 299.
19 C. G. Jung, "The psychology of the child archetype," *CW* 9i: 302.
20 H. Hesse, *Demian*, London: Panther Books, 1969, p. 7.
21 C. G. Jung, *Psychology and Religion*, *CW* 11: 146.

22 E. Casey, *Spirit and Soul: Essays in Philosophical Psychology*, Dallas: Spring Publications, 1991, p. 39.

23 W. Giegerich, *The Soul's Logical Life: Towards a Rigorous Notion of Psychology*, Frankfurt am Main: Peter Lang, 1998.

24 Giegerich, *The Soul's Logical Life*, p. 67.

25 Giegerich, *The Soul's Logical Life*, p. 67: "'Sublation' is the translation of the Hegelian term *Aufhebung* in the threefold sense of a) negating and cancelling, b) rescuing and retaining, c) elevating or raising to a new level. [Jung's] psychology is sublated (*aufgehoben*) religion inasmuch as it negates the immediate religious interpretation *with which* the contents of the inner experience *come*, but it also preserves the religious contents and atmosphere, however, only as a 'moment' of the new Notion of the reality of the soul."

26 C. G. Jung, *Letters,* vol. ii: *1951–1961*, ed. G. Adler and A. Jaffé, trans. R. F. C. Hull, Princeton, NJ: Princeton University Press, 1975, p. 90.

27 C. G. Jung, "Psychological comments on 'The Tibetan Book of the Great Liberation' and 'The Tibetan Book of the Dead'," *CW* 11: 766.

28 Cf. P. Kugler, "Involuntary Poetics," *New Literary History: A Journal of Theory and Interpretation* 15 (1983–4): "Both Jung and Lacan have demonstrated the insistence of the letter in the unconscious. Their work bears witness to the fact that it is language, not the ego, that places demands upon us, language who calls us for literary exaltations, that insists that we speak."

29 Jung does not use the Saussurean terminology of signifier and signified. Yet, in his early work with the word association experiment, he does demonstrate the difference between the signifying chain of associated words that make up a complex and the conceptual and empirical referents of those words. Jung's more usual term is "image." Images, for Jung, are imagos, which is to say, they are subjectively conditioned and, thus, discontinuous with their apparent objects of reference. The following statement is typical of Jung's recognition of the discontinuity between psychic images and the referent objects (empirical and conceptual) they would seem to signify: "I am conscious that I am moving in a world of images and that none of my reflections touches the essence of the unknowable." His *Answer to Job*, *CW* 11: 556.

30 C. G. Jung, *Answer to Job*, *CW* 11: 757.

31 C. G. Jung, *The Undiscovered Self*, *CW* 10: 511.

32 Cited in C. G. Jung, *Aion: Researches into the Phenomenology of the Self*, *CW* 9ii: 347.

33 Cf. C. G. Jung, "Religion and psychology: a reply to Martin Buber," *CW* 18: 1509.

34 Cf. Jung, *Aion*, *CW* 9ii: 9.

35 Jung, *Letters*, vol. ii, pp. 4–5.

36 Jung, *C. G. Jung Speaking*, pp. 249–50.

37 Paraphrasing Jung from a personal interview conducted on 28 February 1959, Miguel Serrano writes: "So far, I [Jung] have found no stable or definite centre in the unconscious and I don't believe such a centre exists. I believe that the thing which I call the Self is an ideal centre. . . ." M. Serrano, *Jung and Hesse: A Record of Two Friendships*, New York: Schocken Books, 1968, p. 50.

38 While Jung does speak of the phallus as one of the infinite possible symbols of the self (*CW* 9ii: 357), the following passage is more to the point: "any judgement and any statement about [the self] is incomplete and has to be supplemented (but not nullified) by a conditioned negative. If I assert, 'the self exists,' I must supplement this by saying, 'But it seems not to exist.' For the sake of completeness I must also invert the proposition and say, 'the self does not exist, but yet seems to exist'." *CW* 11, p. 262n.

39 Cited in a similar context by D. Miller, "Theologia imaginalis," in M. Parisen (ed.), *Angels and Mortals: Their Co-Creative Power*, Madras and London: Quest Books, 1990, p. 174.

40 With an eye for resemblances I am here roughly equating Rilke's "inflection," Hillman's "de-literalizing", Derrida–Lacan's "deconstruction," Hegel's "logical negation," Giegerich's "logical movement," and Jung's notion of "immanent–transcendent." This is not to deny the differences between the various projects which these terms operationalize. They are many and significant. For instance, when comparing the vexing evasiveness of the spirit Mercurius in the unconscious (Jung) with the gap between signifier and signified (Lacan, Derrida) we must bear in mind that for Jung the image is a *manifestation* or *emanation* of what, in Lacan's view, we are always already divided from by an irrevocable rupture. Likewise, Giegerich's "logical movement" is a sublating of the image which Hillman's "deliteralizing" would always stick to. Nevertheless, these ideas are all indicative of the psychological spirit, the move away from positivity and into reflection.

41 Cf. C. G. Jung, *Answer to Job*, *CW* 11: 357–470.

42 C. G. Jung, *The Psychology of the Transference*, *CW* 16: 449.

43 Jung, *Memories, Dreams, Reflections*, p. 62.

44 Cf. M. Buber, *Eclipse of God: Studies in the Relation between Religion and Philosophy*, New York: Harper & Row, 1952.

45 C. G. Jung, "Religion and psychology: a reply to Martin Buber," *CW* 18: 1505.

46 C. G. Jung, *Answer to Job*, *CW* 11: 758.

47 John 3:8.

48 Cited by M.-L. Von Franz in her translation in *Psychotherapy*, Boston: Shambhala, 1993, p. 178. See also Jung, *Letters*, vol. ii, p. 57.

49 Jung, *Letters*, vol. i, p. 377. Cf. p. 118.

50 S. Freud, "Recommendations for physicians on the psycho-analytic method of treatment," in *Collected Papers*, vol. ii, trans. J. Riviere, London: Hogarth Press and the Institute of Psycho-Analysis, 1950, p. 324.

51 E. Dickinson, *The Letters of Emily Dickinson*, 3 vols., ed. T. Johnson and T. Ward, Cambridge: Belknap Press of Harvard University Press, 1958, L459a.

52 Cited in P. Kugler, "Childhood seduction: material and immaterial facts," in S. Marlan (ed.), *Fire in the Stone: The Alchemy of Desire*, Wilmette: Chiron, 1997, p. 59.

53 Cited in J. Kerr, *A Most Dangerous Method: The Story of Jung, Freud, and Sabina Spielrein*, New York: Alfred A. Knopf, 1994, p. 375.

54 Cited in Kugler, "Childhood seduction," p. 61.

55 Cited in E. Taylor, *William James on Exceptional Mental States: the 1898 Lowell Lectures*, Amherst: University of Massachusetts Press, 1984, p. 54.

56 *Hysteron proteron* is a Greek term which refers to an inverting of the logical order of explanation such that the consequent is taken as the antecedent. It is usually regarded as a fallacy in logic. Applied to psychology, however, it suggests the movement from immediately given psychological phenomena to thought which mediates apperception of these phenomena from the outset. For a discussion of this principle in relation to psychological thinking see Giegerich, *The Soul's Logical Life*, pp. 21, 62.

57 C. Bollas, *The Mystery of Things*, London: Routledge, 1999, p. 181.

58 Jung, *C. G. Jung Speaking*, p. 294.

59 Cf. Giegerich, *The Soul's Logical Life*

Chapter 1: "That Girl"

1 C. Bollas, *Hysteria*, London: Routledge, 2000, p. 142.

2 C. G. Jung, "On the psychology of the trickster figure," *CW* 9i: 485.

3 Bollas, *Hysteria*, text from back cover.

4 Bollas, *Hysteria*, p. 162.

5 Bollas, *Hysteria*, p. 144.

200 Notes

6 J. Keats, *Selected Poems and Letters*, ed. D. Bush, Boston: Houghton Mifflin, 1959, p. 261.

7 Bollas, *Hysteria*, p. 29.

8 W. B. Yeats, "Leda and the Swan," in *W. B. Yeats: Selected Poetry*, ed. A. N. Jeffares, London: Pan Books, 1974, lines 12–15.

9 C. G. Jung, "The realities of practical psychotherapy," *CW* 16: 543.

10 Here I am de-emphasizing the passages in Jung's writings where the anima and animus are biologically accounted for in terms of men and women having a minority of genes belonging to the other sex (*CW* 9i: 58, 512; *CW* 18: 429). These arguments are not psychological in the strict sense. Pushing off from sex and gender in their biological positivity, Jung writes elsewhere that "[w]hen projected, the anima always has a feminine form with definite characteristics. This empirical finding does not mean that the archetype is constituted like that *in itself*" (*CW* 9i: 142).

11 Animus means spirit even as anima means soul. It is beyond the scope of the present work, with its emphasis upon the logically negative femininity of hysteria and anima, to discuss the animus in the fuller sense of its meaning. It is enough to note with James Hillman that "we cannot take any stand regarding anima without . . . taking up an animus position" and that "[t]here is no *other* vantage point toward either than the other" (1985, p. 171). In our reflections in these pages the animus usually shows up as psycho-analysis (Freudian and Jungian), as the figure of the analyst, and as analytic theory. For Hillman's discussion of the anima/animus relation see his *Anima: An Anatomy of a Personified Notion*, Dallas: Spring Publications, 1985, pp. 167–83.

12 C. G. Jung, *The Psychology of the Transference*, CW 16: 398.

13 Bollas, *Hysteria*, p. 25: "The most prominent paradox of the hysteric . . . is the exchange of carnal sexuality – specifically, the genital drive – for spiritual sexuality. Where once the body and its drives prevailed upon the self to accept the animal within, the hysteric vigorously refuses this logic, but uncannily inverts carnal excitation into spiritual excitation."

14 Bollas, *Hysteria*, p. 49.

15 Bollas, *Hysteria*, p. 16.

16 Bollas, *Hysteria*, p. 86.

17 C. G. Jung, *Aion: Researches into the Phenomenology of the Self*, CW 9ii: 20–4.

18 T. S. Eliot, *Collected Poems 1909–1962*, London: Faber & Faber, 1974, p. 219.

19 Jung writes, "The most striking feature about the anima-type is that the maternal element is entirely lacking." "Mind and earth," *CW* 10: 75. Again, "a personalistic interpretation always reduces her [i.e., the anima] to the personal mother or some other female person. The real meaning of the figure naturally gets lost in the process. . . . " "The psychological aspects of the kore," (*CW* 9i: 356–7).

20 C. G. Jung, "Psychological aspects of the mother archetype," *CW* 9i: 158.

21 Bollas, *Hysteria*, p. 168.

22 Bollas, *Hysteria*, p. 168.

23 Bollas, *Hysteria*, p. 169.

24 W. McGuire (ed.), R. Manheim and R. F. C. Hull (trans.) *The Freud/Jung Letters: The Correspondence between Sigmund Freud and C. G. Jung*, Princeton, NJ: Princeton University Press, 1974, pp. 12–13.

25 Bollas, *Hysteria*, pp. 117–18.

26 Bollas analyzes hysterical transference by leading it back to identifications the patient made during childhood to the mother's interior object world or desire. Juliet Mitchell writes in a similar vein about hysterical identification, although without linking this, in the manner of Bollas, to Winnicott's theory of the false self. "Freud," she writes, "was later dismissive of the common observation that hysterics identify with other people to an unusual degree, asserting instead that this property of hysteria was superficial:

hysterics do not simply identify with the other person; instead, they identify with what the other person desires (or, more accurately, what they imagine the other person desires). In fact, I think in hysteria both types of identification, that is, with the other person and with their desires, takes place, although it is easy to neglect the element of desire." What Bollas, Freud, and Mitchell describe as hysterical identification corresponds roughly to what Jung describes in his theory of the anima/animus. Jung's anima/animus concept is a synthetic, perspective, or teleological approach to what these psychoanalysts call hysterical identification. The desires of the other that are being identified with, according to Jung, may be those of the collective unconscious. Insofar as the other person is identified with this greater other, or carrying its projected contents in the eye of the beholder, they have the mediating function of an anima or animus. For the above reference to Mitchell see her *Mad Men and Medusas: Reclaiming Hysteria*, New York: Basic Books, 2000, p. 57. Cf. Jung on people who are "anima types" – *CW* 17: 339; *CW* 9i: 355, 169.

27 Without referring to anima/animus, Jung succinctly sums up a main dynamic associated with these mediating figures when he writes: "The kind of sexuality described by Freud is that unmistakable sexual obsession which shows itself whenever a patient has reached the point where he needs to be forced or tempted out of the wrong attitude or situation" ("Freud and Jung: contrasts," *CW* 4: 780).

28 C. G. Jung, *Letters*, vol. i, ed. G. Adler, London: Routledge & Kegan Paul, 1973–4, p. 31.

29 C. G. Jung, *The Psychology of the Transference*, *CW* 16: 534.

Chapter 2: Sex and Religion

1 C. Bollas, *Hysteria*, London: Routledge, 2000, pp. 28–9.
2 C. G. Jung, "Psychological aspects of the mother archetype," *CW* 9i: 159.
3 C. G. Jung, *Memories, Dreams, Reflections*, ed. A. Jaffé, trans. R. and C. Winston, New York: Pantheon, 1963, pp. 150–1.
4 Jung, *Memories, Dreams, Reflections*, pp. 149–50.
5 S. Freud, *On the History of the Psycho-Analytic Movement* (1914), *SE* 14: 62.
6 Bollas, *Hysteria*, p. 57.
7 Bollas, *Hysteria*, p. 16.
8 Bollas, *Hysteria*, p. 163.
9 Jung, *Memories, Dreams, Reflections*, p. 150.
10 Jung, *Memories, Dreams, Reflections*, p. 151.
11 Bollas, *Hysteria*, pp. 29, 59–60, 79.
12 Bollas, *Hysteria*, p. 107.
13 Bollas, *Hysteria*, p. 99.
14 Bollas, *Hysteria*, p. 112.
15 Bollas, *Hysteria*, p. 80.
16 Bollas, *Hysteria*, p. 81.
17 Matthew 19:12.
18 Jung, *Memories, Dreams, Reflections*, p. 168.
19 C. G. Jung, *The Psychology of the Transference*, *CW* 16: 419.
20 Jung, *The Psychology of the Transference*, *CW* 16: 454.
21 Jung, *The Psychology of the Transference*, *CW* 16: 420.
22 Jung, *The Psychology of the Transference*, *CW* 16: 383.
23 S. Freud, *New Introductory Lectures on Psycho-Analysis*, trans. W. J. H. Sprott, London: Hogarth Press, 1933, p. 380.
24 Bollas, *Hysteria*, p. 69.
25 Jung, *The Psychology of the Transference*, *CW* 16: 504. To be possessed by the anima

is to be possessed by the archetypal content that "she" mediates. We may think, for example, of someone who is utterly wrapped up in perfection fantasies or narcissistically attached to an idea.

26 C. G. Jung, "The philosophical tree," *CW* 13: 457.
27 Jung, *Memories, Dreams, Reflections*, p. 167.
28 Jung, *The Psychology of the Transference*, *CW* 16: 465.
29 S. Freud and K. Abraham, *A Psycho-Analytic Dialogue: The Letters of Sigmund Freud and Karl Abraham, 1907–1926*, ed. H. C. Abraham and E. L. Freud, trans. B. Marsh and H. C. Abraham, New York: Basic Books, 1965, p. 141.
30 Jung, *The Psychology of the Transference*, *CW* 16: 391.
31 Jung, *The Psychology of the Transference*, *CW* 16: 390.
32 C. G. Jung, "The archetypes of the collective unconscious," *CW* 9i: 50.

Chapter 3: Nega-Nativity

1 C. Bollas, *Hysteria*, London: Routledge, 2000, p. 18.
2 C. G. Jung, *The Relations between the Ego and the Unconscious*, *CW* 7: 250.
3 C. G. Jung, "The spirit mercurius," *CW* 13: 299.
4 Cf. W. Giegerich, *The Soul's Logical Life: Towards a Rigorous Notion of Psychology*, Frankfurt am Main: Peter Lang, 1998, pp. 123–33.
5 C. G. Jung, *Letters;* vol. i *1906–1950*, ed. G. Adler and A. Jaffé, trans. R. F. C. Hull, Princeton, NJ: Princeton University Press, 1973, p. 556.
6 C. G. Jung, *The Psychology of the Transference*, *CW* 16: 469.
7 Jung, *The Psychology of the Transference*, *CW* 16: 420.
8 S. T. Coleridge, *Notebooks of Samuel Taylor Coleridge*, vol. ii, ed. K. Coburn and M. Christensen, New York: Pantheon, 1957–1991, item 2670 – for "psychoanalysis." S. T. Coleridge, *Aids to Reflection*, in *Samuel Taylor Coleridge*, ed. H. Jackson, Oxford: Oxford University Press, 1985, p. 672 – for "tautegorical."
9 Giegerich, *The Soul's Logical Life*, pp. 119–23.
10 Giegerich, *The Soul's Logical Life*, p. 203.
11 C. Bollas, *The Shadow of the Object: Psychoanalysis of the Unthought Known*, London: Free Association Books; New York: Columbia University Press, 1987, p. 70.
12 Bollas, *Hysteria*, p. 164.
13 Bollas, *Hysteria*, p. 77.
14 W. B. Yeats, *W. B. Yeats: Selected Poetry*, ed. N. Jeffares, London: Pan Books, 1974, p. 100.
15 C. G. Jung, *The Undiscovered Self*, *CW* 10: 585.
16 C. G. Jung, "Commentary on 'the secret of the golden flower'," *CW* 13: 54.
17 C. G. Jung, *Memories, Dreams, Reflections*, ed. A. Jaffé, trans. R. and C. Winston, New York: Pantheon, 1963, p. 90, italics mine.
18 J. Milton, "On the Morning of Christ's Nativity," stanza 19, in A. Allison, *et al.* (eds.), *The Norton Anthology of Poetry*, 3rd edn, New York and London: W. W. Norton, 1983, p. 155.
19 Jung, *Memories, Dreams, Reflections*, pp. 11–12.
20 D. W. Winnicott, "Review of *Memories, Dreams, Reflections*," in C. Winnicott, R. Shepherd, and M. Davis (eds.), *Psycho-Analytic Explorations*, Cambridge, MA: Harvard University Press, 1989, p. 489.
21 S. T. Coleridge, *Biographia Literaria*, ed. J. Engell and W. J. Bate, Princeton, NJ: Princeton University Press, 1984, pp. 80–1.
22 M.-L. von Franz, *C.G. Jung: His Myth in Our Time*, Toronto: Inner City Books, 1998, pp. 183–4.
23 Enoch 7:2.
24 Genesis 6:1–4.

25 Matthew 18:20.
26 Giegerich, *The Soul's Logical Life*, pp. 55–60.
27 J. Field (M. Milner), *On Not Being Able to Paint*, London: Heinemann, 1950.
28 Giegerich, *The Soul's Logical Life*, p. 56.
29 Giegerich, *The Soul's Logical Life*, p. 57.
30 T. S. Eliot, "The Hollow Men," in *Collected Poems 1909–1962*, London: Faber & Faber, 1974, p. 92.
31 C. G. Jung, *The Tavistock Lectures: On the Theory and Practice of Analytical Psychology*, *CW* 18: 296.
32 C. Bollas, *Forces of Destiny: Psychoanalysis and Human Idiom*, London and New Jersey: Jason Aronson, 1989, pp. 213–14.
33 Bollas, *Forces of Destiny*, pp. 213–14.
34 F. Nietzsche, *Joyful Wisdom*, New York: Frederick Ungar, 1960, p. 168.
35 Yeats, *W. B. Yeats: Selected Poetry*, p. 100.
36 Bollas, *Hysteria*, p. 61.
37 Bollas, *Hysteria*, p. 62.
38 Bollas, *Hysteria*, p. 61.
39 Bollas, *Hysteria*, p. 62.
40 John 14:1.
41 J. Hillman, *The Soul's Code: In Search of Character and Calling*, New York: Warner Books, 1996, p. 184.
42 M. H. Abrams *et al.* (eds.) *The Norton Anthology of English Literature*, 3rd edn, New York: W. W. Norton, 1962, editor's note, p. 1429.
43 W. Wordsworth, "Ode: Intimations of Immortality From Recollections of Early Childhood," lines 111–15, in Abrams *et al., The Norton Anthology of English Literature*, p. 1432.
44 Wordsworth, "Ode: Intimations of Immortality From Recollections of Early Childhood,", lines 49–57, in Abrams *et al., The Norton Anthology of English Literature*, p. 1431.
45 C. G. Jung, "Introduction to Wickes's *Analyse Der Kinderseele*," *CW* 17: 95.
46 Jung, "Introduction to Wickes's *Analyse Der Kinderseele*," *CW* 17: 97.
47 Cited by F. Summers, *Object Relations Theories and Psychopathology: A Comprehensive Text*, Hillsdale: Analytic Press, 1994, p. 139.
48 C. G. Jung, "The psychology of the child archetype," *CW* 9i: 273.
49 C. G. Jung, "Psychological aspects of the mother archetype," *CW* 9i: 161 n. 21.

Chapter 4: The Dove in the Consulting Room

1 C. Bollas, *Hysteria*, London, Routledge, 2000, p. 179.
2 C. G. Jung, "A psychological approach to the dogma of the trinity," *CW* 11: 261.
3 C. G. Jung, *Analytical Psychology: Notes of the Seminar given in 1925*, ed. W. McGuire, Princeton, NJ: Princeton University Press, 1989, p. 80.
4 Bollas, *Hysteria*, p. 150.
5 C. G. Jung, *The Psychology of the Transference*, *CW* 16: 460.
6 Bollas, *Hysteria*, p. 155.
7 Bollas, *Hysteria*, p. 156.
8 Bollas, *Hysteria*, p. 152.
9 Bollas, *Hysteria*, pp. 158–60.
10 Bollas, *Hysteria*, p. 158.
11 Bollas, *Hysteria*, p. 158.
12 Bollas, *Hysteria*, p. 159.
13 Apocryphal insertion at Luke 6:4.

14 C. G. Jung, "The psychology of the child archetype," *CW* 9i: 302.
15 Here we may recall the passage from Monoïmos we quoted in the introduction.
16 Bollas, *Hysteria*, p. 179.
17 Bollas, *Hysteria*, p. 162.
18 C. G. Jung, *Memories, Dreams, Reflections*, ed. A. Jaffé, trans. R. and C. Winston, New York: Pantheon, 1963, p. 333.
19 John 10:34. Cf. *Answer to Job*, *CW* 11: 755.
20 E. Dickinson, *The Letters of Emily Dickinson*, 3 vols., ed. T. Johnson and T. Ward, Cambridge: Belknap Press of Harvard University Press, 1958, L459a.
21 J. Donne, "Holy Sonnets," no. 14, line 1. In M. H. Abrams, *et al.* (eds.), *The Norton Anthology of English Literature*, 3rd edn, New York: W. W. Norton, 1962, p. 613.
22 P. Kugler, "Clinical authority: some thoughts out of season," *Quadrant* 23/2.
23 C. G. Jung, *Mysterium Coniunctionis*, *CW* 14: 205.
24 G. Bachelard, *On Poetic Imagination and Reverie, Selections from the Works of Gaston Bachelard*, trans. C. Gaudin, Indianapolis: Bobbs-Merrill, 1971, pp. 14f.
25 J. Milton, *Paradise Lost, Collected Works*, in H. Darbishire (ed.), Oxford: Oxford University Press, 1952–5, iv. 75.
26 C. G. Jung, "On the nature of the psyche," *CW* 8: 429.
27 C. G. Jung, "Archetypes of the collective unconscious," *CW* 9i: 50.
28 Jung, "The psychology of the child archetype," *CW* 9i: 271.

Chapter 5: Listening Cure

1 C. G. Jung, "Analytical psychology and *Weltanschauung*," *CW* 8: 737.
2 C. Bollas, *Cracking Up: The Work of Unconscious Experience*, New York: Hill & Wang, 1995, p. 17.
3 C. G. Jung, "Archetypes of the collective unconscious," *CW* 9i: 11.
4 J. Hasting (designer), *Annunciation*, London: Phaidon Press, 2000.
5 Hasting, *Annunciation*, p. 20.
6 T. Reik, *Listening with the Third Ear*, New York: Farrar, Straus, 1948.
7 K. Abraham, "The ear and auditory passage as erotogenic zones," in *Selected Papers on Psycho-Analysis*, London: Maresfield Reprints, 1927, pp. 244–7.
8 C. Bollas, *Hysteria*, London: Routledge, 2000, p. 62.
9 John 1:14
10 Bollas, *Hysteria*, p. 43.
11 Bollas, *Hysteria*, p. 96.
12 Bollas, *Hysteria*, p. 166.
13 Bollas, *Hysteria*, p. 166.
14 Bollas, *Hysteria*, p. 166.
15 Bollas, *Hysteria*, p. 150.
16 Bollas, *Hysteria*, p. 150.
17 W. Blake, "Jerusalem," in N. Frye (ed.) *Selected Poetry and Prose of Blake*, New York: Random House, 1953, p. 302.
18 Though this term refers to Mary's exemption from Original Sin, Bollas, I believe, uses it with the miraculous conception of Christ in mind – a typical conflation of the two equally non-sexual events.
19 Bollas, *Hysteria*, p. 150.
20 Bollas, *Hysteria*, p. 150.
21 Bollas, *Hysteria*, p. 149.
22 Bollas, *Hysteria*, p. 162.
23 B. Walker, *The Encyclopedia of the Occult, the Esoteric, and the Supernatural*, Briarcliff Manor, NY: Stein and Day, 1980, p. 76.

24 Bollas, *Hysteria*, p. 156.
25 Bollas, *Hysteria*, p. 43.
26 Bollas, *Hysteria*, p. 43.
27 Bollas, *Hysteria*, p. 150.
28 Bollas, *Hysteria*, p. 43.
29 Bollas, *Hysteria*, p. 43.
30 Bollas, *Hysteria*, p. 149.
31 Bollas, *Hysteria*, p. 150.
32 Bollas, *Hysteria*, p. 72.
33 Hebrews 10:31.
34 C. G. Jung, "The Swiss line in the European spectrum," *CW* 10: 917.
35 Cf. J. Hillman, "On the necessity of abnormal psychology: Ananke and Athene," in J. Hillman (ed.), *Facing the Gods*, Irving, TX: Spring Publications, 1980, p. 33, note 6.
36 Cf. J. Hillman, *Archetypal Psychology: A Brief Account*, Dallas: Spring Publications, 1983, p. 13.
37 Bollas, *Hysteria*, p. 60.
38 D. W. Winnicott, "A point of technique," in C. Winnicott, R. Shepherd, and M. Davis (eds.), *Psycho-Analytic Explorations*, Cambridge; MA: Harvard University Press, 1989, p. 26.
39 Bollas, *Cracking Up*.
40 J. Donne, "The Canonization," lines, 26–7, in M. Abrams *et al.* (eds.), *The Norton Anthology of English Literature*, 3rd edn, New York: W. W. Norton, 1962, p. 591.
41 J. Campbell, *The Masks of God*, vol i: *Primitive Mythology*, New York: Viking Press, 1959, p. 121.
42 Job 19:26.
43 F. Nietzsche, *Twilight of the Idols*, in *Twilight of the Idols and The Anti-Christ*, trans. R. J. Hollingdale, Harmondsworth: Penguin Books, 1968, p. 38.
44 W. Shakespeare, *King Lear*, Act II, Scene 4, lines 54–6. The mother, or *hysterica passio*, refers to a hysterical attack in which a wind from the belly rises up to the heart and, then, on to the throat.
45 M. Klein, "Early stages of the Oedipus conflict," in *Love, Guilt and Reparation and Other Works 1921–1945*, London: Hogarth Press and the Institute of Psycho-Analysis, 1975, p. 188.
46 C. G. Jung, *Symbols of Transformation*, *CW* 5: 654.
47 S. Freud, "Abstracts of the scientific works of Dr. Sigm. Freud, 1877–1897," *SE* 3: 244.
48 Jung, *Symbols of Transformation*, *CW* 5: 654.
49 Perhaps the pre-oedipal psyche can be thought of as that part of the archetypal unconscious that is unmediated by collective culture, Lacan's symbolic order, the father.
50 C. G. Jung, "On the relation of analytical psychology to poetry," *CW* 15: 129.
51 For an excursus on this point see my *God Is a Trauma: Vicarious Religion and Soul-Making*, Dallas: Spring Publications, 1989, pp. 42–4.
52 C. G. Jung, *Psychology and Alchemy*, *CW* 12: 32.
53 D. W. Winnicott, "Fear of breakdown," in C. Winnicott, R. Shepherd, and M. Davis (eds.), *Psycho-Analytic Explorations*, Cambridge, MA: Harvard University Press, 1989, pp. 87–95.
54 Cited in a similar connection in P. Rudnytsky, *Freud and Oedipus*, New York: Columbia University Press, 1987, p. 12.
55 Cited by Noah Pikes, "Giving voice to hell," in *Spring 55: A Journal of Archetype and Culture*, Putnam: Spring Journal, 1994, p. 58.
56 J. Campbell, *The Masks of God,* vol. iv: *Creative Mythology*, Harmondsworth: Penguin Books, 1968, p. 94.

57 S. Freud and J. Breuer, *Studies on Hysteria*, trans. J. Strachey, New York: Basic Books, 1957, p. 181.
58 J. Derrida, *Writing and Difference*, trans. A. Bass, Chicago: University of Chicago Press, 1978, p. 293.

Chapter 6: Speech and Language in Analytical Psychology

1 C. G. Jung, *Symbols of Transformation*, *CW* 5: 373.
2 C. Bollas, *The Mystery of Things*, London: Routledge, 1999, p. 40.
3 C. G. Jung, "Association, dream, and hysterical symptom," *CW* 2: 793–862.
4 Jung, "Association, dream, and hysterical symptom," *CW* 2: 850.
5 C. G. Jung, "On the psychology and pathology of so-called occult phenomena," *CW* 1: 1–150.
6 C. G. Jung, "The psychopathological significance of the association experiment," *CW* 2: 882.
7 C. Bollas, *Hysteria*, London: Routledge, 2000, p. 97.
8 Cf. J. Grotstein, "The numinous and immanent nature of the psychoanalytic subject," *Journal of Analytical Psychology* 43/1 (1998), pp. 41–68.
9 Cited by P. Kugler, *The Alchemy of Discourse: An Archetypal Approach to Language*, Lewisburg: Bucknell University Press, 1982, p. 98.
10 Cited by Kugler, *The Alchemy of Discourse*, p. 17.
11 Kugler, *The Alchemy of Discourse*, p. 25.
12 Kugler, *The Alchemy of Discourse*, p. 27.
13 Kugler, *The Alchemy of Discourse*, pp. 19–20.
14 Kugler, *The Alchemy of Discourse*, p. 23.
15 Kugler, *The Alchemy of Discourse*, p. 23.
16 P. Berry, *Echo's Subtle Body: Contributions to an Archetypal Psychology*, Dallas: Spring Publications, 1982, p. 90.
17 T. S. Eliot, "The Love-Song of J. Alfred Prufrock," in *Collected Poems 1909–1962*, London: Faber & Faber, 1974, p. 17.
18 Kugler, *The Alchemy of Discourse*, p. 25.
19 Kugler, *The Alchemy of Discourse*, p. 24.
20 Bollas, *Hysteria*, p. 49.
21 Bollas, *Hysteria*, p. 47.
22 E. Neumann, *The Great Mother: An Analysis of the Archetype*, trans. R. Manheim, Princeton, NJ: Princeton University Press, 1963, p. 139.
23 C. G. Jung, *Dream Analysis*, Zurich: C.G. Jung Institute, 1958, vol. ii, pp. 53–4. Cited by R. Lockhart in *Words as Eggs: Psyche in Language and Clinic*, Dallas: Spring Publications, 1983, p. 91.
24 Cited in D. Miller, *Hells and Holy Ghosts: A Theopoetics of Christian Belief*, Nashville: Abingdon Press, 1989, p. 107.
25 Miller, *Hells and Holy Ghosts*, p. 111.
26 Cited by Miller, *Hells and Holy Ghosts*, p. 117.
27 Cited by Miller, *Hells and Holy Ghosts*, p. 117 The reference is to Kugler's *The Alchemy of Discourse*, p. 22.
28 Miller, *Hells and Holy Ghosts*, p. 114.
29 C. G. Jung, "The psychology of the child archetype," *CW* 9i: 302.
30 John 3:8.
31 N. Frye, "Reflections in a mirror," in M. Krieger (ed.), *Northrop Frye in Modern Criticism*, New York: Columbia University Press, 1966, p. 143.
32 Bollas, *Hysteria*, pp. 149, 150, 43.

Chapter 7: My Fair Hysteria

1 C. G. Jung, "Archetypes of the collective unconscious," *CW* 9i: 62.
2 C. Bollas, *Cracking Up: The Work of Unconscious Experience*, New York: Hill & Wang, 1995, pp. 45–6.
3 Jung writes "the self comprises infinitely more than a mere ego. . . . It is as much one's self, and all other selves, as the ego. Individuation does not shut one out from the world, but gathers the world to oneself." "On the nature of the psyche," *CW* 8: 432.
4 W. B. Yeats, "Leda and the Swan," line 14, in *W. B. Yeats: Selected Poetry*, ed. A. N. Jeffares, London: Pan Books, 1974, p. 127.
5 C. G. Jung, *Memories, Dreams, Reflections*, ed. A. Jaffé, trans. R. and C. Winston, New York: Pantheon, 1963, p. 28.
6 Jung, *Memories, Dreams, Reflections*, p. 167.
7 C. G. Jung, *Analytical Psychology: Notes of the Seminar Given in 1925*, ed. W. McGuire, Princeton, NJ: Princeton University Press, p. 27.
8 C. G. Jung, *The Psychology of the Transference*, *CW* 16: 401. Also "A psychological view of conscience," *CW* 10: 850.
9 Jung, *Analytical Psychology*, pp. 27–8.
10 Jung, *Memories, Dreams, Reflections*, p. 186.
11 S. Shamdasani, "A woman called Frank," in *Spring 50: A Journal of Archetype and Culture*, Dallas: Spring Publications, 1990, pp. 26–56.
12 Jung, *Memories, Dreams, Reflections*, p. 187.
13 Cf. C.G. Jung, *Psychology and Alchemy*, *CW* 12: 11.
14 Cf. W. Giegerich, *The Soul's Logical Life: Towards a Rigorous Notion of Psychology*, Frankfurt am Main: Peter Lang, 1998, pp. 66–72.
15 Bollas, *Cracking Up*, pp. 52–3.
16 Bollas, *Cracking Up*, p. 53.
17 John 3:8.
18 C. Bollas, *Being a Character: Psychoanalysis and Self Experience*, London: Routledge, 1992, pp. 66–100.
19 C. Bollas, *Free Association*, Cambridge: Icon Books, 2002, pp. 45–51.
20 Bollas, *Being a Character*, p. 67.
21 Bollas, *Being a Character*, p. 68.
22 Bollas, *Being a Character*, p. 70.
23 Bollas, *Being a Character*, p. 69.
24 W. McGuire (ed.) R. Manheim and R. F. C. Hull (trans.) *The Freud/Jung Letters: The Correspondence between Sigmund Freud and C. G. Jung*, Princeton, NJ: Princeton University Press, 1974, pp. 216–19.
25 S. Freud, "Leonardo da Vinci and a memory of his childhood," *SE* 11: 136.
26 S. Freud, "Dostoevsky and parricide," *SE* 21: 177.
27 J. Masson (ed. and trans.), *The Complete Letters of Sigmund Freud and Wilhelm Fliess 1887–1904*, Cambridge, MA, and London: Belknap Press of Harvard University Press, 1985, p. 261.
28 Bollas, *Being a Character*, pp. 73–4.
29 Bollas, *Being a Character*, p. 88.
30 Bollas, *Being a Character*, p. 88.
31 In the third dream, the anima of generative chaos is no longer imaged. Perhaps (and here I follow Giegerich) the image-based, anima consciousness which constitutes itself through the negation of sensuous, object-based, empirical perception, is here itself being negated and sublated into thought. In that case, it may not merely be a new idea or attitude that is being generated, but a new logical status.
32 C. G. Jung, *Mysterium Coniunctionis*, *CW* 14: 422.
33 Cf. A. Molino (ed.) *Freely Associated: Encounters in Psychoanalysis with Christopher*

Bollas, Joyce McDougall, Michael Eigen, Adam Phillips, Nina Coltart, New York: Free Assocation Books, 1997, p. 33.
34 Bollas, *On Being a Character*, pp. 16–65.
35 Cf. J. Hillman, *The Thought of the Heart & the Soul of the World*, Dallas: Spring Publications, 1992, and Robert Sardello, "Saving the things or how to avoid the bomb," *Spring 1985: An Annual of Archetypal Psychology and Jungian Thought*, Dallas: Spring Publications, 1985, pp. 28–41.
36 G. Bachelard, *The Poetics of Reverie: Childhood, Language, and the Cosmos*, trans. D. Russell, Boston: Beacon Press, 1969, pp. 153–4.
37 Bollas, *Being a Character*, p. 59.
38 D. Winnicott, "The use of an object and relating through identifications," in C. Winnicott, R. Shepherd and M. Davis (eds.), *Psycho-Analytic Explorations*, Cambridge, MA: Harvard University Press, 1989, pp. 218–27.
39 Cf. Bollas's chapters "The structure of evil," in *Cracking Up* and "Cruising in the homosexual arena" and "The fascist state of mind," in *Being a Character*.
40 Bollas, *Cracking Up*, pp. 180–220.
41 C. G. Jung, *Symbols of Transformation*, CW 5: 655.
42 N. Micklem, "On hysteria: the mythical syndrome," in *Spring 1974: An Annual of Archetypal Psychology and Jungian Thought*, New York: Spring Publications, 1974, p. 153.
42 Micklem, "On hysteria," p. 153.
44 W. Stevens, "An ordinary evening in New Haven," in H. Stevens (ed.), *The Palm at the End of the Mind*, New York: Vintage Books, 1972, p. 338.
45 Giegerich, *The Soul's Logical Life*, p. 124.
46 C. G. Jung, *Psychological Types*, CW 6: 377.
47 E. Wind, *Pagan Mysteries of the Renaissance*, New York: Norton, 1968, p. 238.
48 Bollas, *Hysteria*, pp. 144–5.
49 C. Bollas, *The Mystery of Things*, London: Routledge, 1999, pp. 67–8.
50 S. Freud, "The passing of the Oedipus-complex,' *CP* 2: 273.
51 Cf. W. Giegerich, "On the neurosis of psychology or the third of the two," in *Spring 1977: An Annual of Archetypal Psychology and Jungian Thought*, Zurich: Spring Publications, 1977, pp. 153–74.
52 Bollas, *Cracking Up*, p. 25.
53 M. Heidegger, *Basic Writings*, New York: Harper & Row, 1977, pp. 236–7.
54 Bollas, *Being a Character*, p. 64.
55 Bollas, *The Mystery of Things*, p. 86.
56 Bollas, *The Mystery of Things*, p. 157.

Chapter 8: Voicing the Weather Oracle

1 C. G. Jung, "The structure of the psyche," *CW* 8: 331.
2 C. Bollas, *Hysteria*, London: Routledge, 2000, p. 1.
3 Adam Phillips in conversation with Anthony Molino, in A. Molino (ed.), *Freely Associated: Encounters in Psychoanalysis with Christopher Bollas, Joyce McDougall, Michael Eigen, Adam Phillips, Nina Coltart*, New York: Free Association Books, 1997, p. 149.
4 Bollas, *Hysteria*, p. 1.
5 Letter to Miguel Serrano, 14 September 1960, in *C. G. Jung Letters,* vol. ii: *1951–1961*, ed. G. Adler and A. Jaffé, trans. R. F. C. Hull, Princeton, NJ: Princeton University Press, 1975, p. 595.
6 P. Gay, "Sigmund Freud," *Time Magazine* 153/12 (29 March 1999), pp. 38–41.
7 W. H. Auden, *W. H. Auden: Collected Poems*, ed. E. Mendelson, New York: Random House, 1976, p. 217.

8 C. Bollas, *The Shadow of the Object: Psychoanalysis of the Unthought Known*, New York: Columbia University Press, 1987, pp. 99–172.

9 Bollas, *The Shadow of the Object*, p. 115.

10 Bollas, *The Shadow of the Object*, pp. 115–16.

11 C. G. Jung, "Archetypes of the unconscious," *CW* 9i: 57.

12 Cf. J. Hillman, "Anima mundi: the return of the soul to the world," in *Spring: An Annual of Archetypal Psychology and Jungian Thought*, Dallas: Spring Publications, 1982, pp. 71–93.

13 Freud to Oskar Pfister, 9 October 1918, in E. Freud and H. Meng (eds.) *Psycho-Analysis and Faith: The Letters of Sigmund Freud and Oskar Pfister*, New York: Basic Books, 1963, p. 63.

14 W. McGuire (ed.), *The Freud/Jung Letters: The Correspondence between Sigmund Freud and C.G. Jung*, trans. R. Manheim and R. F. C. Hull, Princeton, NJ: Princeton University Press, 1974, p. 525.

15 Cf. C. G. Jung, "Spirit and life," *CW* 8, and "Mind and earth," *CW* 10.

16 C. G. Jung, "Some crucial points in psychoanalysis: a correspondence between Dr Jung and Dr Loÿ," *CW* 4: 658.

17 C. G. Jung, "On the psychology of the unconscious," *CW* 7: 18.

18 C. G. Jung, *Memories, Dreams, Reflections*, ed. A. Jaffé, trans. R. and C. Winston, New York: Pantheon, 1963, pp. 233–4.

19 J. Hillman, *Re-Visioning Psychology*, New York: Harper & Row, 1975, p. 49.

20 G. Bachelard, *The Poetics of Reverie: Childhood, Language, and the Cosmos*, trans. D. Russell, Boston: Beacon Press, 1971, p. 173–4.

21 Cf. J. Hillman, *The Dream and the Underworld*, New York: Harper Colophon, 1979, p. 32.

22 C. G. Jung, "The psychology of the child archetype," *CW* 9i: 273.

23 S. Freud, *Group Psychology and the Analysis of the Ego*, in S. Freud, *Civilization, Society and Religion*, Pelican Freud Library, 12, Harmondsworth: Penguin Books, 1985, p. 119.

24 Freud, *Group Psychology and the Analysis of the Ego*, p. 117.

25 Freud, *Group Psychology and the Analysis of the Ego*, p. 117.

26 M.-L. Von Franz, *Projection and Re-Collection in Jungian Psychology: Reflections of the Soul*, trans. W. Kennedy, La Salle: Open Court, 1980, pp. 122–42.

27 J. Hillman, *The Myth of Analysis: Three Essays in Archetypal Psychology*, New York: HarperPerennial, 1978, pp. 50–5.

28 Bollas, *Hysteria*, p. 168.

29 M. Williams, "The indivisibility of the personal and collective unconscious," in M. Fordham (ed.), *Analytical Psychology: A Modern Science*, London: Heinemann, 1973, p. 79.

30 R. Evans, *Conversations with Carl Jung and Reactions from Ernest Jones*, New York: Van Nostrand Reinhold, 1964, p. 35.

31 S. Freud, "Hysterical phantasies and their relation to bisexuality," *CP* 2: 57. Cited by Hillman, in his *The Myth of Analysis*, p. 261.

32 For William James psychoanalysis was a dangerous method because of it reliance on symbolism.

33 Jung, *Memories, Dreams, Reflections*, p. 168.

34 C. G. Jung, "On psychic energy," *CW* 8: 92.

35 E. Humbert, "Jung and the question of religion," in *Spring 1985: An Annual of Archetypal Psychology and Jungian Thought*, Dallas: Spring Publications, 1985, p. 115.

36 P. Wheelwright, *Heraclitus*, Princeton, NJ: Princeton University Press, 1959, frag. 75.

37 C. G. Jung, *The Tavistock Lecture*, *CW* 18: 187. Italics mine.

38 S. Freud, "On narcissism: an introduction," *CP* 4: 58.

39 Freud, *Group psychology and the analysis of the ego*, pp. 143–4.

40 If hysteria is synonymous with the anima, the ego-ideal corresponds, at the same time, to the animus.

41 Freud, "On narcissism: an introduction," *CP* 4: 59.

42 I refer to the film, *Chinese Box*, Wayne Wang (director), 1998.

43 Cf. G. Hogenson, "The Baldwin effect: a neglected influence on C. G. Jung's evolutionary thinking," *Journal of Analytical Psychology*, 46/4 (2001), pp. 591–611.

44 J. Hillman, *Loose Ends: Primary Papers in Archetypal Psychology*, Dallas: Spring Publications, 1978, p. 192.

45 E. Neumann, *Depth Psychology and a New Ethic*, trans. E. Rolfe, New York: Putnams, 1969, p. 130.

46 Cited by J. Hillman, "Oedipus revisited," in J. Hillman and K. Kerényi, *Oedipus Variations: Studies in Literature and Psychoanalysis*, Dallas: Spring Publicaitions, 1991, p. 92.

47 Jung, *Memories, Dreams, Reflections*, p. 215.

48 W. Giegerich, *The Soul's Logical Life: Towards a Rigorous Notion of Psychology*, Frankfurt am Main: Peter Lang, 1998, p. 71.

49 C. G. Jung, *The Psychology of the Transference*, *CW* 16: 367.

50 E. Neumann, *The Origins and History of Consciousness*, trans. R. F. C. Hull, Princeton, NJ: Princeton University Press, 1970, p. 336.

51 Neumann, *The Origins and History of Consciousness*, p. 349.

52 Oedipus's double lineage – i.e., his having two sets of parents – is "positivity-negating" in the same way that the appearance of a second moon in the dream discussed in Chapter 7 negated the dream-ego's positive certainty with respect to the first moon.

53 Further to the above note we may add that, just as the doubled moon is no longer identical with what the first moon literally and singly had been in its positivity, so the doubling of the family motif in the Oedipus story is an "interiorizing, family-negating movement."

54 J. Joyce, *A Portrait of the Artist as a Young Man*, Harmondsworth: Penguin Books, 1988, p. 253.

55 D. H. Lawrence, "Healing," in *D. H. Lawrence: Selected Poems*, New York: Viking Press, 1959, p. 114.

56 Hillman, *Re-Visioning Psychology*, p. 104.

57 S. Freud, *The Interpretation of Dreams*, *SE* 4: 363.

58 A. Cameron, *The Identity of Oedipus the King: Five Essays on the "Oedipus Tyrannus,"* New York: New York University Press, 1984, p. 21.

59 C. G. Jung, "Psychological aspects of the mother archetype," *CW* 9i: 178.

60 Hillman, *Re-Visioning Psychology*, p. 192.

61 Hillman, *Re-Visioning Psychology*, p. 193.

62 Bollas, *Hysteria*, p. 1.

63 L. Schapira, *The Cassandra Complex: Living with Disbelief – A Modern Perspective on Hysteria*, Toronto: Inner City Books, 1988, p. 15.

64 Schapira, *The Cassandra Complex*, p. 16.

65 Schapira, *The Cassandra Complex*, p. 147.

66 Cited in Schapira, *The Cassandra Complex*, p. 53.

67 Cited in Schapira, *The Cassandra Complex*, p. 53.

68 Giegerich, *The Soul's Logical Life*, back cover text.

69 Hillman, *The Myth of Analysis*, p. 186.

Chapter 9: The Jungian Thing

1 C. G. Jung, "Basis postulates of analytical psychology," *CW* 8: 673.

2 C. Bollas, *Hysteria*, London: Routledge, 2000, p. 44.

3 Cited in S. Hoeller, *Jung and the Lost Gospels*, Wheaton: Theosophical Publishing House, 1989, p. 198.

4 Cf. W. Giegerich, *The Soul's Logical Life: Towards a Rigorous Notion of Psychology*, Frankfurt am Main: Peter Lang, 1998, p. 270.

5 J. Keats, *Lamia*, line 233, in M. H. Abrams, *et al.* (eds.), *The Norton Anthology of English Literature*, 3rd edn, New York: W. W. Norton, 1962, p. 1873.

6 D. H. Lawrence, "Snake," in *D. H. Lawrence: Selected Poems*, New York: Viking Press, 1959, pp. 95–8.

7 S. Freud, "The unconscious," *CP* 4: 134.

8 S. Freud, *New Introductory Lectures on Psycho-Analysis*, ed. E. Jones, trans. W. J. H. Sprott, London: Hogarth Press, no. 24, p. 106.

9 Wolfgang Giegerich's emphasis on the killing sublation of imagination is not the same as this move from image to concept that we are critiquing here. Giegerich would have us think images rather than simply imagining them. Such thinking retains the image within or beneath itself. By thinking a number of images all at once, consciousness is released from the positivistic pictorial quality of the images that were its starting point. But this is not to substitute concepts for images. Concepts, being particular ideas, still present the negativity of thought in too positivistic a form. In the movement that constitutes the soul's logical life, concepts need to be further negated, even absolutely so, through the rescue of the images which they kill, much as we did in the case of Bollas's conceptualization of hysteria when we confronted it with a fuller account of the story of the Holy Family.

10 Bollas, *Hysteria*, p. 113.

11 Bollas, *Hysteria*, p. 7.

12 Bollas, *Hysteria*, p. 43.

13 Bollas, *Hysteria*, p. 112.

14 Cf. J. Mitchell, *Mad Men and Medusas: Reclaiming Hysteria*, New York: Basic Books, 2000, pp, 34, 208, 209, 242.

15 Mitchell, *Mad Men and Medusas*, pp. 63, 267–8.

16 Mitchell, *Mad Men and Medusas*, p. 209.

17 Mitchell, *Mad Men and Medusas*, p. 209.

18 Mitchell, too, writes of the hysteric wanting mother. For her, however, the hysteric "wants the mother that the sibling has taken." *Mad Men and Medusas*, p. 66.

19 Mitchell, *Mad Men and Medusas*, p. 209.

20 Mitchell, *Mad Men and Medusas*, p. 216.

21 Mitchell, *Mad Men and Medusas*: "Loss is a condition of symbolization and representation. The hysteric cannot allow the loss (it is simply too terrifying), therefore he cannot have a symbol or representation of the body" (p. 211). "[The things being equated] stand for each other, are metaphors for each other, yes, but they cannot be symbols since nothing has been acknowledged as missing" (p. 213).

22 C. G. Jung, "Spirit and life," *CW* 8: 620.

23 C. G. Jung, *Letters,* vol. i: *1906–1950*, ed. G. Adler and A. Jaffé, trans. R. F. C. Hull, Princeton, NJ: Princeton University Press, 1973, p. 143.

24 W. Wordsworth, *The Prelude*, in *Wordsworth's Prelude*, ed. E. de Selincourt, Oxford and London: Oxford University Press, 1959, lines 260–1.

25 C. G. Jung, *Memories, Dreams, Reflections*, ed. A. Jaffé, trans. R. and C. Winston, New York: Pantheon, 1963, p. 12.

26 Angelus Silesius (Johann Scheffler) 1642–77. Cited by Jung in *Mysterium Coniunctionis*, *CW* 14: 444.

27 Wordsworth, *The Prelude*, Book II, lines 279–81.

28 Jung, "Spirit and life," *CW* 8: 618.

29 C. G. Jung, "Psychological aspects of the mother archetype, "*CW* 9i: 187.

30 C. G. Jung, "The soul and death," *CW* 8: 815.
31 Cf. C. G. Jung, "The transcendent function," *CW* 8: p. 68: "the unconscious is not this thing or that; it is the Unknown as it immediately affects us."
32 C. G. Jung, *Aion: Researches into the Phenomenology of the Self*, *CW* 9ii: 316 n. 63.
33 C. G. Jung, *Symbols of Transformation*, *CW* 5: 182. Cf. *CW* 9i: 283, 289; *CW* 9ii: 223, 257.
34 C. G. Jung, "Some crucial points in psychoanalysis: a correspondence between Dr Jung and Dr Loÿ," *CW* 4: 665.
35 C. G. Jung, "Foreword to Suzuki's *Introduction to Zen Buddhism*," *CW* 11: 897.
36 C. G. Jung, "Synchronicity: an acausal connecting principle," *CW* 8 : 964. Cf. *CW* 15: 127.
37 C. G. Jung, "The structure of the psyche," *CW* 8: 316.
38 C. G. Jung, *Dream Analysis: Notes on the Seminar Given in 1928–1930*, ed. W. McGuire, Princeton, NJ: Princeton University Press, 1984, p. 204.
39 Jung, *Memories, Dreams, Reflections*, p. 225.
40 J. Lacan, *Ecrits: A Selection*, trans. A. Sheridan, New York: W. W. Norton, 1977.
41 C. G. Jung, *Letters*, vol. ii: *1951–1961*, ed. G. Adler and A. Jaffé, trans. R. F. C. Hull, Princeton, NJ: Princeton University Press, 1975, p. 578.
42 Jung, *Symbols of Transformation*, *CW* 5: 396.
43 C. G. Jung, "The development of the personality," *CW* 17: 303.
44 P. Kugler, *The Alchemy of Discourse: Image, Sound and Psyche*, Einsiedeln: Daimon Verlag, 2002, p. 81.
45 C. G. Jung, *Psychological Types*, *CW* 6: 78.
46 Jung, *Psychological Types*, *CW* 6: 78.
47 Kugler, *The Alchemy of Discourse: Image, Sound and Psyche*, p. 81.
48 Kugler, *The Alchemy of Discourse: Image, Sound and Psyche*, p. 81.
49 Matthew 18:3.
50 C. G. Jung, *Mysterium Coniunctionis*, *CW* 14: 377.
51 Jung, *Memories, Dreams, Reflections*, p. 3.
52 C. G. Jung, *The Visions Seminars*, vol. i, Zurich: Spring Publications, 1976, p. 23.
53 Jung, *The Psychology of the Transference*, *CW* 16: 449.
54 Jung, *The Psychology of the Transference*, *CW* 16: 396.
55 Jung, *Memories, Dreams, Reflections*, p. 182.
56 C. Bollas, "The psychoanalyst and the hysteric," in *The Shadow of the Object: Psychoanalysis of the Unthought Known*, New York: Columbia University Press, 1987, pp. 189–99.
57 Cf. H. Corbin, "The question of comparative philosophy: convergences in Iranian and European thought," in *Spring 1980: An Annual of Archetypal Psychology and Jungian Thought*, Dallas: Spring Publications, 1980, p. 20.
58 C. G. Jung, "The symbolic life," *CW* 18: 608–96.
59 Cf. C. G. Jung, "Analytical psychology and *Weltanschauung*," *CW* 8: 713.
60 Mitchell, *Mad Men and Medusas*, pp. 267, 277–8
61 "The Gospel of Thomas," section 77, in W. Barnstone (ed.), *The Other Bible*, New York: Harper & Row, 1984, p. 305.
62 Jung, *Mysterium Coniunctionis*, *CW* 14: 770.
63 Mitchell, *Mad Men and Medusas*, pp. 200–1, 226, 230–1.
64 S. Freud, "From the history of an infantile neurosis" *CP* 3: 565.
65 Bollas, *Hysteria*, p. 85.
66 Bollas, *Hysteria*, pp. 72–3.
67 "Flectere si nequeo superos, Acheronta movebo," cited by S. Freud, *The Interpretation of Dreams*, Pelican Freud Library, 4, trans. J. Strachey, Harmondsworth: Penguin Books, 1976, p. 31.

68 C. G. Jung, "The state of psychotherapy today," *CW* 10: 367.
69 J. Kristeva, "Credo in unum Deum," in D. Capps (ed.), *Freud and Freudians on Religion: A Reader*, New Haven and London: Yale University Press, 2001, p. 314.
70 For a discussion of what he calls the "anthropological fallacy" see Giegerich, *The Soul's Logical Life*, p. 133.
71 C. G. Jung, "On the nature of the psyche," *CW* 8: 423.
72 Jung, *Memories, Dreams, Reflections*, p. 339.
73 Cited by C. G. Jung, "The holy men of India," *CW* 11: 959.
74 Jung, *Memories, Dreams, Reflections*, p. 335.
75 Jung, *Memories, Dreams, Reflections*, p. 336.
76 Jung, *Psychological Types*, *CW* 6: 814.
77 Jung, "The transcendent function," *CW* 8: 148.
78 Jung, *Psychological Types*, *CW* 6: 814.
79 Jung, *Letters*, vol. i, pp. 142–3.
80 C. G. Jung, "The meaning of psychology for modern man," *CW* 10: 305.
81 W. B. Yeats, "The Circus Animals' Desertion," in *W. B. Yeats: Selected Poetry*, ed. A. N. Jeffares, London: Pan Books, 1974, p. 202.
82 Jung, *Memories, Dreams, Reflections*, p. 349.
83 Jung, *Memories, Dreams, Reflections*, p. 349.

Chapter 10: The Advent of the Notion

1 C. G. Jung, *Memories, Dreams, Reflections*, ed. A. Jaffé, trans. R. and C. Winston, New York: Pantheon, 1963, p. 333.
2 C. Bollas, *Cracking Up: The Work of Unconscious Experience*, New York: Hill & Wang, 1995, pp. 18–19.
3 L. Cohen, "Anthem," on *The Future*, produced by L. Cohen, S. Lindsey, B. Ginn, L. Ungar, R. De Mornay, and Y. Goren, Sony Music Entertainment, 1992, liner notes, p. 6.
4 W. Giegerich, *The Soul's Logical Life: Towards a Rigorous Notion of Psychology*, Frankfurt am Main: Peter Lang, 1998, p. 178.
5 C. G. Jung, *Letters*, vol. ii *1951–1961*, ed. G. Adler and A. Jaffé, trans. R. F. C. Hull, Princeton, NJ: Princeton University Press, 1975, p. 394. Cited by Giegerich, *The Soul's Logical Life*, p. 178.
6 Giegerich, *The Soul's Logical Life*, p. 178.
7 C. G. Jung, *The Tavistock Lectures: On the Theory and Practice of Analytical Psychology*, *CW* 18: 279. Cited by Giegerich, *The Soul's Logical Life*, p. 75.
8 Giegerich, *The Soul's Logical Life*, p. 178. For Giegerich, the rupture in the soul refers to a specific event in history – the early nineteenth century. In the West, this was a time in which a "before" of myths and Gods was decisively separated from an "after" in which these are gone. My approach differs in that while I also regard the rupture brought about during the nineteenth century as crucial in the manner discussed by Giegerich (e.g., with respect to the question of the logical form of consciousness), I see the movement of history as being articulated through a whole series of ruptures. While I do not take a perennial-philosophy-type position, I do retain something of that position under sublation.
9 N. Tinbergen, *The Study of Instinct*, London: Oxford University Press, 1951.
10 J. Campbell, *The Masks of God*, vol. i: *Primitive Mythology*, New York: Viking Press, 1959, p. 34.
11 Genesis 24:2.
12 W. Giegerich, "Killings: psychology's Platonism and the missing link to reality," in *Spring 54: A Journal of Archetype and Culture*, Putnam, CT: Spring Journal, 1993, p. 10.

13 Giegerich, "Killings," p. 11.
14 Revelation 13:8; 1 Peter 1:18–20.
15 Cohen, "Anthem."
16 S. Freud, "Overview of the transference neuroses," in I. Grubrich-Simitis (ed.), *A Phylogenetic Fantasy: Overview of the Transference Neuroses*, Cambridge, MA: Belknap Press of Harvard University Press, 1987, p. 13.
17 Freud, "Overview of the transference neuroses," p. 13.
18 Freud, "Overview of the transference neuroses," pp. 13–14.
19 S. Freud, *The Ego and the Id*, trans. J. Riviere, New York: W. W. Norton, 1962, p. 19.
20 Freud, *The Ego and the Id*, p. 28.
21 Cf. S. Freud, "From the history of an infantile neurosis," in *CP* 3: 578.
22 I. Grubrich-Simitis, "Metapsychology and metabiology: on Sigmund Freud's draft overview of the transference neuroses," in Grubrich-Simitis, *A Phylogenetic Fantasy: Overview of the Transference Neuroses*, p. 93.
23 S. Freud, *Group Psychology and the Analysis of the Ego*, in S. Freud, *Civilization, Society and Religion: Group Psychology, Civilization and its Discontents and Other Works*, Pelican Freud Library 12, Harmondsworth: Penguin Books, 1985, p. 169.
24 W. McGuire (ed.) *The Freud/Jung Letters: The Correspondence between Sigmund Freud and C. G. Jung*, trans. R. Manheim and R. F. C. Hull, Princeton, NJ: Princeton University Press, 1974, p. 228.
25 Cited in J. Kerr, *A Most Dangerous Method: The Story of Jung, Freud, and Sabina Spielrein*, New York: Alfred A. Knopf, 1994, p. 491.
26 For Kerr's argument connecting Spielrein with Jung's notion of the anima see *A Most Dangerous Method*, pp. 506–7.
27 Kerr, *A Most Dangerous Method*, p. 507.
28 Cited by Kerr, *A Most Dangerous Method*, p. 491.
29 S. Spielrein, "Destruction as the cause of coming into being," reprinted in *Journal of Analytical Psychology*, 39/2 (1994), pp. 155–86.
30 Kerr, *A Most Dangerous Method*, pp. 320–1.
31 McGuire, *The Freud/Jung Letters*, p. 294.
32 C. G. Jung, *Letters*, vol. i: *1906–1950*, ed. G. Adler and A. Jaffé, trans. R. F. C. Hull, Princeton, NJ: Princeton University Press, 1973, p. 19.
33 Cohen, "Anthem."
34 C. G. Jung, "The letters of C. G. Jung to Sabina Spielrein," trans. B. Wharton, *Journal of Analytical Psychology*, 46/1 (2001), pp. 173–99.
35 Cited in A. Carotenuto, *A Secret Symmetry: Sabina Spielrein between Jung and Freud*, New York: Random House, 1982, pp. 53ff., 62ff., 68ff., 82ff. For Spielrein's account of how she was "awakened as from a dream" by thoughts concerning the living Siegfried symbol and decided to write to Jung about how to interpret it see p. 88.
36 C. Bollas, *Hysteria*, London: Routledge, 2000, p. 162.
37 Jung, "The letters of C. G. Jung to Sabina Spielrein," p. 192.
38 For a passage dealing with the two worlds and the anima see *CW* 7: 507. For related references see *CW* 4: 381, 778; *CW* 5: 221; *CW* 6: 337, 347, *CW* 7: 311, 397; *CW* 8: 327; *CW* 9i: 260. See also *Memories, Dreams, Reflections*, p. 335; *Analytical Psychology: Notes of the Seminar Given in 1925*, pp. 78–9, 86.
39 C. G. Jung, "The transcendent function," *CW* 8: 131–93.
40 Carotenuto, *A Secret Symmetry*, pp. 78, 86–7.
41 See Spielrein's account of such wild self-analytic experience in Carotenuto, *A Secret Symmetry*, p. 88.
42 Spielrein had worried that her inner figure, Siegfried, would harm her actual child.
43 Jung, "The letters of C. G. Jung to Sabina Spielrein," p. 194.
44 Cited in Carotenuto, *A Secret Symmetry*, p. 73.

45 Jung, "The letters of C. G. Jung to Sabina Spielrein," p. 192.
46 Cf. H. Kohut, *The Restoration of the Self*, New York: International Universities Press, 1977 and H. Kohut, *How Does Analysis Cure?*, ed. A. Goldberg and P. Stepansky, Chicago: University of Chicago Press, 1984.
47 S. Freud, *Three Essays on the Theory of Sexuality*, *SE* 7: 226 n.
48 Freud, *Three Essays on the Theory of Sexuality*.
49 T. Flournoy, *From India to the Planet Mars: A Case of Multiple Personality with Imaginary Languages*, ed. S. Shamdasani, Princeton, NJ: Princeton University Press, 1994.
50 C. G. Jung, *On the Psychology and Pathology of So-called Occult Phenomena*, *CW* 1: 134–6.
51 C. G. Jung, "The state of psychotherapy today," *CW* 10: 367.
52 C. G. Jung, "The relations between the ego and the unconscious, *CW* 7: 216.
53 Jung, *Memories, Dreams, Reflections*, p. 335.
54 F. Nietzsche, *Thus Spoke Zarathustra*, trans. R. Hollingdale, Harmondsworth: Penguin Books, 1969, p. 46.
55 Giegerich, *The Soul's Logical Life*, pp. 123–5.
56 C. G. Jung, *The Visions Seminars*, vol. i, Zurich: Spring Publications, 1976, p. 156.
57 Jung, *Letters*, vol. ii, p. 138.
58 McGuire, *The Freud/Jung Letters*, p. 294.
59 Freud, *The Ego and the Id*, p. 47.
60 C. G. Jung, "On the nature of the psyche," *CW* 8: 398.
61 S. Freud, *New Introductory Lectures on Psycho-Analysis*, Pelican Freud Library 2, trans. J. Strachey, Harmondsworth: Penguin Books, 1973, p. 99.
62 C. G. Jung, "The symbolic life," *CW* 18: 617.
63 Jung, *Letters*, vol. ii, p. 138.
64 C. G. Jung, "The archetypes of the collective unconscious," *CW* 9i: 50.
65 C. G. Jung, "On psychic energy," *CW* 8: 92.
66 Kerr, *A Most Dangerous Method*, p. 125.
67 Carotenuto, *A Secret Symmetry*, p. 89.
68 M. Marini, *Jacques Lacan: The French Context*, trans. A. Tomiche, New Brunswick, NJ: Rutgers University Press, 1992, p. 83.
69 J. Mitchell, *Psychoanalysis and Feminism: A Radical Reassessment of Freudian Psychoanalysis*, New York: Basic Books, 2000, pp. 357–416.
70 Carotenuto, *A Secret Symmetry*, p. 86.
71 Jung, *Memories, Dreams, Reflections*, pp. 180–1.
72 "*Auseinandersetzung*" is an untranslatable German word meaning having it out with, discussing, analyzing, and eventually coming to terms with the other. In Jungian usage, the "other" would usually be the unconscious.
73 C. G. Jung, *Answer to Job*, *CW* 11: 617.
74 Cited by J. P. Bienvenu, "Healing through the search for truth," oral presentation to the Canadian Psychoanalytic Society, Toronto, Ontario, April 2001.
75 C. G. Jung, "The psychology of the child archetype," *CW* 9i: 302.
76 Jung, *Memories, Dreams, Reflections*, p. 337. The last italics is my emphasis.
77 W. Giegerich, "Comment" to P. Kugler and J. Hillman, "The autonomous psyche: a communication to Goodheart from the bi-personal field of Paul Kugler and James Hillman," *Spring 1985: An Annual of Archetypal Psychology and Jungian Thought*, Dallas: Spring Publications, 1985, pp. 172–4.
78 Jung, *Memories, Dreams, Reflections*, p. 337.
79 C. G. Jung, "Some crucial points in psychoanalysis," *CW* 4: 665.
80 Galatians 2:20. Cited by Giegerich to make a similar point in *The Soul's Logical Life*, p. 70.

81 Jung, *Memories, Dreams, Reflections*, p. 333.
82 Jung, *Memories, Dreams, Reflections*, p. 338.
83 Jung, *Memories, Dreams, Reflections*, pp. 255–6.
84 Freud, *Beyond the Pleasure Principle*, trans. J. Strachey, New York: W. W. Norton, 1961, pp. 31–7.
85 Freud, *Beyond the Pleasure Principle*, pp. 20–7.
86 Freud, *Beyond the Pleasure Principle*, p. 21.
87 Campbell, *The Masks of God,* vol. i: *Primitive Mythology*, pp. 38–49.
88 Jung, "Psychological aspects of the mother archetype," *CW* 9i: 183.
89 W. Giegerich, "The 'patriarchal neglect of the feminine principle': a psychological fallacy of Jungian theory," *Harvest: Journal for Jungian Studies*, 45/1 (1999), p. 10.
90 Giegerich, "The 'patriarchal neglect of the feminine principle': a psychological fallacy of Jungian theory," pp. 10f.
91 Giegerich, "The 'patriarchal neglect of the feminine principle': a psychological fallacy of Jungian theory," pp. 11f.
92 P. Teilhard de Chardin, *The Phenomenon of Man*, London: William Collins & Sons, 1959, pp. 64–70.
93 C. G. Jung, *Analytical Psychology: Notes of the Seminar given in 1925*, ed. W. McGuire, Princeton: Princeton University Press, 1989, pp. 27–8.
94 S. Freud, "A disturbance of memory on the Acropolis," *CP* 5: 310.
95 Freud, *Group Psychology and the Analysis of the Ego*, p. 118.
96 W. Giegerich, "Jung's betrayal of his truth: the adoption of a Kant-based empiricism and the rejection of Hegel's speculative thought," *Harvest: Journal for Jungian Studies*, 44/1 (1998), pp. 46–64.
97 S. Freud, "Formulations regarding the two principles in mental functioning," *CP* 4. C. G. Jung, "Two kinds of thinking," in *Symbols of Transformation*, *CW* 5.
98 Giegerich, *The Soul's Logical Life*, p. 90.
99 Cf. Giegerich: "the cure of neurosis consists in the cure of a consciousness fixated on continuity, unity, positivity, self-identity; it consists in allowing the split to *come home to* consciousness and to permeate the logical form of its constitution, in order for consciousness to become something that can give the disunity (in ourselves, in the world, in life) as well as the individual dissociated partial truths each their own legitimate place". *The Soul's Logical Life*, p. 25.

Final Thoughts: The status of hysteria in the vision of psychology

1 S. Freud, "Fragment of an analysis of a case of hysteria," *CP* 3:15.
2 C. G. Jung, "Psychology and literature," *CW* 15: 148.
3 J. Hinson Lall, "Astrological divination in psychotherapy," *Spring 66: A Journal of Archetype and Culture*, Putnam: Spring Journal, 1999, p. 51.
4 Jung, "Psychology and literature," *CW* 15: 148.
5 Xanthippe was Socrates' ill-tempered wife. We include her here to darken an otherwise too idealized portrayal of the anima of the love-episode.
6 Cf. W. Giegerich, *The Soul's Logical Life: Towards a Rigorous Notion of Psychology*, Frankfurt am Main: Peter Lang, 1998, p. 204.
7 S. Freud, *The Question of Lay Analysis*, trans. J. Strachey, New York: W. W. Norton, 1950, p. 64.
8 For a discussion of the importance of the notion of truth for psychology see Giegerich, *The Soul's Logical Life*, pp. 220–32, 274.
9 C. G. Jung, *The Psychology of the Transference*, *CW* 16: 449.

Bibliography

Abraham, K. "The ear and auditory passage as erotogenic zones," in *Selected Papers on Psycho-Analysis*, London: Maresfield Reprints, 1927, pp. 244–7.

Abrams, M. H. *et al.* (eds.) *The Norton Anthology of English Literature*, 3rd edn., New York: W. W. Norton, 1962.

Allison, A. *et al.* (eds.) *The Norton Anthology of Poetry*, 3rd edn., New York and London: W. W. Norton, 1983.

Auden, W. H. *W. H. Auden: Collected Poems*, ed. E. Mendelson, New York: Random House, 1976.

Bachelard, G. *The Poetics of Reverie: Childhood, Language, and the Cosmos*, trans. D. Russell, Boston: Beacon Press, 1969.

Bachelard, G. *On Poetic Imagination and Reverie, Selections from the Works of Gaston Bachelard*, trans. C. Gaudin, Indianapolis: Bobbs-Merrill, 1971.

Barnstone, W. (ed.) *The Other Bible*, New York: Harper & Row, 1984.

Berry, P. *Echo's Subtle Body: Contributions to an Archetypal Psychology*, Dallas: Spring Publications, 1982.

Bienvenu, J.-P. "Healing through the search for truth," oral presentation to the Canadian Psychoanalytic Society, Toronto, Ontario, April 2001.

Blake, W. "Jerusalem," in N. Frye (ed.), *Selected Poetry and Prose of Blake*, New York: Random House, 1953.

Bollas, C. *The Shadow of the Object: Psychoanalysis of the Unthought Known*, London: Free Association Books; New York: Columbia University Press, 1987.

Bollas, C. *Forces of Destiny: Psychoanalysis and Human Idiom*, London and New Jersey: Jason Aronson, 1989.

Bollas, C. *Being a Character: Psychoanalysis and Self Experience*, London: Routledge, 1992.

Bollas, C. *Cracking Up: The Work of Unconscious Experience*, New York: Hill & Wang, 1995.

Bollas, C. *The Mystery of Things*, London: Routledge, 1999.

Bollas, C. *Hysteria*, London: Routledge, 2000.

Bollas, C. *Free Association*, Cambridge, UK: Icon Books, 2002.

Breuer, J. and Freud, S. *Studies on Hysteria*, trans. J. Strachey, New York: Basic Books, 1957.

Buber, M. *Eclipse of God: Studies in the Relation between Religion and Philosophy*, New York: Harper & Row, 1952.

Cameron, A. *The Identity of Oedipus the King: Five Essays on the "Oedipus Tyrannus,"* New York: New York University Press, 1984.

Campbell, J. *The Masks of God*, vol. i: *Primitive Mythology*, New York: Viking Press, 1959.

Campbell, J. *The Masks of God,* vol. iv: *Creative Mythology*, Harmondsworth: Penguin Books, 1968.

Capps, D. (ed.) *Freud and Freudians on Religion: A Reader*, New Haven and London: Yale University Press, 2001.

Cardinal, M. *The Words to Say It*, Cambridge, MA: Van Vactor & Goodheart, 1983.

Casey, E. *Spirit and Soul: Essays in Philosophical Psychology*, Dallas: Spring Publications, 1991.

Cohen, L. "Anthem," on *The Future*, produced by L. Cohen, S. Lindsey, B. Ginn, L. Ungar, R. De Mornay, and Y. Goren, Sony Music Entertainment, 1992, liner notes.

Coleridge, S. T. *Notebooks of Samuel Taylor Coleridge*, 4 vols., ed. K. Coburn and M. Christensen, New York: Pantheon, 1957–1991.

Coleridge, S. T. *Biographia Literaria*, ed. J. Engell and W. J. Bate, Princeton, NJ: Princeton University Press, 1984.

Coleridge, S. T. *Aids to Reflection*, in *Samuel Taylor Coleridge*, ed. H. Jackson, Oxford: Oxford University Press, 1985.

Coltart, N. *How to Survive as a Psychotherapist*, New Jersey: Jason Aronson, 1993.

Corbin, H. "The question of comparative philosophy: convergences in Iranian and European thought," in *Spring 1980: An Annual of Archetypal Psychology and Jungian Thought*, Dallas: Spring Publications, 1980.

Derrida, J. *Writing and Difference*, trans. A. Bass, Chicago: University of Chicago Press, 1978.

Dickinson, E. *The Letters of Emily Dickinson*, 3 vols., ed. T. Johnson and T. Ward, Cambridge, MA: Belknap Press of Harvard University Press, 1958.

Eliot, T. S. *Collected Poems 1909–1962*, London: Faber & Faber, 1974.

Erikson, E. "Shared visions," in D. Capps (ed.), *Freud and Freudians on Religion: A Reader*, New Haven: Yale University Press, 2001.

Evans, R. *Conversations with Carl Jung and Reactions from Ernest Jones*, New York: Van Nostrand Reinhold, 1964.

Field, J. (Marion Milner) *On Not Being Able to Paint*, London: Heinemann, 1950.

Flournoy, T. *From India to the Planet Mars: A Case of Multiple Personality with Imaginary Languages*, ed. S. Shamdasani, Princeton, NJ: Princeton University Press, 1994.

Freud, S. *The Standard Edition of the Complete Psychological Works of Sigmund Freud*, 24 vols., ed. and trans. J. Strachey *et al.*, London: Hogarth Press and the Institute of Psycho-Analysis, 1953–73.

Freud, S. "Abstracts of the scientific works of Dr. Sigm. Freud, 1877–1897," *SE* 3.

Freud, S. *Three Essays on the Theory of Sexuality*, *SE* 7.

Freud, S. *On the History of the Psycho-Analytic Movement*, *SE* 14.

Freud, S. "Leonardo da Vinci and a memory of his childhood," *SE* 11.

Freud, S. "Dostoevsky and parricide," *SE* 21.

Freud, S. *Collected Papers*, 5 vols., trans. J. Riviere and A. and J. Strachey, London: Hogarth Press and the Institute of Psycho-Analysis, 1950.

Freud, S. "The passing of the Oedipus-complex," *CP* 2.

Freud, S. "Recommendations for physicians on the psycho-analytic method of treatment," *CP* 2.

Freud, S. "Hysterical phantasies and their relation to bisexuality," *CP* 2.

Freud, S. "From the history of an infantile neurosis," *CP* 3.

Freud, S. "Fragment of an analysis of a case of hysteria," *CP* 3.

Freud, S. "On narcissism: an introduction," *CP* 4.

Freud, S. "Mourning and melancholia," *CP* 4.

Freud, S. "The unconscious," *CP* 4.

Freud, S. "Formulations regarding the two principles in mental functioning," *CP* 4.

Freud, S. "Analysis terminable and interminable," *CP* 5.

Freud, S. "A disturbance of memory on the acropolis," *CP* 5.

Freud, S. *The Question of Lay Analysis*, trans. J. Strachey, New York: W. W. Norton, 1950.

Freud, S. *Beyond the Pleasure Principle*, trans. J. Strachey, New York: W. W. Norton, 1961.

Freud, S. *The Ego and the Id*, trans. J. Riviere, New York: W. W. Norton, 1962.

Freud, S. *New Introductory Lectures on Psycho-Analysis*, trans. J. Strachey, Pelican Freud Library, 2, Harmondsworth: Penguin Books, 1973.

Freud, S. *The Interpretation of Dreams*, trans. J. Strachey, Pelican Freud Library, 4, Harmondsworth: Penguin Books, 1976.

Freud, S. *Group Psychology and the Analysis of the Ego,* in *Civilization, Society and Religion*, trans. J. Strachey, Pelican Freud Library, 12, Harmondsworth: Penguin Books, 1985.

Freud, S. *A Phylogenetic Fantasy: Overview of the Transference Neuroses*, ed. E. Grubrich-Simitis, trans. A. and P. T. Hoffer, Cambridge, MA, and London: Belknap Press of Harvard University Press, 1987.

Freud, S. *New Introductory Lectures on Psycho-Analysis*, trans. W. J. H. Sprott, London: Hogarth Press, 1933.

Freud, S. and Abraham, K. *A Psycho-Analytic Dialogue: The Letters of Sigmund Freud and Karl Abraham, 1907–1926*, ed. H. C. Abraham and E. L. Freud, trans. B. Marsh and H. C. Abraham, New York: Basic Books, 1965.

Freud, S. and Pfister, O. *Psychoanalysis and Faith: The Letters of Sigmund Freud and Oskar Pfister*, London: Hogarth Press and the Institute of Psycho-Analysis, 1963.

Frye, N. "Reflections in a mirror," in M. Krieger (ed.), *Northrop Frye in Modern Criticism*, New York: Columbia University Press, 1966.

Gay, P. "Sigmund Freud," *Time* 153/12, (29 March 1999), pp. 38–41.

Giegerich, W. "On the neurosis of psychology or the third of the two," in *Spring 1977: An Annual of Archetypal Psychology and Jungian Thought*, Zurich: Spring Publications, 1977.

Giegerich, W. "Killings: psychology's Platonism and the missing link to reality," in *Spring 54: A Journal of Archetype and Culture*, Putnam, CT: Spring Journal, 1993, pp. 5–18.

Giegerich, W. "Jung's betrayal of his truth: the adoption of a Kant-based empiricism and the rejection of Hegel's speculative thought," *Harvest: Journal for Jungian Studies* 44/1 (1998), pp. 46–64.

Giegerich, W. *The Soul's Logical Life: Towards a Rigorous Notion of Psychology*, Frankfurt am Main: Peter Lang, 1998.

Giegerich, W. "The 'patriarchal neglect of the feminine principle': a psychological fallacy of Jungian theory," *Harvest: Journal for Jungian Studies* 45/1 (1999), pp. 7–30.

Grotstein, J. "The numinous and immanent nature of the psychoanalytic Subject," in *Journal of Analytical Psychology* 43/1 (1998), pp. 41–68.

Grubrich-Simitis, I. (ed.) *A Phylogenetic Fantasy: Overview of the Transference Neuroses*, Cambridge, MA: Belknap Press of Harvard University Press, 1987.

Grubrich-Simitis, I. "Metapsychology and metabiology: on Sigmund Freud's draft overview of the transference neuroses," in I. Grubrich-Simitis (ed.), *A Phylogenetic Fantasy: Overview of the Transference Neuroses*, Cambridge, MA: Belknap Press of Harvard University Press, 1987.

Hasting, J. (designer) *Annunciation*, London: Phaidon Press, 2000.

Heidegger, H. *Basic Writings*, New York: Harper & Row, 1977.

Hesse, H. *Demian*, trans. W. J. Strachan, London: Panther Books, 1969.

Hillman, J. *Re-Visioning Psychology*, New York: Harper & Row, 1975.

Hillman, J. "An inquiry into image," in *Spring 1977: An Annual of Archetypal Psychology and Jungian Thought*, Zurich: Spring Publications, 1977.

Hillman, J. *The Myth of Analysis: Three Essays in Archetypal Psychology*, New York: HarperPerennial, 1978.

Hillman, J. *The Dream and the Underworld*, New York: Harper Colophon, 1979.

Hillman, J. "On the necessity of abnormal psychology: Ananke and Athene," in J. Hillman (ed.), *Facing the Gods*, Irving, TX: Spring Publications, 1980.

Hillman, J. "Silver and the white earth (part one)," in *Spring: An Annual of Archetypal Psychology and Jungian Thought*, Dallas: Spring Publications, 1980.

Hillman, J. "Silver and the white earth (part two)," in *Spring: An Annual of Archetypal Psychology and Jungian Thought*, Dallas: Spring Publications, 1981.

Hillman, J. "Anima mundi: the return of the soul to the world," in *Spring: An Annual of Archetypal Psychology and Jungian Thought*, Dallas: Spring Publications, 1982.

Hillman, J. *Archetypal Psychology: A Brief Account*, Dallas: Spring Publications, 1983.

Hillman, J. *Anima: An Anatomy of a Personified Notion*, Dallas: Spring Publications, 1985.

Hillman, J. "The great mother, her son, her hero, and the puer," in P. Berry (ed.), *Fathers and Mothers*, Dallas: Spring Publications, 1991.

Hillman, J. *The Thought of the Heart and the Soul of the World*, Dallas: Spring Publications, 1992.

Hillman, J. *The Soul's Code: In Search of Character and Calling*, New York: Warner Books, 1996.

Hillman, J. and Kerényi, K. *Oedipus Variations: Studies in Literature and Psychoanalysis*, Dallas: Spring Publications, 1991.

Hinson Lall, J. "Astrological divination in psychotherapy," in *Spring 66: A Journal of Archetype and Culture*, Putnam, CT: Spring Journal, 1999.

Hoeller, S. *Jung and the Lost Gospels*, Wheaton: Theosophical Publishing House, 1989.

Hogenson, G. "The Baldwin effect: a neglected influence on C. G. Jung's evolutionary thinking," *Journal of Analytical Psychology*. 46/4 (2001), pp. 591–611.

Humbert, E. "Jung and the question of religion," in *Spring 1985: An Annual of Archetypal Psychology and Jungian Thought*, Dallas: Spring Publications, 1985.

Jones, E. "The Madonna's conception through the ear: a contribution to the relation between aesthetics and religion," in E. Jones, *Psycho-Myth, Psycho-History*, vol. ii, New York: Stonehill, 1974.

Jones, E. "A psycho-analytic study of the Holy Ghost concept," in his *Psycho-Myth, Psycho-History*, vol. ii, New York: Stonehill, 1974.

Joyce, J. *A Portrait of the Artist as a Young Man*, Harmondsworth: Penguin Books, 1988.

Jung, C. G. Except where indicated, references are by volume and paragraph number to the *Collected Works of C. G. Jung*, 20 vols., ed. H. Read, M. Fordham and G. Adler, trans. R. F. C. Hull, London: Routledge & Kegan Paul; Princeton, NJ: Princeton University Press, 1953–77.

Jung, C. G. *Memories, Dreams, Reflections*, ed. A. Jaffé trans. R. and C. Winston, New York: Pantheon, 1963.

Jung, C. G. *Letters*, vol. i: *1906–1950*, ed. G. Adler and A. Jaffé, trans. R. F. C. Hull, Princeton, NJ: Princeton University Press, 1973.

Jung, C. G. *Letters*, vol. ii: *1951–1961*, ed. G. Adler and A. Jaffé, trans. R. F. C. Hull, Princeton, NJ: Princeton University Press, 1975.

Jung, C. G. *The Visions Seminars*, vols. i and ii, Zurich: Spring Publications, 1976.

Jung, C. G. *C. G. Jung Speaking: Interviews and Encounters*, ed. W. McGuire and R. F. C. Hull, Princeton, NJ: Princeton University Press, 1977.

Jung, C. G. *Analytical Psychology: Notes of the Seminar given in 1925*, ed. W. McGuire, Princeton, NJ: Princeton University Press, 1989.

Jung, C. G. *The Psychology of the Unconscious: A Study of the Transformations and Symbolisms of the Libido*, trans. B. Hickle, Bollingen Series 20, Princeton, NJ: Princeton University Press, 1991.

Jung, C. G. "The letters of C. G. Jung to Sabina Spielrein," trans. B. Wharton, *Journal of Analytical Psychology*, 46/1 (2001), pp. 173–99.

Keats, J. *Selected Poems and Letters*, ed. D. Bush, Boston: Houghton Mifflin, 1959.

Kerr, J. *A Most Dangerous Method: The Story of Jung, Freud, and Sabina Spielrein*, New York: Alfred A. Knopf, 1994.

Klein, M. "Early stages of the oedipus conflict," in *Love, Guilt and Reparation and Other Works 1921–1945*, London: Hogarth Press and the Institute of Psycho-Analysis, 1975.

Kohut, H. *The Restoration of the Self*, New York: International Universities Press, 1977.

Kohut, H. *How Does Analysis Cure?*, ed. A. Goldberg and P. Stepansky, Chicago: University of Chicago Press, 1984.

Kristeva, J. "Credo in unum deum," in D. Capps (ed.), *Freud and Freudians on Religion: A Reader*, New Haven and London: Yale University Press, 2001.

Kugler, P. *The Alchemy of Discourse: An Archetypal Approach to Language*, Lewisburg: Bucknell University Press, 1982.

Kugler, P. "Involuntary poetics," *New Literary History: A Journal of Theory and Interpretation* 15 (1983–4).

Kugler, P. "Clinical authority: some thoughts out of season," *Quadrant: Journal of the C.G. Jung Foundation for Analytical Psychology* 23/2 (1990).

Kugler, P. "Childhood seduction: material and immaterial facts," in S. Marlan (ed.), *Fire in the Stone: The Alchemy of Desire*, Wilmette: Chiron, 1997.

Kugler, P. *The Alchemy of Discourse: Image, Sound and Psyche*, Einsiedeln: Daimon Verlag, 2002.

Kugler, P. and Hillman, J. "The autonomous psyche: a communication to Goodheart from the bi-personal field of Paul Kugler and James Hillman," in *Spring 1985: An Annual of Archetypal Psychology and Jungian Thought*, Dallas: Spring Publications, 1985.

Lacan, J. *Ecrits: A Selection*, trans. A. Sheridan, New York: W. W. Norton, 1977.

Lawrence, D. H. *D. H. Lawrence: Selected Poems*, New York: Viking Press, 1959.

Lockhart, R. *Words as Eggs: Psyche in Language and Clinic*, Dallas: Spring Publications, 1983.

McGuire, W. (ed.) *The Freud/Jung Letters: The Correspondence between Sigmund Freud and C. G. Jung*, trans. R. Manheim and R. F. C. Hull, Princeton, NJ: Princeton University Press, 1974.

McLynn, F. *Carl Gustav Jung: A Biography*, New York: St Martin's Press, 1996.

Marini, M. *Jacques Lacan: The French Context*, trans. A. Tomiche, New Brunswick, NJ: Rutgers University Press, 1992.

Masson, J. (ed. and trans.) *The Complete Letters of Sigmund Freud and Wilhelm Fliess 1887–1904*, Cambridge, MA, and London: Belknap Press of Harvard University Press, 1985.

Miller, D. *The New Polytheism: The Rebirth of the Gods and Goddesses*, Dallas: Spring Publications, 1981.

Miller, D. *Hells and Holy Ghosts: A Theopoetics of Christian Belief*, Nashville: Abingdon Press, 1989.

Miller, D. "Theologia imaginalis," in M. Parisen (ed.), *Angels and Mortals: Their Co-Creative Power*, Madras and London: Quest Books, 1990.

Milton, J. *Paradise Lost*, in *Collected Works*, ed. Helen Darbishire, Oxford: Oxford University Press, 1952–5.

Mitchell, J. *Psychoanalysis and Feminism: A Radical Reassessment of Freudian Psychoanalysis*, New York: Basic Books, 2000.

Mitchell, J. *Mad Men and Medusas: Reclaiming Hysteria*, New York: Basic Books, 2000.

Mogenson, G. *God Is a Trauma: Vicarious Religion and Soul-Making*, Dallas: Spring Publications, 1989.

Molino, A. (ed.) *Freely Associated: Encounters in Psychoanalysis with Christopher Bollas, Joyce McDougall, Michael Eigen, Adam Phillips, Nina Coltart*, London: Free Association Books, 1997.

Neumann, E. *Depth Psychology and a New Ethic*, trans. E. Rolfe, New York: Putnam, 1969.

Neumann, E. *The Origins and History of Consciousness*, trans. R. F. C. Hull, Princeton, NJ: Princeton University Press, 1970.

Nietzsche, F. *Joyful Wisdom*, New York: Frederick Ungar, 1960.

Nietzsche, F. *Twilight of the Idols*, in *Twilight of the Idols and The Anti-Christ*, trans. R. J. Hollingdale, Harmondsworth: Penguin Books, 1968.

Nietzsche, F. *Thus Spoke Zarathustra*, trans. R. J. Hollingdale, Harmondsworth: Penguin Books, 1969.

Pikes, N. "Giving voice to hell," in *Spring 55: A Journal of Archetype and Culture*, Putnam, CT: Spring Journal, 1994.

Reik, T. *Listening with the Third Ear*, New York: Farrar, Straus, 1948.

Rudnytsky, P. *Freud and Oedipus*, New York: Columbia University Press, 1987.

Ryrie, C. *The Ryrie Study Bible*, Chicago: Moody Press, 1976.

Sardello, R. "Saving the things or how to avoid the bomb," in *Spring 1985: An Annual of Archetypal Psychology and Jungian Thought*, Dallas: Spring Publications, 1985.

Schapira, L. *The Cassandra Complex: Living with Disbelief – A Modern Perspective on Hysteria*, Toronto: Inner City Books, 1988.

Serrano, M. *Jung and Hesse: A Record of Two Friendships*, New York: Schocken Books, 1968.

Shakespeare, W. *King Lear*, in *The Complete Works of William Shakespeare*, London: Rex Library, 1973.

Shamdasani, S. "A woman called Frank," in *Spring 50: A Journal of Archetype and Culture*, Dallas: Spring Publications, 1990.

Shaw, G. B. *Pygmalion: A Romance in Five Acts*, ed. D. Laurence, Harmondsworth: Penguin Books, 1957.

Spence, D. *Narrative Truth and Historical Truth: Meaning and Intepretation in Psychoanalysis*, New York: W. W. Norton, 1984.

Spielrein, S. "Destruction as the cause of coming into being," trans. K. McCormick, reprinted in *Journal of Analytical Psychology* 39/2 (1994), pp. 155–86.

Stevens, W. "An ordinary evening in New Haven," in H. Stevens (ed.), *The Palm at the End of the Mind*, New York: Vintage Books, 1972.

Summers, F. *Object Relations Theories and Psychopathology: A Comprehensive Text*, Hillsdale, NJ: Analytic Press, 1994.

Teilhard de Chardin, P. *The Phenomenon of Man*, London: William Collins & Sons, 1959.

Tinbergen, N. *The Study of Instinct*, London: Oxford University Press, 1951.

Taylor, E. *William James on Exceptional Mental States: The 1898 Lowell Lectures*, Amherst: University of Massachusetts Press, 1984.

von Franz, M.-L. *Projection and Re-Collection in Jungian Psychology: Reflections of the Soul*, trans. W. Kennedy, La Salle: Open Court, 1980.

von Franz, M.-L. *Psychotherapy*, Boston: Shambhala, 1993.

von Franz, M.-L. *C. G. Jung: His Myth in Our Time*, Toronto: Inner City Books, 1998.

Walker, B. *The Encyclopedia of the Occult, the Esoteric, and the Supernatural*, Briarcliff Manor, NY: Stein and Day, 1980.

Wheelwright, P. *Heraclitus*, Princeton, NJ: Princeton University Press, 1959.

Williams, M. "The indivisibility of the personal and collective unconscious," in M. Fordham (ed.), *Analytical Psychology: A Modern Science*, London: Heinemann, 1973.

Wind, E. *Pagan Mysteries in the Renaissance*, New York: Norton, 1968.

Winnicott, D. W. "Review of *Memories, Dreams, Reflections*," in C. Winnicott, R. Shepherd, and M. Davis (eds.), *Psycho-Analytic Explorations*, Cambridge, MA: Harvard University Press, 1989.

Winnicott, D. W. "A point of technique," in C. Winnicott, R. Shepherd, and M. Davis (eds.), *Psycho-Analytic Explorations*, Cambridge, MA: Harvard University Press, 1989.

Winnicott, D. "Fear of breakdown," in C. Winnicott, R. Shepherd and M. Davis (eds.), *Psycho-Analytic Explorations*, Cambridge, MA: Harvard University Press, 1989.

Winnicott, D. "The use of an object and relating through identifications," in C. Winnicott, R. Shepherd and M. Davis (eds.), *Psycho-Analytic Explorations*, Cambridge, MA: Harvard University Press, 1989.

Winnicott, D. and Khan, M. "Review of *Psychoanalytic Study of the Personality*," in C. Winnicott, R. Shepherd, and M. Davis (eds.), *Psycho-Analytic Explorations*, Cambridge, MA: Harvard University Press, 1989.

Wordsworth, W. "The Prelude," in E. de Selincourt (ed.), *Wordsworth's Prelude*, Oxford and London: Oxford University Press, 1959.

Yeats, W. B. *W. B. Yeats: Selected Poetry*, ed. A. N. Jeffares, London: Pan Books, 1974.

Index